ON YOUR OWN

A Personal Budgeting Simulation
Instructions and Source Documents Booklet

Mary Queen Donnelly
Dean of Institutional Advancement
Jackson Academy
Jackson, MS

THOMSON
™
SOUTH-WESTERN

Australia · Canada · Mexico · Singapore · Spain · United Kingdom · United States

THOMSON
—★— ™
SOUTH-WESTERN

On Your Own: A Personal Budgeting Simulation, 2E

Mary Queen Donnelly

Editor-in-Chief:
Jack Calhoun

**Vice President/
Executive Publisher:**
Dave Shaut

Team Leader:
Karen Schmohe

Executive Editor:
Eve Lewis

Director of Marketing:
Carol Volz

Senior Marketing Manager:
Nancy Long

Marketing Coordinator:
Yvonne Patton

Project Manager:
Carol Sturzenberger

Consulting Editor:
Cinci Stowell

Editor:
Kim Kusnerak

Production Manager:
Tricia Boies

Manufacturing Coordinator:
Kevin Kluck

Compositor:
electro-publishing

Printer:
Globus Printing
Minster, OH

Design Project Manager:
Stacy Jenkins Shirley

Cover/Envelope/Internal Designer:
Joe Pagliaro

Cover/Envelope Photo:
Courtesy of © Matton

Permissions Editor:
Linda Ellis

For more information, contact
South-Western
5191 Natorp Boulevard
Mason, Ohio 45040.
Or you can visit our Internet site at:
http://www.swlearning.com

For permission to use material from this
text or product, contact us by
Phone: 1-800-730-2214
Fax: 1-800-730-2215
http://www.thomsonrights.com

The names of all products mentioned herein are used for identification purposes only and may be trademarks or registered trademarks of their respective owners. South-Western disclaims any affiliation, association, connection with, sponsorship, or endorsement by such owners.

About the Author
Mary Queen Donnelly is Dean of Institutional Advancement at Jackson Academy, Jackson, MS. She was formerly Director of Guidance at Marist School, Atlanta, GA, and at St. Mary's Dominican High School, New Orleans, LA. She has taught in the high school classroom for over 20 years and counseled students from a wide variety of economic, demographic, and family situations.

Expect More From South-Western...
...And Get It!

Economic Education for Consumers 2E

Make your students "super-informed" consumers! This text has exciting features, engaging lessons, and multimedia ancillaries to help economic, consumer, and personal finance concepts come to life.

Text	0-538-43579-8
Student Workbook	0-538-43581-X
Interactive Study Guide CD	0-538-43586-0

Instructor Support and Other Materials Available

Managing Your Personal Finances 4E

Discover new ways to maximize earning potential, develop strategies for managing resources, explore skills for the wise use of credit, and gain insight into the different types of investing. This text will inform your students of their financial responsibilities as citizens, students, family members, consumers, and active participants in the business world.

Text	0-538-69958-2
Student Activity Guide	0-538-69961-2
Planning Tools CD	0-538-43448-1

Instructor Support and Other Materials Available

Banking and Financial Systems

This exciting new text gives an overview of banking and financial services, including career opportunities. It presents a survey of the principles and practices of banking and credit in the United States. Appropriate for the National Academy Foundation's (NAF's) Academy of Finance courses.

Text	0-538-43241-1
Module (includes ExamView CD, Instructor's Resource CD, Video, and Annotated Instructor's Edition)	0-538-43242-X

Instructor Support and Other Materials Available

Family Financial Management 6E

This comprehensive money management simulation is presented in an extended family setting, presenting situations for every stage of life—from young adult to preparing for retirement. Students learn to calculate net worth, plan monthly budgets, complete banking transactions, pay utility bills, perform credit transactions, make housing payments, plan for large purchases, and reconcile monthly bank statements. Data disks allow students to use commercial spreadsheet software to work with statements of net worth, cash proofs, budgets, receipts and payments, bank reconciliations, and credit card statements.

Envelope Simulation	0-538-67501-2
Data Disk: Windows 0-538-68115-2	Macintosh 0-538-68116-0

Instructor Support and Other Materials Available

Fundamentals of Insurance

Explore health and property insurance, insurance rates, claims procedures, careers in insurance, and annuities. The extensive use of hands-on activities helps students understand the importance of insurance and how it affects them today and through their retirement years. Appropriate for the National Academy Foundation's (NAF's) Academy of Finance courses.

Text	0-538-43201-2
Module (includes ExamView CD, Instructor's Resource CD, Video, and Annotated Instructor's Edition)	0-538-43248-9

Instructor Support and Other Materials Available

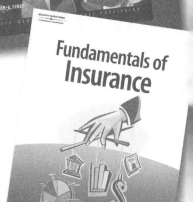

THOMSON
SOUTH-WESTERN

Join us on the Internet at
www.swlearning.com

Preface

This is the story of Mark Smith. When Mark's parents told him he had to make it on his own, he didn't have much to go on. First, he checked out what he did have. He had a high school diploma. He had a job that paid minimum wage. And he had a good friend, Kim Nguyen, who knew a lot about living on your own.

Nonetheless, life wasn't easy for Mark. As you will learn, he made some mistakes. More than once, he made a poor decision. However, Mark did two things right: He was honest with himself and he wasn't afraid to ask for help.

Kim helped him the most. Through Kim, he learned that certain skills are needed to make it in life. Education is basically learning "how to":

- How to interpret information
- How to calculate with numbers
- How to bounce back from setbacks
- How to take on a challenge
- How to stick with it
- How to manage time
- How to benefit from mistakes
- How to stand up for your beliefs

However, to be on your own, you need to learn:

- How to keep records
- How to maintain a bank account
- How to budget your money
- How to set goals for yourself
- How to save money for future goals
- How to build a good credit record
- How to read and interpret an apartment lease
- How to buy a used car
- How to interpret insurance policies
- How to apply for a job
- How to use your consumer rights and responsibilities

And last, but not least,

HOW TO BE ON YOUR OWN!

Mary Queen Donnelly

Acknowledgments

Putting together a simulation such as *On Your Own*, 2nd Edition, requires teamwork. At this time, I wish to acknowledge my team. First and foremost, I am grateful to my editors, Carol Sturzenberger, Project Manager, and Cynthia Stowell, Consulting Editor. Both contributed in a major way toward the production of this project. As always, I am grateful to Eve Lewis, Executive Editor at South-Western Educational Publishing. I thank my headmaster at Jackson Academy, Peter Jernberg, for allowing me flex time in order to work on the second edition of *On Your Own*.

Numerous colleagues and professionals in their respective fields provided their expertise, talents, and time. Their contributions were essential to the successful outcome of this work. Special thanks to:

Don Breazeale

Lenwood Brooks V

Ellen Buntyn

Bob Donnelly

Michael Donnelly

Janet Ellis

Rusty Healy

Jan Kling

Nancy Mize

Mary Lacy Montgomery

Jackye Shanks-Moore

Billy W. Queen

Bill Queen, Jr.

James R. Queen

Josie Shanks

Table of Contents

Chapter 1

SETTING UP A FILE

PHOTO: © GETTY IMAGES/
PHOTODISC

Mark Smith walked along the streets of his neighborhood, thinking what a difference a day makes. Yesterday he didn't have a care in the world. He had just celebrated his nineteenth birthday. He was happy living at home with his parents and three younger sisters. He had a fairly good job at Antwan's Auto Parts, and he planned to attend City Community College in order to improve his prospects for the future.

That was before Mark's dad gave him the bad news. Mark would have to move out as soon as possible and support himself as best he could. His mother had been given a pink slip at 5 p.m. as she was preparing to go home for the day. Because of the poor economy, she was laid off—indefinitely.

Mr. Smith reminded Mark of the importance of education for all the children in the family. He reminded Mark how he had encouraged him to stay in school and graduate. He told Mark how proud he was that he had done just that.

Mr. Smith said he wanted the same for Mark's sisters. He wanted them to stay in school and get a high school diploma. He said that he couldn't afford to feed all the family members on one salary. Without Mrs. Smith's salary, the family would have to make some changes.

Mark didn't know where to start. He felt overwhelmed. He had to find an apartment—one he could afford. He barely had enough money for bus fare now, and that had been about all he had to pay for so far, except his own entertainment. He had never bought groceries on his own. He didn't have a checking account. However, Mark knew his dad was right. Mark had been given the opportunity to get a high school education. He was 19; he should be able to support himself.

Mark slowly strolled to the bus stop. He got on the bus and settled into a seat without looking to see who was sitting beside him.

"Hi, Mark! Long time no see." It was Kim Nguyen. Mark hadn't seen Kim since high school graduation. Her parents had come to the United States to escape poverty in their home country. They could barely speak English when Kim was younger. Mark really admired Kim and her family. They had overcome obstacles that Mark couldn't imagine anyone overcoming. Now he had his own story to tell, and Kim listened carefully.

"First, you need to get organized," Kim said later, as they sat eating a sandwich. Mark felt better already. This woman was a genius.

"You must start a filing system. It's the only way to get organized and stay organized," she said.

"First, get a crate or a box, something to store your files in," she said. "No need to spend money on a fancy filing system. Save your money for more important matters.

"Next, buy file folders. A box of 100 file folders is very inexpensive and well worth your money. I prefer letter-size, but you can also get them in legal size. Letter-size fits most boxes and can usually be found in different colors at discount stores."

Find out where you can buy file folders. Acquire 20 file folders. If possible, buy a multi-pack that includes green, red, yellow, and blue folders. Or, arrange with classmates to buy different colors and then trade, so that each of you has some of each of these four colors. Later in this chapter, you will set up a filing system with your folders. You'll need 12 green folders, 5 red folders, 2 yellow folders, and 1 blue folder to start your system. If you can't obtain these colors, then folders of any color will work.

How to Set Up an Effective Filing System

Kim explained to Mark that a filing system can be neatly divided into four categories:

1. *Financial:* Records of financial transactions and documents (bank records, canceled checks, budget records, investment records)

2. *Personal:* Records of important personal documents (birth certificate; social security card; diplomas; school transcripts; academic certificates; apartment lease; insurance policies; deeds; passport; marriage/divorce papers; health records; financial documents such as bonds, retirement plans and similar documents; and current will)

3. *Self Improvement:* Plans and programs for self improvement (personal goals, career goals, certification programs, class schedules, college catalogs, fitness programs)

4. *Leisure:* Enjoying life (maps, travel plans, recreational tips, Web sites)

For quick access, Kim suggested a color-coded filing system. She recommended the colors she uses in her own filing system: green, red, yellow, and blue for the dividers. Kim uses folders that match the divider colors, but she said that regular manila folders are fine, too.

Kim said Mark should start his file right away. However, she warned against making a lot of labels for files that he might not need. "At first, just begin with the four main categories. You can add folders as you need them," Kim said.

Financial File

The *Financial File* (color-coded *green* for money!) should contain *financial transactions*: bills to be paid, checking and savings account records, loan payment records, credit card receipts, and your paycheck pay statements.

This file is very helpful for keeping an accurate budget, which you'll learn more about in Chapter 3. If you use electronic banking for financial transactions, it's very important to keep receipts of financial transactions. In addition, you'll need some receipts and financial records to prepare your yearly income tax. These documents also serve as proof of the accuracy of your tax report. If you are audited, the Internal Revenue Service examines your financial records. Therefore, you should keep income tax records for six years after the last filing date.

Personal File

The *Personal File* (color-coded *red*) should include important personal documents you will need over the years. For example, this file would contain medical records, apartment lease, insurance papers, diplomas, vehicle records, and warranties. It would also contain your *vital records*—documents you will need from time to time throughout your life, such as your birth certificate, as well as papers needed by your loved ones after your death, such as your will.

For added security, you may want to keep the originals of these records in a bank safe-deposit box and keep *copies* in your Personal File at home. It would be very inconvenient to have to go to the safe-deposit box every time you need to check one of the documents for information. Also, you might not be able to get to your safe-deposit box on the day you need the information, as the bank could be closed.

Self Improvement File

The *Self Improvement File* (color-coded *yellow*) should contain records of your personal and career goals, as well as information on schools, workshops, seminars, and programs that will enable you to accomplish these goals. It is a good idea to revisit these goals about once a year and perhaps keep a journal of your plans. *Remember: An idea is not a plan until you write it down.*

Self improvement may pertain to job opportunities or other types of personal self improvement. You may read about a new company moving into town or discover a fitness program that you like. Or, you may find a program to help you stop smoking. At the time, you may not be able to afford it, or the program may not begin until months later. This is the information you want to keep on file so you can find it later when you need it.

Leisure File

The *Leisure File* (color-coded *blue*) is one that most people don't think is important enough to keep. Yet it's a file that saves a lot of time, energy, and often money. For example, suppose you read a magazine article about a vacation in the Blue Ridge Mountains. It describes all sorts of bargains: inexpensive cabins, discounted transportation, places to go, and things to do. All the arrangements can be made at a particular Web site. At the time, you can't afford to take the trip. But maybe months later you have the opportunity to go. Maybe a year later, a friend is planning just such a trip and invites you to go along. Of course, you won't remember so much as the name of a highway if you don't keep the article containing the information and Web address in your file.

Call this your fun file. You don't want to keep everything—just information that really appeals to you. Some people gather information on hotels and recreational opportunities on the Internet and save the Web addresses on a floppy disk. You can keep the disk in your Leisure file.

According to Kim, being able to enjoy your leisure time is the reason you keep the other three files. Kim keeps information on travel and vacations, books, sports, gardening, recreation, hobbies—anything that serves as leisure for her.

B Student Activity

1. Name the four major categories of an effective filing system:
   a. _Financial file_
   b. _Personal file_
   c. _Self Improvement file_
   d. _Leisure file_

2. Under what major filing category should you keep the following?
   a. Canceled check records _Financial_
   b. Apartment lease _Personal_
   c. Paralegal course information _Self Improvement_
   d. Disney World vacation package _Leisure_
   e. Credit card receipts _Financial_

3. Give two reasons why everyone should set up a filing system.
   a. _Stay organized_
   b. _quickly easily retrieve_

How to Use This Simulation

Before you go any further, you need to make sure you thoroughly understand the items in your *On Your Own* simulation. We'll examine each item and show how it will be used in the following chapters.

Outer Envelope

The *On Your Own* simulation is packaged in a sturdy envelope. You will place the filing system you develop in this envelope, along with your *Financial Management Record Booklet* and the checkbook. The envelope provides a convenient way to keep all your materials together and organized. When this class is over, you may want to purchase an expandable folder or plastic crate to hold your filing system. Then you can continue to expand your system, as needed.

Instructions and Source Documents Booklet

You are reading out of the *Instructions and Source Documents Booklet* at this very moment. Turn now to the Table of Contents. Notice how the booklet is organized. There are 11 chapters. Chapter 1 is an introductory chapter. It helps you get organized by showing you how to set up a filing system.

As you look through the Table of Contents, you can see that you will work through all the basic skills you need in order to lead a productive life. You'll learn how to manage your money. You will learn how to pursue a career, to obtain financial security, and to manage credit. You will find out how to cover risks of loss of property, health, or life. In the last chapter, you'll learn about your consumer rights and responsibilities.

Now flip through Chapter 2 of the *Instructions and Source Documents Booklet*. Notice that there are Student Activities throughout the chapter. The purpose of these activities is to make sure you understand the information you need in order to perform the transactions required of Mark. In some of the Student Activities, you'll be given directions to record Mark's transactions. As you handle Mark's transactions, you'll be mastering these skills for yourself.

Each chapter contains a section called *On Your Own for Life*. In these sections, you will be completing activities for yourself. These activities will help you develop the skills you need in order to have a productive life.

The back of this *Instructions and Source Documents Booklet* contains a Source Documents section with all the forms, receipts, bills, invoices, and any other documents you will need in order to take care of Mark's transactions. Notice that each form is numbered (Form 2-1, Form 2-2, etc.) and perforated along the left side. Don't tear out any forms until you are instructed to do so. You'll see samples of the forms in the chapters of the *Instructions and Source Documents Booklet*. However, the forms you'll actually use are in the Source Documents section.

You should handle actual forms for two reasons: (1) to become acquainted with the way they look and (2) to practice using forms like those you'll encounter in real life. We tend to avoid things that are unfamiliar. Having seen and used the forms, you'll be familiar with them and will be more likely to put them to good use for yourself.

Checkbook

Look at the simulated *Checkbook*. Simulated means that the checkbook isn't real. In other words, you can't use the checkbook for real cash money. However, it looks like a real checkbook. It has checks in it that you will use for Mark. It has deposit slips and a check register, all of which you will learn how to use in Chapter 2. By using this simulated checkbook, you will learn how to use your own checkbook.

Outgoing File

Inside your simulation is a manila envelope. This is your *Outgoing File*. You will file all the forms or checks that are mailed or given to someone else in the *Outgoing File*. You'll file these documents in numerical order as you complete them. For example, you'll file Form 2-4 behind Form 2-3. The purpose of keeping these documents on file is to make sure you have filled them out properly.

Tabbed Dividers

The four color-coded, tabbed dividers in your simulation will help you organize a filing system. In Student Activity C of this chapter, you will use the four dividers to organize your file folders according to the four basic categories of a filing system: Financial (green), Personal (red), Self Improvement (yellow), and Leisure (blue). You will keep track of all forms, documents, and financial records by filing them in the proper category. You'll be given instructions whenever you have to file.

You'll create sub-categories within the main categories of your filing system. For example, in your Financial File you'll include individual folders labeled *Bills to Be Paid, Banking,* and *Budget.*

After you have filed for Mark and yourself throughout the 11 chapters, you will have developed valuable organizational skills. You'll be in the habit of filing on a regular basis. Plus, you'll discover how easy it is to find and retrieve information and documents that may otherwise be lost or thrown away.

Folder Label Sheet

A page of pre-printed folder labels is provided at the front of the Source Documents section in this *Instructions and Source Documents Booklet.* You will cut out the labels and tape them to your folder tabs to create your filing system.

Financial Management Records Booklet

Mark's *Financial Management Records Booklet* is really the monthly record of his income and expenditures. It's a record of how well he's managing to stay within his planned budget. You will manage Mark's monthly budget by entering his monthly income and expenditures.

You will learn how to plan and keep a budget in Chapter 3. As you proceed through Chapter 3 and the other chapters, you'll record Mark's financial transactions in his *Financial Management Records Booklet*. You'll be given the necessary instructions each time you are required to record information for Mark.

By managing Mark's *Financial Management Records Booklet*, you'll acquire the skills to plan and manage your own budget. To live within your financial resources, you must learn how to manage a budget.

Student Activity

In this activity, you will set up a filing system using the 20 file folders you acquired in Student Activity A. A sheet of folder labels appears at the front of the Source Documents section in this *Instructions and Source Documents Booklet*.

1. Tear out the sheet of folder labels. Notice that the labels are marked for the appropriate color category.

2. Cut out the individual labels and tape them to your file folders. If you have colored folders, tape the labels to the appropriately colored folder.

3. Insert your file folders behind the corresponding colored dividers in the simulation's envelope. Place the folders in alphabetical order within each of the four file categories. Alphabetical order helps you find the folders quickly.

4. Write "Outgoing File" on the manila envelope. Place it in front of the Financial divider.

5. Store the *Checkbook* and *Financial Management Records Booklet* in the front of your filing system.

How to Know Where to File

Many people have trouble with a filing system because they don't know where to file things. To put it another way, they don't know what category to use.

Kim set up a file *index* that helps her to be consistent when filing. It is similar to a table of contents. It helps Kim remember where she filed a particular document. She keeps her index in the front of her file for easy reference.

A file index for the files you just set up is provided in the Source Documents section of this *Instructions and Source Documents Booklet.* Find and remove Form 1-1 from the back of this booklet. Notice that the folder labels are listed in alphabetical order under each category. Also, notice that certain labels are subdivided, such as *Checking Account.* The main category is always written first on the label followed by a dash (—) and the subdivision. For example, *Checking Account—ATM Receipts; Checking Account—Bank Statements;* and *Checking Account—Canceled Checks.* Place the file index (Form 1-1) in the front of the first divider in your filing system.

Usually, you need to subdivide a folder into separate folders if it is too full or if an additional file folder helps you find items more quickly. For instance, you may not remember that you filed your bank statements with your canceled check records. Or, you may have so many canceled checks in the *Checking Account* folder that you need another folder to hold other paperwork related to your checking account.

The point is that you should customize your filing system to fit your individual needs. After establishing the four major categories (Financial, Personal, Self Improvement, and Leisure), you want to make (label) file folders to store only the documents and information that you presently have to file. Add additional file folders as you need them.

You already set up a basic filing system in Student Activity C. When you finish this course, you will have the basis for a filing system that will serve you for life.

How to Know When to File

Kim told Mark that many people get discouraged because they don't set aside a definite time to file. Most people don't want to stop and file every time an item needs to be filed. On the other hand, if you avoid filing for a long time, the job becomes mind-boggling.

Kim recommended that Mark set a definite time to file his bills in the file folder. She pays her bills and files them twice a month, on the days she gets paid (on the 15th of the month and on the last day of each month). In between these times, she keeps the bills in the Bills to Be Paid folder.

You will be filing for Mark *immediately* after each transaction, so that you'll learn how and where to file. As you develop your own filing system, you need to schedule a definite time to file, as Kim did. If you don't file right away, don't wait longer than a two-week period. If you wait longer than two weeks, you'll defeat the value of your filing system. You will have a bunch of disorganized papers lying around.

How to Set Up Annual Files

Kim suggested that Mark go through his files at the end of each year and dispose of those papers that are outdated or that he no longer needs or wants.

File each annual income tax report, along with supporting documents (receipts/invoices), in a separate file folder or in a large manila-clasp envelope. Indicate the year of filing right on the folder or envelope. Store these files so you can retrieve them if and when needed. It would be wise to keep your entire filing system in a fireproof box. You can purchase a fireproof box at a reasonable cost at a discount store.

Examining your files each year reminds you of what you have filed so far. Also, clearing files encourages you to throw away items that are no longer useful.

You can often re-use your file folders year after year. It is work to set up an efficient filing system. You don't want to go through that every year.

D Student Activity

1. Do you have a filing system now? _No_

2. How often do you think you should file once you have a system set up? _every week_

3. What is the value of "cleaning out" files annually?
you know whats knew, not holding onto things you don't know. reuse files

On
Your
Own *For Life*

Leisure files are very specific to each person's recreational preferences. Therefore, the use of leisure files has not been included in the activities you perform for Mark. However, you should begin collecting materials about leisure activities that interest you. As you progress through *On Your Own*, gather information of interest to you and file it in the Leisure File created in Student Activity C.

Check Up

When you are on your own, you have to get organized. Keeping track of your important papers, your financial transactions, and your plans for the future are the first steps in getting organized.

Having completed the Student Activities in this chapter, you should have mastered the skills listed below. Put a checkmark next to the skills you have mastered. If you aren't sure of a skill, review that section of the chapter.

- ☐ How to set up an effective filing system
- ☐ How to use this simulation
- ☐ How to know where to file
- ☐ How to know when to file
- ☐ How to set up annual files

Now that you have mastered the skills listed above, move on to Chapter 2, *Opening a Checking Account.*

Chapter 2

OPENING A CHECKING ACCOUNT

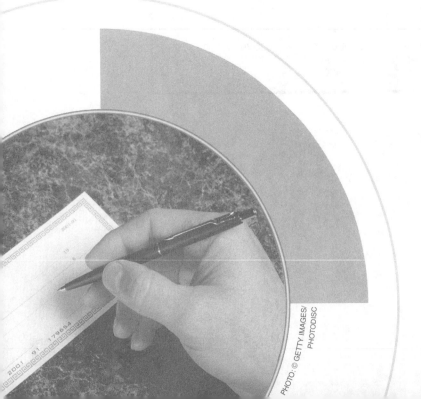

PHOTO: © GETTY IMAGES/ PHOTODISC

Mark and Kim took a day to check out financial institutions and the services offered to customers. "For the sake of convenience, it's a good idea to look at financial institutions located near your apartment or workplace," said Kim. Since Mark didn't have a clue where he would (or could) get an apartment, he decided to look at banks close to his present employer, Antwan's Auto Parts.

How to Compare Banking Services

Kim explained to Mark that the main types of financial institutions offering checking accounts are commercial banks, savings and loan associations, and credit unions. By far, commercial banks are the most popular banking institutions. Banks offer services such as checking accounts, savings accounts, small consumer loans, credit cards, safe-deposit boxes, and other consumer services.

In the past, savings and loan associations specialized in handling savings deposits and loaning money for the purchase of a home. However, in 1981 Congress authorized savings and loan associations to offer services that were previously provided only by commercial banks.

The credit union is another type of financial institution offering a broad range of services. Kim explained that a credit union wasn't available to Mark at this point in his life. A credit union is a nonprofit organization that offers membership only to the members of a particular group, such as teachers in a school system, workers in a factory, or store employees. A credit union offers services similar to those from a savings and loan association.

PHOTO: © GETTY IMAGES/PHOTODISC

Kim made one point very clear. Mark should make sure to open a checking account in an institution that is *insured*. The federal government offers insurance to financial institutions through an agency called the Federal Deposit Insurance Corporation (FDIC). The FDIC insures accounts in most commercial banks and in many savings and loan associations. The agency was established in 1933 to protect the money consumers deposit in a financial institution. At the present time, the maximum amount of insurance coverage is $100,000 per depositor in any one institution.

The Savings Association Insurance Fund (SAIF), an agency of the FDIC, insures deposits in savings and loan associations. SAIF is backed by the full faith and credit of the U.S. government. SAIF insures all the funds of a single depositor up to $100,000, according to SAIF and FDIC rules. If a customer has three different individual accounts at one insured institution, all accounts are added together and the total amount is insured up to $100,000.

The National Credit Union Administration (NCUA) protects customer accounts up to $100,000 per depositor in federally chartered credit unions.

"It's important," said Kim, "to look for the FDIC, SAIF, or NCUA symbols on the window, the entrance door, and the publications of the financial institution with which you're interested in dealing. If you see the symbol, you know your money is insured."

A Student Activity

1. In the past, what was the main difference between commercial banks and savings and loan associations? *Commercial offers many services. S&L only offer saving & loans*

2. At the present time, can Mark open an account at a credit union? Give a reason for your answer.

3. Identify the following:
   a. FDIC *Federal Deposit Insurance Corp.*
   b. SAIF *Savings Ass. Insurance fund*
   c. NCUA *National Credit Union Administration*

How to Open a Checking Account

Mark checked out several institutions around Antwan's Auto Parts, where he works, before deciding to open an account at National Bank. Ms. Keisha Reed, a bank officer there, had been very helpful. She pointed out several services that appealed to Mark.

Initial Deposit

"If you agree, let's open the account. You do have money with you?" Ms. Reed smiled.

Mark quickly got out his wallet and pulled out $100, which left about $50 in his pocket. "How much do I need?" he asked.

"That's sufficient for an initial deposit," said Ms. Reed. "Usually $50 to $100 is enough to open a checking account. You don't want to put all your cash into the account; yet you want enough in your account to cover the checks you plan to write. On the other hand, there are times when you'll want to pay cash instead of writing a check."

Mark explained that he gets his paycheck every Friday. He would deposit more on the following Friday.

Signature Card

Ms. Reed pulled out a signature card and filled it out for Mark. A **signature card** is verification of the ownership of an account. It is signed by those who have the privilege of using the bank account. Some banking institutions will not permit a minor to sign the signature card unless it is signed jointly by a parent or guardian. Examine Mark's signature card in Figure 2-1 as Ms. Reed explains the items on the card.

ACCOUNT NUMBER	TYPE OF ACCOUNT		
04452294	☐ JOINT ☑ INDIVIDUAL	☐ NOW ☐ SUPER NOW	☑ REGULAR ☐ ECONOMY PLAN

We, the undersigned, hereby open an account with National Bank, and do authorize, empower, and direct the said bank to open an account with us in the name set forth below, and we hereby agree and notify said Bank that each or either of us, or the survivor of either of us, the undersigned, may, at any and all times, endorse and deposit to the credit of said account any check, draft or other voucher payable to the order of each or either of us and draw and receive from said Bank the whole or any part of said money now deposited, or which may hereafter be deposited to the credit of said account. Checks, drafts, and other items drawn on this office of this bank not paid for any reason as of close of business day on which they have been deposited may be charged back to the customer. This bank will act only as the agent of the customer from which it receives such items, and will assume no responsibility or liability except for its own negligence, nor will it assume any responsibility or liability for any items lost in the mail.

SIGNATURE			
Mark L. Smith			

SIGNATURE			

HOME ADDRESS		HOME PHONE	BUSINESS PHONE
1040 Peachtree Atlanta GA 30319-1396		555-1254	555-8763
EMPLOYER		OCCUPATION	
Antwan's Auto Parts		Salesperson	
EMPLOYER'S ADDRESS	30317-6247	SOCIAL SEC. NO.	DATE
7890 Makeshift Drive Atlanta GA		636-00-4854	11/29/--
ACCEPTED BY			
Keisha Mae Reed			

Figure 2-1

Mark's Signature Card for a Checking Account

Account Number

Ms. Reed asked Mark to notice the space for the account number. Mark's **account number** identifies his specific bank account. His account number is 04452294. The same number will be printed on the bottom of all Mark's checks. Ms. Reed said that Mark's checks will be contained in a checkbook and will be mailed to him as soon as the checks are printed.

Mark's account number will be printed after a bank number. The numbers at the bottom of his checks will look like this: 025000779:04452294. When he is asked for his account number, he'll give only the second set of numbers: 04452294.

B Student Activity

Read the following paragraph that was copied from Mark's signature card (Figure 2-1). Answer true or false to the statements below.

We, the undersigned, hereby open an account with National Bank, and do authorize, empower, and direct the said bank to open an account with us in the name set forth below, and we hereby agree and notify said Bank that each or either of us, or the survivor of either of us, the undersigned, may, at any and all times, endorse and deposit to the credit of said account any check, draft or other voucher payable to the order of each or either of us and draw and receive from said Bank the whole or any part of said money now deposited, or which may hereafter be deposited to the credit of said account. Checks, drafts, and other items drawn on this office of this bank not paid for any reason as of close of business day on which they have been deposited may be charged back to the customer. This bank will act only as the agent of the customer from which it receives such items, and will assume no responsibility or liability except for its own negligence, nor will it assume any responsibility or liability for any items lost in the mail.

T 1. If Mark opens an account with someone else, his co-signer can write a check on the account by simply signing his or her name to the check.

T 2. The bank can charge Mark for checks he writes that exceed the amount he has in the bank.

F 3. The bank agrees to sue a customer who owes Mark money.

F 4. The bank assumes responsibility for checks Mark puts in the mail.

T 5. The bank accepts responsibility for any errors the bank makes regarding Mark's account.

Individual and Joint Accounts

Ms. Reed pointed out that Mark's signature card lists either an individual account or a joint account. She explained that an **individual account** has only one holder. If Mark opens an individual account, he is the only one who can make withdrawals from the account.

A **joint account** is held between two or more individuals and grants each person who signs the signature card all the rights and privileges attached to the account. Ms. Reed said she and her husband have a joint account, which means that each of them can make withdrawals, without the other's knowledge or permission, at any time.

Ms. Reed said the names on her joint account are recorded as follows:

Keisha Mae Reed *or*
Dontae C. Reed

She said that she or her husband may withdraw money or make deposits to the account without the signature of the other. However, if the names on a joint account are connected by the word *and,* both signatures are required for any withdrawals. For example:

Keisha Mae Reed *and*
Dontae C. Reed

Ms. Reed said that the signature card usually lists the types of accounts available: regular, and various types of interest-bearing accounts. Mark wanted a regular account. Most interest-bearing accounts require a large balance to be kept in the account at all times. Mark can't afford to do this at the present time.

C Student Activity

1. Explain the difference between an individual account and a joint account. Individual has one holder and a joint is held between 2 or more individuals and grants ea. person who signs rights

2. Explain the significance of recording signatures on a joint account as follows: Keisha Mae Reed *or* Dontae C. Reed
   Either signature needed.

   Keisha Mae Reed *and* Dontae C. Reed
   Both signature needed

3. The numbers printed on the bottom of Mark's checks are: 025000779:04452294. What is his account number?
   04452294

4. Can anyone open a checking account if he or she has enough money for an initial deposit? Yes

5. Give a reason for your answer to Question 4.

How to Keep Accurate Records

Ms. Reed explained that a **checkbook** contains checks that are used for making payments in place of cash. The National Bank will process each of Mark's checks and subtract the amount from his checking account.

"You should keep an accurate record of how much money is in your account," Ms. Reed said. "Accurate records are important because you are charged a fee if you have insufficient funds in your account to cover your withdrawal. Your checkbook can also be an effective way of keeping records of your expenditures for other reasons, such as budgeting."

Ms. Reed showed Mark some samples of checkbooks. There was quite a variety. Some had illustrations or designs on the checks. "The more elaborate checks cost more," Ms. Reed said.

Mark noticed that some checkbooks have check stubs for keeping records. The **check stub** is attached to each check. It is used for recording the balance of the account, the amount of each check written, to whom the check is written, deposits made to the account, the date, and any charges made by the bank. Figure 2-2 is an example of a check and check stub.

Figure 2-2

Check Stub and Check

Ms. Reed showed Mark another type of checkbook that has a check register. She said the **check register** is a separate form that has space to keep track of the amount of each check, the check number, the balance, deposits to the account, date of the transaction, and description of the transaction. Mark chose to use the check register style. Figure 2-3 shows a blank page from Mark's check register.

Figure 2-3

Mark's Check Register

NUMBER	DATE	DESCRIPTION OF TRANSACTION	AMOUNT OF PAYMENT	✓	AMOUNT OF DEPOSIT	BALANCE FORWARD	
		TO					
		FOR				Bal.	
		TO					
		FOR				Bal.	
		TO					
		FOR				Bal.	
		TO					
		FOR				Bal.	
		TO					
		FOR				Bal.	
		TO					
		FOR				Bal.	

Check registers vary in format, but they usually contain the same basic columns. Use the *Amount of Deposit* column to record any money added to the account. Use the *Amount of Payment* column to record any money deducted from the account. You can use the ✓ column when you balance your bank statement, which will be discussed later in this chapter.

Service Charges

Kim explained to Mark that there are service charges for having a checking account. A **service charge** is a fee charged by the financial institution for services provided to the customer. Kim told Mark to check out service charges when comparing financial institutions.

One common service charge is for returning canceled checks. **Canceled checks** are a customer's checks that the bank has processed and deducted from the customer's account. Ms. Reed said that National Bank, like many other banks, no longer returns canceled checks unless the customer asks for them. "This cuts down on the service charge," she said. "However, National Bank does mail a *copy* of all canceled checks with the bank statement each month."

Mark decided that he wanted a photocopy of his canceled checks so he could file the record in his Financial file in his new filing system. The filing system was beginning to make sense!

Personalized Checks

Mark chose personalized checks with his name and address printed on them. He used his parents' home address since he didn't have a permanent residence yet. Kim had cautioned him not to put his home phone number on his checks, although some people do this. Kim said she didn't like to have that much personal information on her checks. "Never have your social security number printed on your checks," she added.

Ms. Reed gave Mark a few bank checks to use until his personalized checks arrived in the mail. She said he would find it easier to cash his personalized checks, and they provided better records because they were numbered. But she realized he might need a check before he received his own.

When Mark's personalized checks arrived in the mail, he noticed several identification numbers. One of Mark's blank checks is shown in Figure 2-4.

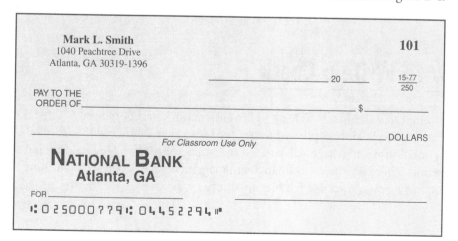

Figure 2-4

Mark's Check

On the right side of each check is a number that identifies the bank on which it is drawn. The American Bankers Association (ABA) assigns a number to each commercial bank in the country. On Figure 2-4 you can see this ABA number, 15-77/250, on the right side of the check. The numbers above the line indicate the city or state in which the bank is located and the bank's individual number. The number below the line is a Federal Reserve number, used in routing checks through the system.

The numbers at the bottom of the check identify the bank and Mark's account number. These numbers are printed with magnetic ink so the checks can be processed electronically. The check number (#101, #102, etc.) is located in the upper-right corner of the check.

Student Activity

Write the word(s) that correctly completes each definition given below.

1. In one style of checkbook, a **check stub** is attached to each check and is used for recording the balance of the account, the amount of each check written, deposits made to the account, and any charges made by the bank.

2. A **check register** is a separate form for recording the same information as listed in Question 1.

3. A **service charge** is a fee charged by the financial institution for services provided to the customer.

4. **Cancelled checks** are checks that the financial institution has processed and deducted from the customer's account.

How to Write a Check

Mark wanted to write his first check to his father. Mark had borrowed $20 from his father last week. He was pleased to be able to repay his father with a check. It was a small thing, maybe, but Mark felt in control of his life. He knew he had only begun. There was more to financial management than opening a checking account. But it was a start. He felt like an adult.

Completing the Check Register

Mark remembered Ms. Reed cautioning him to fill out his check register either before or immediately after writing a check. The time taken to record the transaction would prevent him from forgetting to whom and for what amount he had written the check.

Mark did just that. He was careful to record the date, the number of the check, the name of the person being paid, a description of the transaction, the amount of payment, and the balance after deducting the amount of the check. The **balance** is the amount of money on deposit in the account at that time. Every time Mark writes a check, he must deduct the check amount from the previous balance in order to calculate the new balance. Mark had $100 in his account before he wrote the $20 check to his father.

Writing the Check

Before writing his first check to his dad, Mark went over the following procedure with Kim:

1. Using a pen, write in the date. Include the month, day, and year.

2. After *Pay to the Order of,* write the name of the *payee* (the person or business being paid). There is no need to use titles, such as Ms., Mr., or Dr.

3. Write the amount of the check in numbers. Cents should be written as a fraction of 100. For example, write 33 cents as 33/100. If there are no cents, write 00/100. Begin the amount close to the dollar sign ($). That way, no one can change the amount by adding another number just after the dollar sign.

4. Write the amount in words, except for the cents. Again, write the cents as a fraction. Start writing at the beginning of the amount line so there is no extra space before the written amount. Draw a wavy line after the written amount to the word *Dollars*. You do not want to leave room for someone to change the amount.

5. You can use the line marked *For* to make a note about the purpose of the check transaction. You don't have to fill in the purpose, but it helps when recording expenditures in your budget.

6. Sign your name in the same way it appears on your signature card.

Kim mentioned a few precautionary measures.

- Never write checks in pencil or with an erasable ink pen.

- If you make a mistake, write the word VOID across the check and the entry in the check register. (The word VOID means "not valid.") Begin a new check. Don't try to correct your error on the original check.

- In general, do not write checks for *Cash*. If you lose the check, anyone can cash it. A check written for *Cash* is the same as cash money.

Student Activity

Mark owes his father $20. Now that he has the money, he wants to pay it back.

1. Remove the checkbook from your simulation envelope. Record in the check register the initial $100.00 deposit Mark made to open his checking account on November 29, 20--.

2. Record the necessary information in the check register for Check 101 for $20.00 to Mark's father, Michael Smith. The date is December 3, 20--. Write *Entertainment* as the description, since Mark used the money to go out with his friends. Calculate the new balance in Mark's checking account.

3. Write Check 101.

4. Tear out Check 101. Mark will be giving this check to his father, so file it in the Outgoing File envelope in your packet. Mark will receive this check with his bank statement at the end of the month.

Compare your check register and completed check with Mark's check register and check shown in Figures 2-5 and 2-6.

Figure 2-5

Transactions Recorded in Mark's Check Register

NUMBER	DATE	DESCRIPTION OF TRANSACTION	AMOUNT OF PAYMENT	✓	AMOUNT OF DEPOSIT	BALANCE FORWARD	
	20-- 11/29	TO FOR *Initial cash deposit*			100 00	Bal. 100	00
		TO *Michael Smith*				20	00
101	12/3	FOR *Entertainment*	20 00			Bal. 80	00
		TO FOR				Bal.	
		TO FOR				Bal.	
		TO FOR				Bal.	
		TO FOR				Bal.	

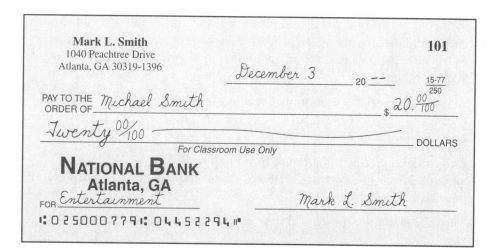

Figure 2-6

Mark's Completed Check

How to Deposit Money in a Checking Account

Mark plans to deposit $240.01 of his paycheck every week in his checking account and keep $85 in cash. When depositing money, you must fill out a deposit slip. A **deposit slip** is a form to be completed when you deposit money in your account. Personalized deposit slips are included in the back of checkbooks. They are preprinted with the customer's name, address, and account number. Mark learned that the bank had extra deposit slips if he forgot his checkbook, but he preferred his personalized slips. A copy of Mark's personalized deposit slip is shown in Figure 2-7.

Figure 2-7

Mark's Deposit Slip

When you make a deposit, complete a deposit slip as follows:

1. Write the date, using the current month, day, and year.

2. Write the total value of any cash you're depositing. Cash includes bills and coins.

3. Write the bank's number (the number above the line on the right side of the check) and the amount of each check you're depositing. Use a separate line for each check. Usually, there are more lines on the back of the deposit slip if you need them.

4. Add the cash and check amounts to get the *Total.* If you are depositing only checks and want some cash back, write the amount you want in cash on the *Less Cash Received* line.

5. Deduct the *Cash Received* amount from the *Total* to get the *Net Deposit* amount. This is the amount that the bank will add to your checking account balance.

6. Enter the amount of the deposit in your check register and calculate your new balance.

When you make a deposit, you should always get a receipt. At Mark's bank, the bank teller stamps a duplicate copy of the deposit slip and returns it to the depositor. You should keep these receipts as proof of your deposits.

How to Endorse a Check

When you cash or deposit a check made out to you, you must **endorse** the check. To endorse a check, sign your name on the back. An endorsement consisting of just a signature is called a **blank endorsement**. When Mark endorsed his payroll check, he used a blank endorsement, as shown in Figure 2-8.

Figure 2-8

Mark's Blank Endorsement of His Payroll Check

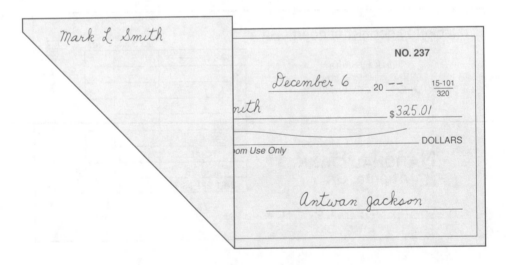

Always sign your name at the top left end of the back of the check. Never endorse a check until you are ready to cash or deposit it. Some banks require you to add your account number below your endorsement. A blank endorsement is the most common form of endorsement.

Payroll checks come in the form of a voucher check. A **voucher check** is a check divided into two parts by a perforation. One part is your payroll check, which you can cash or deposit just like a personal check. The other part is your voucher, or pay statement. The pay statement serves as a record of your pay and all deductions. (You will learn more about deductions from pay in Chapter 3.)

Student Activity

Mark deposited his payroll checks and wrote more checks in December.

1. Remove Mark's payroll check (Form 2-1) from the Source Documents section of this *Instructions and Source Documents Booklet*. Cut along the dotted line to detach the pay statement from the check. Then file the pay statement in the Financial (green) file labeled *Income Records.* Endorse the check for Mark, using a blank endorsement.

2. On December 6, 20--, Mark wanted to deposit $240.01 of his $325.01 payroll check and receive $85.00 in cash. Remove a deposit slip from the back of the checkbook and fill out the deposit slip for Mark. Enter the deposit in the check register in the front of Mark's checkbook and calculate the new balance for Mark's checking account. File Mark's paycheck and deposit slip in the Outgoing File.

3. On December 8, 20--, Mark bought a Christmas present for his parents. He found a toaster oven they wanted for $29.99 at Lacy's Department Store. With tax, the bill came to $31.78. Enter the transaction in Mark's check register and calculate the new balance. Write Check 102 to Lacy's for $31.78. After *For,* write *Gift.* File the check in the Outgoing File.

4. Record the following additional December transactions for Mark. Write the checks, complete the deposit slips, record the transactions in the check register, calculate the new balance, and file the documents as directed in Items 2 and 3 above.

   a. On December 10, Mark wrote Check 103 to Linens, Linens, Linens for $39.57 for sheets for his new apartment.

   b. On December 12, he wrote Check 104 to Service Merchandise for $22.50 for dishes. (*Note:* This transaction completes the first page of the check register.)

   c. On December 13, Mark received his payroll check (Form 2-2 in the back of this *Instructions and Source Documents*

Continued

Booklet). As he did previously, he deposited $240.01 of his $325.01 payroll check and received $85.00 in cash. Detach the pay statement and file it in the *Income Records* file. Endorse Mark's paycheck and prepare the checking account deposit slip.

d. On December 14, he wrote Check 105 to HalMart for $43.28 for clothes.

e. On December 19, Mark wrote Check 106 to Lacy's Department Store for $45.75 for Christmas gifts for his sisters.

f. On December 20, Mark received his payroll check (Form 2-3 in the back of this *Instructions and Source Documents Booklet)*. He deposited $240.01 of the amount and received $85.00 in cash. Detach the pay statement and file it in the *Income Records* file. Endorse Mark's paycheck and prepare the checking account deposit slip.

g. On December 27, Mark received his payroll check (Form 2-4 in the back of this *Instructions and Source Documents Booklet)*. He deposited $240.01 of it and received $85.00 in cash.

h. On December 30, Mark wrote Check 107 to Service Merchandise for $59.10 for small appliances for his apartment.

i. On December 31, he wrote Check 108 to Fay's Drugstore for $15.21 for personal items. This transaction completes the second page of the check register. Record the ending balance in the Balance Forward block on the next page.

How to Interpret and Reconcile a Bank Statement

Just as Ms. Reed promised, Mark received his bank statement at the end of December. The **bank statement** is a record of all deposits, withdrawals, and service charges for your checking account since the last statement. It is also a record of your balance (cash on deposit in your account) at the time the statement was prepared. Mark's bank statement, dated December 26, is shown in Figure 2-9.

Figure 2-9

Mark's Bank Statement

NATIONAL BANK
Atlanta, GA

STATEMENT OF ACCOUNT

Mark L. Smith
1040 Peachtree Drive
Atlanta, GA 30319-1396

ACCOUNT NUMBER	04452294
STATEMENT DATE	Dec. 26, 20--

BALANCE LAST STATEMENT	TOTAL AMOUNT WITHDRAWALS	NO. OF WITHDRAWALS	NO. OF DEPOSITS	TOTAL AMOUNT DEPOSITS	SERVICE CHARGE	BALANCE THIS STATEMENT
0.00	202.88	6	4	820.03	4.00	613.15

CHECK	AMOUNT	DEPOSITS	DATE	BALANCE
		100.00	11/29	100.00
101	20.00		12/05	80.00
		240.01	12/06	320.01
102	31.78		12/10	288.23
103	39.57		12/12	248.66
		240.01	12/13	488.67
104	22.50		12/16	466.17
105	43.28		12/17	422.89
		240.01	12/20	662.90
106	45.75		12/23	617.15
	4.00 SC		12/26	613.15

SC – SERVICE CHARGE
CC – CHECK CHARGE
MC – MISCELLANEOUS CHARGE
RT – RETURNED CHECK
ATD – AUTOMATED TELLER DEPOSIT
ATW – AUTOMATED TELLER WITHDRAWAL

Interpreting a Bank Statement

Notice that Mark's bank statement lists the checks by number and amount. His bank statement also shows the deposits made and the service charge for the month. The date column on the bank statement indicates when the bank paid the checks, recorded the deposits, and added any service charges.

Mark examined his check register to see if his checkbook balance agreed with the bank statement balance. He also wanted to make sure that all his deposits had been added to his account and all the checks he had written had been processed. Checks written but not yet processed by the bank are called **outstanding checks**.

Mark determined which checks were outstanding by comparing the canceled checks (returned with the bank statement) with his check register. He placed a checkmark in the ✓ column of the check register next to each check that the bank had processed. Any checks not checked off were outstanding.

Mark also placed a checkmark in the ✓ column of the check register next to each deposit that appeared on the bank statement. Any deposits not checked off were probably made after the date of the bank statement.

Figure 2-10 shows the check register completed by Mark. When he compared his check register with his bank statement (Figure 2-9), the two did not agree.

Figure 2-10

Check Register
Completed by Mark

NUMBER	DATE	DESCRIPTION OF TRANSACTION	AMOUNT OF PAYMENT		✓	AMOUNT OF DEPOSIT		BALANCE FORWARD	
	20-- 11/29	TO FOR Initial cash deposit			✓	100	00	Bal. 100	00
101	12/3	TO Michael Smith FOR Entertainment	20	00	✓			20 00 Bal. 80	00
	12/6	TO FOR Deposit paycheck			✓	240	01	240 01 Bal. 320	01
102	12/8	TO Lacy's Depart. Store FOR Parents' Christmas gift	31	78	✓			31 78 Bal. 288	23
103	12/10	TO Linens, Linens, Linens FOR Sheets for apartment	39	57	✓			39 57 Bal. 248	66
104	12/12	TO Service Merchandise FOR Dishes for apartment	22	50	✓			22 50 Bal. 226	16

	12/13	TO FOR Deposit paycheck			✓	240	01	240 01 Bal. 466	17
105	12/14	TO WalMart FOR Clothes	43	28	✓			43 28 Bal. 422	89
	12/27	TO FOR Deposit paycheck				240	01	240 01 Bal. 662	90
107	12/30	TO Service Merchandise FOR Appliances for apt.	59	10				59 10 Bal. 603	80
108	12/31	TO Fay's Drugstore FOR Personal items	15	21				15 21 Bal. 588	59
		TO FOR						Bal.	
		TO FOR						Bal.	

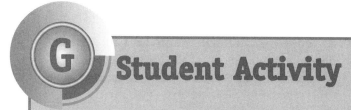

Student Activity

Determine why Mark's check register balance does not agree with his bank statement balance. Answer the following questions.

1. Has Mark forgotten to record any checks in his check register?
   If so, what check number and amount? <u>Check 106   45.75</u>

2. What is the amount of the bank service charge that Mark has not yet deducted? $ <u>4.00</u>

3. According to the records, are there any outstanding checks?
   If so, what check numbers and amounts? <u>107, $59.10</u>
   <u>and   108, $5.21</u>

4. Has Mark forgotten to record any deposits in his check register? <u>yes</u>
   If so, what date and amount? <u>12/20   240.01</u>

5. Were there any deposits that do not appear on the bank statement? <u>yes</u>
   If so, what date and amount? <u>12/27   240.01</u>

6. What is the balance shown on the bank statement? <u>613.15</u>

7. What is the balance shown in Mark's check register? <u>588.59</u>

Reconciling a Bank Statement

Once Mark discovered that his checkbook balance did not match the balance on the bank statement, he completed the reconciliation statement form on the back of his bank statement. Figure 2-11 is a copy of Mark's completed reconciliation statement. (The word "reconcile" means "to settle.")

After Mark completed the reconciliation statement, he corrected his check register. He recorded the check and deposit he had forgotten to enter. Then he entered the service charge and calculated the new balance. He recorded these corrections as shown in Figure 2-12.

When Mark told Kim about his first errors in his check register, Kim said she had a story of her own. When she first opened a checking account, she felt so independent. She wrote several checks that same day.

"Somehow I got the strange notion that I had as much money in the bank as I had checks. It looked simple. Need money—write a check," she laughed.

It wasn't long before Kim received an overdraft notice from her bank. Writing checks for more money than you have on deposit is called **overdrafting** or **overdrawing**. She was $85 overdrawn on her account, which meant she had written checks for $85 more than she had in her account. The bank charged her $25 for every check that "bounced."

If you do not keep an accurate record of each check, deposit, and service charge, you can easily overdraw your account. Both the financial institution and the business to which you write the check will probably charge you a large fee for a check not covered by sufficient funds. In fact, **Insufficient Funds (ISF)** is the bank's name for a "rubber" check.

Figure 2-11

Mark's Reconciliation Statement

YOU CAN EASILY
BALANCE YOUR CHECKBOOK
BY FOLLOWING THIS PROCEDURE

FILL IN THE FOLLOWING AMOUNTS FROM YOUR CHECKBOOK AND BANK STATEMENT.

BALANCE SHOWN ON BANK STATEMENT	$ 613.15	BALANCE SHOWN IN YOUR CHECKBOOK	$ 588.59
ADD DEPOSITS NOT ON STATEMENT	$ 240.01	ADD ANY DEPOSITS NOT ALREADY ENTERED IN CHECKBOOK	$ 240.01
TOTAL	$ 853.16	TOTAL	$ 828.60

SUBTRACT CHECKS ISSUED BUT NOT ON STATEMENT

NO.	AMOUNT
107	$ 59.10
108	15.21

SUBTRACT CHECKS, SERVICE CHARGES AND OTHER BANK CHARGES NOT IN CHECKBOOK

ITEM	AMOUNT
Ck 106	$ 45.75
SC	4.00

TOTAL	$ 74.31	TOTAL	$ 49.75
BALANCE	$ 778.85	BALANCE	$ 778.85

THESE TOTALS REPRESENT THE CORRECT AMOUNT OF MONEY YOU HAVE IN THE BANK AND SHOULD AGREE. DIFFERENCES, IF ANY, SHOULD BE REPORTED TO THE BANK WITHIN TEN DAYS AFTER THE RECEIPT OF YOUR STATEMENT.

NUMBER	DATE	DESCRIPTION OF TRANSACTION	AMOUNT OF PAYMENT	✓	AMOUNT OF DEPOSIT	BALANCE FORWARD
	12/27	FOR Deposit paycheck			240 01	Bal. 662 90
107	12/30	TO Service Merchandise / FOR Appliances for apt.	59 10			59 10 / Bal. 603 80
108	12/31	TO Fay's Drugstore / FOR Personal items	15 21			15 21 / Bal. 588 59
106	12/19	TO Lacy's Depart. Store / FOR Sisters' Christmas gifts	45 75	✓		45 75 / Bal. 542 84
	12/20	TO / FOR Deposit paycheck		✓	240 01	240 01 / Bal. 782 85

NUMBER	DATE	DESCRIPTION OF TRANSACTION	AMOUNT OF PAYMENT	✓	AMOUNT OF DEPOSIT	BALANCE FORWARD 782 85
	12/31	TO / FOR Service charge	4 00	✓		4 00 / Bal. 778 85
		TO / FOR				Bal.

Figure 2-12

Mark's Corrected Check Register

Student Activity

1. Fill in the blanks with the correct term(s).
   a. A(n) **overdraft** occurs when the amount withdrawn from an account exceeds the account balance.
   b. **endorse** means to sign your name on the back of a check.
   c. **Outstanding Checks** are checks written but not yet processed by the bank.
   d. A(n) **Bank Statement** is the bank's record of all deposits, withdrawals, and service charges for your checking account.
   e. A(n) **deposit slip** is a form used for depositing money in a checking account.
   f. A(n) **check register** is a form that helps customers balance their checkbook record with their bank statement.

2. Remove the canceled checks (Form 2-5) from the back of this *Instructions and Source Documents Booklet*. Compare the canceled checks with the check register you prepared for Mark. Place a checkmark in the ✓ column next to each check that has been processed and returned. Any checks without a checkmark are outstanding. File Mark's copy of his canceled checks in the Financial file *Checking Account—Canceled Check Records*.

3. Compare your check register with the bank statement in Figure 2-9. Place a checkmark in the ✓ column next to each deposit the bank added to Mark's account.

4. Record the service charge in the check register and calculate the new balance. Your checkbook balance at the end of December should be $778.85.

On Your Own *For Life*

1. Contact (or visit) two financial institutions in your community to find out about the kinds of checking account services offered and the cost of these services. Prepare a comparative chart of the services offered by each financial institution.

2. As you gather information from financial institutions on checking accounts, file it in the Financial (green) file labeled *Checking Account*.

Check Up

Having completed the Student Activities in this chapter, you should have mastered the skills listed below. Put a checkmark next to the skills you have mastered. If you aren't sure of a skill, review that section of the chapter.

☐ How to compare banking services

☐ How to open a checking account

☐ How to keep accurate checking account records

☐ How to write a check

☐ How to deposit money in a checking account

☐ How to endorse a check

☐ How to interpret and reconcile a bank statement

Now that you have mastered the skills listed above, move on to Chapter 3, *Setting Up a Budget.*

3 Chapter

SETTING UP A BUDGET

PHOTO: © GETTY IMAGES/
PHOTODISC

Mark could not have been more excited about his new checking account. However, time was closing in on him. He had to move out of his family's home as soon as he could find a place to live.

He knew he couldn't depend on his parents for financial resources any longer. He would have to make it on his own. First, that meant finding an apartment, and he didn't know what kind of apartment he could afford. He went to his trusty friend, Kim, for advice.

"We need to prepare a budget for you," Kim said. "Otherwise you could be in big financial trouble in a very short time. A **budget** is a plan that matches your estimated income with your estimated expenditures. It's always a good idea to prepare a budget before you make any kind of major change in your finances. Your budget helps in decision making," she said.

To explain what she meant, Kim told Mark that she wanted a new car last spring. She was tired of all the repairs on her old car. She also wanted to move to a new apartment in time for summer. She wanted one with a swimming pool. Finally, she really wanted to begin a college program in the fall. She knew there was little chance of advancement in her present job without some community college courses.

Kim knew she couldn't afford to reach all three goals by the summer. In fact, after she completed her budget estimates, she discovered she could afford only one. She decided to enroll in the college classes. She figured that the classes, and eventually a post-secondary degree, would benefit her most in the long run.

"So you see, goals have a lot to do with why and how you set up your budget," Kim said. "My goals happened to be optional. In your case, you have to become financially independent of your parents. Whether our goals are optional or not, we should always clarify goals for ourselves before setting up a budget. Our goals help us decide how to spend and save our money."

How to Determine Budget Goals

Kim explained that most goals fall into three categories:

1. **Short-term goals**: These goals involve immediate needs or desires, such as the ability to pay for food, car repairs, medical emergencies, and apartment rent.

2. **Medium-range goals**: These are goals you hope to achieve within the next few years, such as a college education, a big vacation, a new home, home improvements, or a car. To reach these goals, you will need to save now to pay for future expenses.

3. **Long-range goals**: These are goals you hope to achieve in five, ten, or more years from now. For most people, these goals mean building substantial savings for a comfortable retirement, a change in career, or a change in lifestyle.

Kim suggested that Mark write down his goals and keep them for future reference. "Writing down your goals and keeping them on file is a great motivator for keeping a budget," said Kim. "It can also be a source of satisfaction as you go back and realize what goals you've achieved. I usually re-examine my goals at least twice a year. The process helps me think about what I really want to do and gives me reasons for saving my money. Often, I change my goals after examining my budget."

So Mark sat down and wrote his budget goals. For the moment, they were relatively simple:

1. *Short-term*: Find an affordable apartment with a reasonable deposit; be able to pay daily living expenses.

2. *Medium-range*: Save enough money to enroll in classes at City College in the fall; buy and maintain a used car.

3. *Long-range:* Marry and support a family someday.

How to Determine Net Worth

Kim pointed out that after setting goals, the next step was to determine Mark's net worth. She said to determine your net worth, you have to know how much you own (your **assets**) and how much you owe (your **liabilities**). Subtract your liabilities from your assets and you have your **net worth**.

Mark laughed. "My net worth is one big zero. 0 - 0 = 0."

"Not exactly," Kim said. "You do have a balance in your checking account, which is classified as an asset. Most people our age don't have many financial assets. That's all the more reason for us to keep to a budget so we can live within our income, plan for emergencies, and not fall into debt. If we keep to a budget and think smart, one day we'll have assets. We may not be rich, but we can be financially independent."

Kim offered her list of assets and liabilities as an example of how to determine net worth. Kim's assets and liabilities are shown in Figure 3-1. She explained that the *depreciated value* of something is the amount that someone would probably be willing to pay for it now. For example, Kim estimated that if she were to sell her old car right now, she could probably get $850 for it.

Figure 3-1

Kim's Assets and
Liabilities

Kim's Assets

$379.24	Checking account balance
4,571.98	Savings account balance
1,050.00	Cash value of life insurance policy
850.00	Depreciated value (Blue Book value) of her old car
2,000.00	Depreciated value of her apartment furnishings
500.00	Jewelry

Kim's Liabilities

$600.00	December apartment rent
550.00	Balance of loan from National Bank
135.10	Edison Electric bill
80.00	City Gas Company bill
30.00	City water and sewerage
45.00	TV cable
25.00	Internet
30.00	GA Telephone Company bill
55.00	Cell phone
100.00	Credit card bill

A Student Activity

1. Prepare Kim's Statement of Net Worth.

   a. Remove Form 3-1 from the Source Documents section in the back of this *Instructions and Source Documents Booklet*. Write *Kim Nguyen* on the line above the heading *Statement of Net Worth*.

   b. Complete the Assets section by listing the amount of each asset in the correct space. Add the column and write the total amount next to Total Assets.

   c. Complete the Liabilities section by listing the amount of each liability in the correct space. Add the column and write the total amount next to Total Liabilities.

   d. Calculate Kim's net worth by subtracting the total liabilities from the total assets. The remaining amount is Kim's net worth—the difference between what she owns and what she owes. Write the amount on the line next to Net Worth.

   e. File the completed form in the Financial (green) file labeled *Budget*.

2. On a sheet of paper or in a word-processed document, list your short-term goals (goals for this year), medium-range goals (goals for the next two to five years), and long-range goals (goals for the next five to ten years or more). File your list of goals in the Self Improvement (yellow) file labeled *Goals and Objectives*. At the end of each year, check off the goals you have accomplished. Re-evaluate the remaining goals to determine if any need to be changed or added.

How to Determine Total Monthly Income

Kim told Mark he should use his net pay or take-home pay when preparing a monthly budget. Basing a budget on gross pay is meaningless.

Gross Pay vs. Net Pay (Take-Home Pay)

Gross pay is the salary or wages earned before taxes and deductions have been withheld. **Net pay** is the amount of money you take home after taxes and other deductions have been subtracted from your gross pay. Net pay is the amount you actually have to spend. That is the reason you should base your budget on net pay.

Kim showed Mark how net pay is calculated. She used the pay statement from her payroll check, shown in Figure 3-2.

Reductions (Pre-Tax)			Taxes			Deductions (After Tax)		
Description	Current	YTD	Description	Current	YTD	Description	Current	YTD
			Fed. With. Tax	$102.40	$1024.00	Health Ins.	$27.50	$275.00
			Soc. Sec. Tax	$ 62.00	$ 620.00			
			Medicare	$ 14.50	$ 145.00			
			State With. Tax	$ 26.44	$ 264.40			

	Gross Wages	Less Reductions	=Taxable Wages	Less Taxes	Less Deductions	=Net Pay
Current	$1000.00		$1000.00	$205.34	$27.50	$767.16
Year-To-Date	$10,000.00		$10,000.00	$2053.40	$275.00	$7,671.60

Figure 3-2

Kim's Paycheck Pay Statement

Kim receives a paycheck twice a month (biweekly). As you can see, Kim's gross pay is $1,000.00 every two weeks. Certain amounts are automatically deducted from her gross pay.

Payroll Deductions

One of Kim's biweekly payroll deductions is $102.40 for federal income tax. This is known as **withholding.** It is an amount that her employer holds back, or *withholds* from each paycheck and sends to the federal government to pay Kim's income tax.

Kim's biweekly social security tax deduction is $62.00. Social security tax is known as *FICA tax* (the abbreviation for the *Federal Insurance Contributions Act).* **FICA tax** includes a tax for old-age, survivors, and disability (social security) and a tax for hospital insurance (Medicare). Kim's Medicare tax deduction is $14.50. Her biweekly state income tax deduction is $26.44. Kim's health insurance plan costs $55.00 a month, so she has $27.50 deducted per paycheck. All deductions, except Kim's health plan deduction, are required by law.

Deductions for health insurance, life insurance, dental plans, pension plans, and automatic savings are often optional, but it is a good idea to take advantage of these plans. The cost is usually much less than the cost of premiums for an individual plan. You will learn more about optional payroll deductions for health and life insurance in Chapter 8.

All the required deductions, plus Kim's health insurance deduction, total \$232.84. After the deductions of \$232.84 are withheld from Kim's gross pay of \$1,000, her net pay (take-home pay) is \$767.16, twice a month. Therefore, her total monthly net pay is \$1,534.32 (\$767.16 × 2).

Employee Payroll Tax Forms

The percentage of federal income tax withheld is based on an employee's total income, marital status, and withholding allowances. An **allowance** is a number that reduces the amount withheld for taxes, but it does not reduce the tax owed. Upon taking a job, an employee must complete a *Form W-4, Employee's Withholding Allowance Certificate.* The employee indicates the number of allowances that the employer will use to calculate the amount to withhold. Figure 3-3 shows the Form W-4 completed by Kim.

Figure 3-3

Form W-4, Employee's Withholding Allowance Certificate

Form **W-4** Department of the Treasury Internal Revenue Service

Employee's Withholding Allowance Certificate

For Privacy Act and Paperwork Reduction Act Notice, see page 2.

OMB No. 1545-0010

20 --

1 Type or print your first name and middle initial: Kim K. Last name: Nguyen

2 Your social security number: 521 00 3476

Home address (number and street or rural route): 105 Rose Boulevard

3 ☑ Single ☐ Married ☐ Married, but withhold at higher Single rate.

Note: *If married, but legally separated, or spouse is a nonresident alien, check the "Single" box.*

City or town, state, and ZIP code: Township, GA 67811-1113

4 **If your last name differs from that on your social security card, check here. You must call 1-800-772-1213 for a new card.** ☐

5 Total number of allowances you are claiming (from line **H** above **or** from the applicable worksheet on page 2) . . . 5 | 1

6 Additional amount, if any, you want withheld from each paycheck . . . 6 | \$

7 I claim exemption from withholding for 20-- , and I certify that I meet **both** of the following conditions for exemption:

- Last year I had a right to a refund of **all** Federal income tax withheld because I had **no** tax liability **and**
- This year I expect a refund of **all** Federal income tax withheld because I expect to have **no** tax liability.

If you meet both conditions, write "Exempt" here . . . 7

Under penalties of perjury, I certify that I am entitled to the number of withholding allowances claimed on this certificate, or I am entitled to claim exempt status.

Employee's signature (Form is not valid unless you sign it.) Kim K. Nguyen **Date** August 15, 20--

8 Employer's name and address (Employer: Complete lines 8 and 10 only if sending to the IRS.) | 9 Office code (optional) | 10 Employer identification number

Notice in Item #5 that Kim has the option of claiming as many allowances as is legal. Kim claimed one allowance (herself) on her Form W-4.

In January of each year, an employer is required to give copies of a *Form W-2, Wage and Tax Statement,* to each employee. Form W-2 provides a record of wages earned and lists the total amounts of federal income, state income, social security, and Medicare taxes withheld from the employee's pay that year. Keep track of your Form W-2 when you receive it from your employer at the end of the year (January). You will have to attach a copy of it to your income tax return. Kim's Form W-2 is shown in Figure 3-4.

Other Income

Some people earn income from sources other than salary. They may receive income from cutting lawns, babysitting, gifts, and tips. If you regularly receive income from sources other than your employer, you should add this income to your monthly net pay to determine total monthly income for budget purposes. At this time, Kim and Mark have income from salaries only. Therefore, Kim's total monthly net pay ($1,534.32) is her total monthly income used for budgeting.

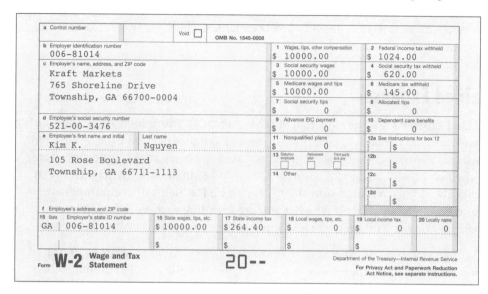

Figure 3-4

Form W-2, Wage and Tax Statement

Student Activity

Answer the following questions on payroll:

1. What is the difference between gross pay and net pay?
_____
_____

2. In Figure 3-2, what is the total amount deducted from Kim's biweekly gross pay?_____

3. What is Kim's marital status as indicated on her Form W-4, Figure 3-3?_____

4. How many allowances did Kim claim on her Form W-4? _____

5. What is a Form W-2? _____
_____

6. How often and when is a Form W-2 issued? _____
_____

7. Determine Mark's monthly net pay. Mark's weekly take-home pay is $325.01. Multiply his weekly net pay by 52 (the number of weeks in a year). The result is his yearly take-home pay. Then divide that total by 12 (the number of months in a year) to determine his net pay for one month. Mark's monthly net pay is $_____.

How to Determine Monthly Expenditures

"Once you determine your total monthly income, you should list your expenditures," Kim said. "These are your living expenses. There are two kinds of living expenses—fixed and variable."

Fixed Expenses

Fixed expenses are amounts that you have already committed to pay. You must pay expenses regularly throughout the year. Examples of fixed expenses are rent, car payments, and insurance premiums. Fixed expenses are an important factor when planning a budget. What may appear to be small monthly payments can quickly add up to a large sum. This is how a budget helps to avoid impulsive or uncontrolled buying. You *see* what you are spending each month. You know whether or not you can make a $25 monthly payment on a DVD player.

Kim's monthly fixed expenses are shown in Figure 3-5. She explained that she has an extra fixed expense due every three months. She pays her annual auto insurance premium in three equal payments, so she has extra fixed expenses in February, June, and October. She has to make financial preparations by putting extra money in her savings or checking accounts to pay her auto insurance during those three months.

"When I looked at my fixed expenses, I knew I couldn't buy a new car now," Kim said. "A car payment would be another fixed expense I can't afford."

Figure 3-5

Kim's Fixed Expenses

Expenses	Due Date	Amount
Apartment rent	1st of every month	$600
Loan payment	5th of every month	55

Variable Expenses

After you determine fixed expenses, the next step is to list all **variable expenses**. These are living expenses that may vary (or be a different amount) each month. Variable expenses include food, clothing, medical care, pet care, transportation, cleaning supplies, personal care products, utilities, savings, school tuition, and recreational activities. These expenses are more difficult to plan for because they may not be the same each month. But there are ways to do that—some of which you'll learn about in this chapter.

How to Prepare a Budget

Mark didn't have any fixed expenses and very few variable expenses while he was living at home and his parents supported him. But he knew that expenses would be very different when he moved out. One fixed expense was going to be rent for an apartment. Also, he was going to have variable expenses, such as food and utilities.

Using Kim's budget estimates of the expenditures he would face when he got his own apartment, Mark decided to prepare a monthly budget. This budget is shown in Figure 3-6.

Figure 3-6

Mark's First Budget

MONTHLY BUDGET

Income (monthly net pay)	**$1,408**
Budget Items	
Savings	$150
Food	300
Clothing	180
Laundry, Cleaning, etc.	20
Rent or Mortgage	700
Electricity	140
Heating	80
Water and Sewerage	30
Telephone/Cell Phone	60
Personal/Household	150
Transit/Auto Expense	50
Home Furnishings	100
Entertainment	200
TV Cable	55
Internet	0
Education/Self Improvement	0
Medical	80
Miscellaneous	30
Total Monthly Costs	**$**

Student Activity

1. Add Mark's estimated monthly expenses in Figure 3-6. What is the total amount he expects to spend for the month? _____

2. Subtract his estimated expenditures from his monthly net pay. Did Mark go over his budget? Explain._____
   _____

3. What is Mark's largest expenditure? _____

4. In your opinion, what figures look unrealistic? Explain. _____
   _____
   _____

5. In your opinion, can Mark support himself on $1,408 per month? Explain. _____
   _____
   _____

6. It's your turn to help Mark with his budget. How can he reduce his costs? From Figure 3-6, list the budget items you would reduce or eliminate. Then show the amounts you would include in the budget for these items.

Budget Item   **Estimated Cost Per Month**

1. _____   _____
2. _____   _____
3. _____   _____
4. _____   _____
5. _____   _____
6. _____   _____
7. _____   _____
8. _____   _____
9. _____   _____
10. _____   _____
11. _____   _____
12. _____   _____
13. _____   _____
14. _____   _____
15. _____   _____
16. _____   _____
17. _____   _____
18. _____   _____

How to Make Budget Decisions

Mark was already discouraged. He didn't know if he could get the kind of apartment he wanted on his budget. He wanted a place as nice as Kim's. It was obvious he didn't have enough money to live the way he wanted.

"So, what's new?" said Kim. "I really wanted a new car. Sometimes what we can't have immediately becomes a short-term or long-term goal. We just need to go back to our budget estimates and see what we can do to make things work. There's always a solution. Look at it this way: At least you're planning ahead on paper. You'd be in big trouble if you had signed a lease for an apartment you can't afford."

That's what Mark liked about Kim. She was so positive. Adjusting a budget requires decision making, Kim said. She suggested that Mark think about getting a roommate for the apartment and sharing the rent and expenses. That way he could have a better apartment for less.

"What about Carlos?" Kim asked. "You two were buddies in high school. I think he's already in an apartment."

Excited about the prospects of a solution, they called Carlos. He didn't sound very happy. It turned out he had been burned by another "friend" who left in the middle of the night without paying his share of the rent. Carlos was left with the entire rent for several months.

However, Carlos was willing to try again if Mark agreed to a separate lease and would sign a written contract with Carlos about other expenses. Mark was a little disappointed by Carlos's lack of trust, but Kim thought Carlos was right. She said that written agreements would protect Mark as well as Carlos. "Sometimes your friends can be your worst enemies when it comes to finances," said Kim.

Mark's adjusted rent would be $350, saving him $350 right off the top. He would also be able to eliminate the furniture rental since Carlos's apartment was fully furnished. Mark realized he had not even budgeted for the rental of furniture. However, Kim told Mark not to get too excited. Although he was certainly saving on such major items as rent, furniture, and utilities, some of the expenditures would not change that much—like food, clothing, personal and household needs, and entertainment.

Kim suggested that Mark stick to his idea of saving a certain amount each month, especially as an emergency fund, because emergencies such as health problems and unexpected repairs can use up reserves fast. Clearly, Mark's parents couldn't afford to pull him out of a crisis.

Mark revised his budget, based on his share of the apartment expenses. He also reduced the amounts he planned to spend for some budget items to bring his spending more in line with his income. His revised budget for a typical month is shown in Figure 3-7.

Figure 3-7

Mark's Revised Budget

REVISED MONTHLY BUDGET

Income (monthly net pay)	**$1,408**
Budget Items	
Savings	$150
Food	220
Clothing	70
Laundry, Cleaning, etc.	20
Rent or Mortgage	350
Electricity	70
Heating	45
Water and Sewerage	15
Telephone/Cell Phone	35
Personal/Household	100
Transit/Auto Expense	50
Home Furnishings	50
Entertainment	125
TV Cable	30
Internet	0
Education/Self Improvement	0
Medical	80
Miscellaneous	0
Total Monthly Costs	**$1,410**

With his revised budget, Mark was short of his estimated budget by only $2.00. However, some months he would get only four paychecks, instead of five, so he decided he would rather have a surplus than a shortfall. So, Mark decided to put only $100 instead of $150 in savings each month. He regretted having to cut savings because a college education was one of his goals, and he would have to pay for it on his own. Still, putting away $100 per month would add up to $1,200 a year in savings. Also, he took $10 out of Home Furnishings, figuring he could wait to purchase those items until he had the money. He could buy some of his apartment furnishings like sheets and dishes this month (December), when he didn't have to pay rent and utilities. He now had $58 to put someplace else in his budget. He added $30 to Personal/Household for a total of $130. He put the $28 in Miscellaneous. Now his budget was *balanced* (Figure 3-8). His expected costs, including savings, equaled his expected income.

Figure 3-8

Mark's Final Budget

FINAL MONTHLY BUDGET

Income (monthly net pay)	**$1,408**
Budget Items	
Savings	$100
Food	220
Clothing	70
Laundry, Cleaning, etc.	20
Rent or Mortgage	350
Electricity	70
Heating	45
Water and Sewerage	15
Telephone/Cell Phone	35
Personal/Household	130
Transit/Auto Expense	50
Home Furnishings	40
Entertainment	125
TV Cable	30
Internet	0
Education/Self Improvement	0
Medical	80
Miscellaneous	28
Total Monthly Costs	**$1,408**

Mark felt good about his budget. He thought it was realistic, and although adjusting the budget had required a lot of work, he realized Kim was right once again. "The piece of paper for your written budget doesn't cost much," she said. "Debt does."

How to Make a Budget Work

Kim said that a budget can make life easier if you keep accurate records and adjust the budget to your personal spending habits. The budget must be realistic or it won't work.

Most people stop budgeting for one of four reasons:

1. Some people try to adopt a budget for a lifestyle that doesn't apply to them. Budget record books in stores may list budget items that don't apply to you. You need to customize the categories to match your budget needs.

2. Some people get bogged down in details and try to record every penny they spend. They become discouraged because the budget takes too much time and energy.

   One way to avoid this problem is to decide ahead of time how you intend to pay for certain items—by cash or check. Then, when depositing your paycheck, take out enough cash for those purchases you intend to pay by cash until your next paycheck. Some people divide up the cash into different envelopes and label them. However, Mark will set up one cash envelope for Transit, Food, Personal/Household, and Entertainment. He will pay for all items in each category out of his cash envelope. When the envelope is empty, he shouldn't purchase any more items in those categories. Mark will need to make note of the cash spent in each category on the cash envelope, and later record the amounts in his *Financial Management Records Booklet. The single most important reason budgets fail is cash spent without a record of where it went.* So set aside the needed amount up front, and don't spend more than that amount.

3. Some people are disorganized and have difficulty keeping practical and accurate records.

   Set a specific time to record your income and expenditures. Most people don't like to record each expenditure when it occurs. You can record cash expenditures immediately or indicate on the outside of your cash envelope what the expenditure was for as you take the cash out of the envelope. Otherwise, you probably won't remember at the end of the week, certainly not at the end of two weeks or a month, where you spent the cash. An account of how you spend your cash is an important safeguard for a successful budget.

   Every payday is a good time to record income and expenditures. Another good time is at the end of the month when you are reconciling your bank statement. Use your check register as a record-keeping tool. If you use a credit card, keep your credit card receipts in a file labeled as such. Mark will keep his credit card receipts in the file labeled Credit Bank Card. Each month when he pays his credit card balance, he will record the amounts on his credit card statement next to the proper budget item in his *Records Booklet*, and will throw away the credit receipts for those expenditures. *Credit cards can be a budget problem as well.* You will learn about credit cards in Chapter 5.

Remember, you have already learned how to record your expenditures by check in your check register. Transfer those expenditures to your budget records every payday or at the end of the month.

4. Some people don't have a good filing system. You do! File away.

Write down your total monthly income, the items of your budget, and your expenditures to make the budget work for you. Mark and Kim went to an office supply store to buy a *Financial Management Records Booklet* for Mark. There were several types available, but Mark preferred the one included in your simulation envelope. Mark will keep all his budget entries in this booklet.

How to Record Income and Expenditures

Look at the sample pages from Mark's *Financial Management Records Booklet* shown in Figure 3-9.

Weekly income is recorded in the boxes at the top of the pages. Income is the *net pay* you receive from your salary, plus any other income. Notice that there are three lines in each box for income. Line 1 is for salary. Line 2 is for other kinds of income (cutting lawns, babysitting, cash gifts, tips). The third line is for recording your total income for the week. Total income is the amount in line 1 plus the amount in line 2.

Notice that there are seven blocks for recording income at the top of the two pages. You will be using the weekly blocks for Mark because he gets paid on a weekly basis. Some months have four weeks, while other months have five weeks. The seventh block provides a place for recording the total income that Mark earns in a particular month. In the middle column of that block, you will record the income Mark budgeted for the month ($1,408.00). In the last column, you will record the difference between Mark's budgeted income and his *actual* income. If his actual income is higher than the amount he budgeted, record the extra amount with a plus sign (+) in front. If his actual income falls short of his budgeted amount, place a minus sign (-) in front of the shortage.

The Expenditures chart is directly below the Income boxes. Notice the Expenditure categories on the left-hand side of the *Records Booklet*. The categories are listed in lines 3 through 20. Extra lines are provided for additional categories, if needed.

These Expenditure categories are ones frequently used in budgets. Sometimes you have to adjust the categories in financial management records booklets to fit your individual needs. This one happened to serve Mark's purposes very well. He will record his expenditures next to the appropriate categories.

The numbers at the top of the Expenditures chart indicate the day of the month. For example, if Mark spends $10.00 for lunch at the Pizza Place on the 3rd of the month, he will record $10.00 in the Food row under the number 3. All other expenditures for that day are recorded in column 3 in the proper Expenditures rows. At the end of the day (or whenever Mark records in his booklet), he will

Record of Income and Expenditures

(Left Page)

	Monthly Income			First Week		Second Week		Third Week
1	Salary			$		$		$
2	Other			$		$		$
	Total Income			$		$		$

	Expenditures	1	2	3	4	5	6	7	8	9	10	11	12	13	14	15	16
3	Savings																
4	Food																
5	Clothing																
6	Laundry, Cleaning, etc.																
7	Rent or Mortgage																
8	Electricity																
9	Heating																
10	Water and Sewerage																
11	Telephone/ Cell phone																
12	Personal/ Household																
13	Transit/ Auto Expense																
14	Home Furnishings																
15	Entertainment																
16	TV Cable																
17	Internet																
18	Education/ Self Improvement																
19	Medical																
20	Miscellaneous																
21																	
22																	
23	Total Expenditures																

(Left Page)

Month of _____

(Right Page)

	Fourth Week		Fifth Week		Income Total	Monthly Budget	Over (+) or Under (-) Budget	
1	$		$					1
2	$		$					2
	$		$					

	17	18	19	20	21	22	23	24	25	26	27	28	29	30	31	Total Spending	Monthly Budget	Over (+) or Under (-) Budget	
3																			3
4																			4
5																			5
6																			6
7																			7
8																			8
9																			9
10																			10
11																			11
12																			12
13																			13
14																			14
15																			15
16																			16
17																			17
18																			18
19																			19
20																			20
21																			21
22																			22
23																			23

(Right Page)

Figure 3-9

Mark's Financial Management Records Booklet

add the Expenditure amounts in column 3 and record the Total Expenditures for that day at the bottom of the chart on line 23.

At the far right of the Expenditures chart are three columns. The first column is for recording the total spending in each category for the month. To determine the total for a category, add all the numbers in the row. In the second column, you will record the amount Mark budgeted to spend for each category. Then you will subtract Mark's *budgeted* spending from his actual spending and record the difference in the last column. If he spent more than he budgeted, record the amount over budget with a plus (+) sign in front. If he spent less than he budgeted, place a minus sign (-) in front of the amount under budget.

For example, Mark budgeted $220.00 for food. Let's say he added his expenses in the Food row (line 4) and found he had actually spent a total of $250.00 on food that month. He records $250.00 in the Total Spending column on line 4. He records $220.00 in the Monthly Budget column on line 4. After subtracting his budgeted spending ($220.00) from his actual spending ($250.00), he records the difference (+$30.00) on line 4 of the last column. The plus sign indicates that he overspent his budget by $30.00 in that category.

At the end of the month, Mark can easily see that he needs to adjust his eating style to fit his budget, or he has to adjust his budget. He has already adjusted his budget twice and doesn't have a lot of options at this point. So, he'll probably cut back on eating out.

Note: If Mark spends money in a category more than once on the same day, he should *total* all expenditures made in that category for the day and record the total in the proper place. For example: Say that on the 5th of the month, Mark eats out twice and buys groceries. He should enter the *total* of both eating-out receipts and the receipt for groceries on line 4, column 5.

How to Form Budget Categories

Mark used the list in Figure 3-10 to determine the categories in which his expenditures belong. As you proceed through Student Activity D and the following chapters, check the list whenever you're unsure about where to record an expenditure. This list of budget categories is also printed in the front of Mark's *Financial Management Records Booklet* for quick reference.

After recording his income and expenditures for the month, Mark could compare the actual amounts spent with the amounts he budgeted.

The budget record in a *Financial Management Records Booklet* helps you see how well you are living within your budget. You can quickly determine in what categories you are overspending. If the differences are large or occur over several months, you may want to adjust your budget amount.

Figure 3-10

Budget Categories

SAVINGS/INVESTMENTS
- Money in Savings Account
- Money in 401K
- Money in Credit Union
- IRA and Other Investments

FOOD
- Groceries
- Eating Out

CLOTHING
- Clothes
- Shoes
- Accessories

LAUNDRY/CLEANING
- Laundromat
- Dry Cleaning
- Alterations, Sewing Needs, Shoe Repair

RENT OR MORTGAGE
- Apartment Rent
- Rental Insurance (furniture, belongings)
- Rent Deposit and Penalties (repairs, late fees)
- Mortgage
- Home Repairs
- Homeowner's Insurance

ELECTRICITY

HEATING

WATER AND SEWERAGE

TELEPHONE/CELL PHONE

PERSONAL /HOUSEHOLD
- Personal Care (hair cuts, makeup, toothpaste, shaving items)
- Small Household Items (cleaning supplies, light bulbs, batteries)
- Bank Fees
- Gifts

TRANSIT/AUTO EXPENSE
- Public Transportation Fares
- Car Rental
- Auto Payments
- Gasoline
- Auto Maintenance
- Auto Repairs
- License, Car Tag, Registration Fees
- Auto Insurance

HOME FURNISHINGS
- Household Items (sheets, dishes, utensils, tools)
- Appliances
- Electrical Equipment (stereo, VCR, TV)
- Furniture
- Furniture Rental

ENTERTAINMENT
- Entertainment (movies, concerts, restaurants, ball games, video rentals)
- Travel

TV CABLE

INTERNET

EDUCATION/SELF IMPROVEMENT
- School Fees and Tuition
- Books, Magazines, Newspapers
- Lessons (music, athletics, language)
- Hobbies

MEDICAL
- Medical and Dental Fees
- Medicine/Doctor Visits
- Major Medical Expense (hospital, emergency room)
- Health Insurance
- Health/Fitness Organizations

MISCELLANEOUS

Student Activity

1. Remove Mark's *Financial Management Records Booklet* from your simulation envelope. Write *December* after *Month of* to indicate that all entries on these pages are for December. Do not write anything in the Monthly Income box. Instead, record Mark's income in the weekly income boxes. One day, Mark may be paid by the month. At that time, he will use the Monthly Income box instead of the weekly boxes.

2. Using the check register that you prepared for Mark in Chapter 2, you will record the expenditures for December. In the following exercises, refer to the categories of expenditures at the front of the booklet or in Figure 3-10 as you determine the proper line on which to record each expenditure.

   a. For the expenditure in Check 101, record the amount, $20.00, in Column 3 (December 3), line 15 (Entertainment).

   b. Record Mark's December 6th weekly net pay, $325.01, in the First Week box on line 1, Salary. Record the same amount on the line for Total Income, the third line in the First Week Income box. Follow this same procedure as you record Mark's net pay each week in the proper box.

   c. Record Mark's cash expenditures under the correct categories in the same manner as you record his check expenditures. Record in the proper categories the following amounts Mark spent in cash on December 6: eating out, $20.00; taxi, $10.00; movie with friend, $25.00.

   d. Record under the proper categories the expenditures in checks 102, 103, and 104. Follow the procedures given in Step (a) above.

   e. Record Mark's $325.01 net pay from his December 13 paycheck in the Second Week income box. Record the following cash expenditures: eating out, $15.00; transit bus card, $10.00; toothpaste, etc., $5.00; concert, $30.00. Follow the procedures given in Steps (b) and (c) above.

   f. Record expenditures in checks 105 and 106.

   g. Record Mark's $325.01 net pay from his December 20 paycheck in the Third Week income box. Record the following cash expenditures: eating out, $15.00; transit bus card, $10.00; haircut, $15.00; evening with friend, $20.00.

Continued

h. Record Mark's $325.01 net pay from his December 27 paycheck in the Fourth Week income box. Record the following cash expenditures: eating out, $5.00; T-shirt, $10.00; transit bus card, $10.00; championship game, $30.00.

i. Record expenditures in checks 107 and 108.

j. Record the bank service charge of $4.00 in the proper expenditure category in the December 31st column.

3. After you have recorded all transactions for the month, total the transactions.

a. Total the expenditures in the date columns and record the total for the day at the bottom of the page on line 23, Total Expenditures.

b. Total the expenditures for each category, lines 3-20. Add all expenditures in a row and record the total in the Total Spending box for that row. Do this for each row. For example: Add all expenditures that Mark made for Food, line 4, and record the total on line 4 under Total Spending.

c. Record Mark's monthly budget for each category in the Monthly Budget column. Use his final budget, shown in Figure 3-8, page 44.

d. For each category row, subtract Mark's Monthly Budget from his Total Spending. Record the result in the Over (+) or Under (–) Budget column. If he spent more than his budget, he is over budget for that category. Write a plus sign (+) next to each over-budget amount. If he spent less that his budget, he is under budget for that category. Write a minus sign (–) in front of each under-budget amount.

e. Add the numbers in Mark's Total Spending column. Record the result at the bottom, line 23. This is the total of all of Mark's actual spending for the month. Add the numbers in his Monthly Budget column, and record the result on line 23. This is his total budgeted spending for the month. Finally, add the numbers in the Over (+) or Under (–) Budget column. This is the total amount he is over or under his budget for the month.

How to Prepare a Yearly Budget

Once you've kept a budget for a year, you may want to prepare a yearly budget so you can see the total amount you plan to spend in each category during the coming year. The yearly budget is helpful to determine your spending habits. December is a good month to plan a budget for the calendar year beginning in January.

When figuring out a yearly budget, follow these steps:

1. Determine your estimated *annual net pay*. If you get paid twice a month (biweekly), then you receive 24 paychecks per year (12 months × 2 paychecks per month). To determine your annual net pay, multiply your biweekly net pay by 24 pay periods. If you get paid weekly, multiply your weekly pay by 52 (weeks) to determine your annual net pay.

> **Example**: $ 500 (biweekly) $230.77 (weekly)
> × 24 (pay periods) × 52 (weeks)
> $12,000 (annual net pay) $12,000 (annual net pay)

2. Determine estimated annual expenditures by multiplying monthly estimated expenditures by 12 months.

> **Example**: $ 450 Monthly Rent
> × 12 Months
> $5,400 Annual Rent Expense

Figure 3-11

Food Expenses for One Year

Month	Actual Food Expense
January	$ 150
February	200
March	215
April	185
May	250
June	175
July	182
August	210
September	220
October	212
November	198
December	203
Total	$2,400

If you have kept a budget for one year, you can determine the average monthly amount spent in each category by dividing the total spent the previous year by 12 months. Determining the average amount spent is especially helpful for items that vary in cost from month to month. For example, Figure 3-11 shows monthly food expenses for a year, including groceries and restaurant food. The total amount spent was $2,400. The average amount spent on food per month was $200 ($2,400/ 12 = $200). The average can be used to determine the monthly allowance for food for the next year's budget.

How to Improve Your Budget Skills

Information about budgeting is available from a variety of sources. Visit your local library and read magazines, newspapers, and books that contain information on money management. Search the Internet for sources of budgeting advice. Consider going to a lecture or participating in a workshop on budgeting

Student Activity

1. Use the method described above to determine Mark's estimated annual net income if he makes $325.01 per week (take home). _____

   _____

2. Using Mark's final monthly budget in Figure 3-8 on page 44, determine his estimated total annual expenditures. _____

   _____

3. If the amount Mark spends on entertainment varies from month to month, how will he estimate a yearly budget for entertainment? _____

   _____

   _____

4. Explain the two steps in planning a yearly budget:

   a. _____

   _____

   b. _____

   _____

and money management. Also, consider purchasing financial management software. Many available programs provide template forms for creating budgets and keeping track of income and expenses. Because they do the arithmetic for you, these programs make money management easier.

Changes occur in your financial and personal situation as well as in the economy. You may be asked to work a number of overtime hours. You might move. You may be ill and miss work, or you may get a different job with a different salary. You will need to adjust your budget as these changes occur. Whether or not major changes occur in your life, it's a good idea to evaluate your budget at least twice a year.

Review your budget goals and your ability to meet them. Adopt reasonable goals based on your income and lifestyle. Money managers often list the following guidelines:

- Try not to pay more than 25 percent of income on housing.

- Try to save or invest at least 10 percent of your income.

- Make sure an adequate amount (normally about 25 percent of assets) is liquid. **Liquid assets** are assets that can quickly be converted to cash. For example, a savings account is a liquid asset. Real estate is not a liquid asset because you have to sell it before you have the cash in hand. This may take quite some time.

- Always establish and write down budget goals: short-term, medium-range, and long-range.

- To estimate the net income from a new job, subtract 20 percent from the proposed salary (gross income). Usually, standard deductions from a paycheck equal around 20 percent. For example, a job advertises a salary of $22,000 per year. Twenty percent of $22,000 is $4,400 ($22,000 × 0.20 = $4,400). Yearly net income would be about $17,600 ($22,000 - $4,400 = $17,600). Also, the Internal Revenue Service provides deduction charts that indicate exact deductions depending on your marital status and gross pay.

On Your Own *For Life*

Choose a job in your community for which you qualify with a high school education. Plan to support yourself totally on the income earned from the job. If you have a part-time job now, you might choose to use the salary you presently earn as a basis for an estimate for a full-time income.

Also, check the counseling office, career center, your school library, or newspaper ads for information about jobs and salary rates. Most libraries have the *Occupational Outlook Handbook*, which contains jobs and salary ranges. Or, you can find this publication online at www.bls.gov/oco. Use the Internet to find job descriptions. Try www.monster.com or www.hotjobs.com.

Prepare a budget based on the income you would receive from the job chosen. If you currently have a full-time job, base your budget on your present net income. Use the budget categories in Figure 3-10, page 49.

If you have never lived on your own before, use Mark's final budget (Figure 3-8, page 44) and his budget estimates in his *Financial Management Records Booklet* to help you estimate the costs of various items for one month. Forms 3-2 and 3-3 in the Source Documents Section of the *Instructions and Source Documents Booklet* are budget worksheets that will help you list and total your monthly estimates. Use the Budget Record (Form 3-4) in the *Instructions and Source Documents Booklet* for your monthly estimates and actual expenditure totals.

Use the following guidelines for estimating monthly costs:

- *Savings*: It's a good idea to include savings—no matter how small— in your budget from the beginning. You want to get in the habit of saving. It's wise to deposit your savings at the beginning of the month. Most people don't have money left to save if they wait until the end of the month. Some people have their employer take money out of their paycheck and automatically deposit it in their savings account so they don't spend it. Write the amount you want to save on your Budget Record (Form 3-4).

- *Food*: Using the Food worksheet (Form 3-2), make a grocery list of items you'll need for one week. (Your first week of grocery shopping will cost more than usual because you will have to buy staples for preparing meals.) Add to the grocery amount the estimated costs of eating out. Then multiply by four to estimate your monthly food expense. Write this estimate on your Budget Record.

- *Clothing*: Clothing is an item that differs from month to month. Most of us buy clothes when we can afford them or when they are on sale. You probably have a fair idea of what your clothes cost, so put down a monthly estimate. If you don't spend it, you can indicate that you are under budget (–) in the clothing category for that month. The main idea is to avoid buying clothes you can't afford. Write the monthly estimate on your Budget Record.

- *Rent or Mortgage*: Check the newspaper for apartments, furnished and unfurnished. Choose one you can afford with your net income in a neighborhood you like. Write the monthly rental cost next to Rent or Mortgage on your Budget Record. In Chapter 6, you will learn about the initial costs, such as rental deposits, for apartment rental.

- *Utilities*: If you are required to pay utilities for your apartment, write down separate estimates for each utility: heating, electricity, water and sewerage, telephone/cell phone, TV cable, and Internet access. Some apartment owners pay for water. Some pay for water, heat, and electricity. Most apartment owners don't pay for any utilities. Ask someone to help you with an estimate of the cost of monthly utilities for the apartment you select. Write the monthly estimate for utilities on your Budget Record.

- *Personal/Household*: If you aren't on your own already, pretend you will be once you get a full-time job. Using your Personal/Household worksheet (Form 3-3), make a list of your personal needs and costs. Write this estimate on your Budget Record.

- *Personal/Household*: If you aren't on your own already, pretend you will be once you get a full-time job. Using your Personal/Household worksheet (Form 3-3) from the *Instructions and Source Documents Booklet*, make a list of your personal needs and costs. Write this estimate on your Budget Record.

- *Transit/Auto Expense*: If you will be using public transportation, check the bus fares in your area. If you have a car, you'll need to add several or all of the following items to this category: car payment, gas, repairs, maintenance (oil change, tune ups, etc.) auto insurance, license fee, and taxes.

- *Home Furnishings*: Make a list of the items you'll need to furnish your own apartment. Determine the items you can borrow from friends and family. For all other furnishings, estimate a cost to buy. Consider buying used furnishings to hold costs down. Write the total cost estimate on your Budget Record.

- *Entertainment*: This category is usually the most difficult to maintain and yet the one that frequently destroys a budget. Most of the time we pay cash for entertainment, which is one of the reasons we don't have an accurate record. Putting cash into an envelope designated for "entertainment only" can help. When you run out of cash in that envelope, that's the end of entertainment until the next paycheck. Estimate your monthly entertainment costs and enter the amount on your Budget Record.

- *Medical*: Be sure you include health insurance and medical costs. Illness strikes all age groups. Lack of health coverage can have disastrous financial consequences.

- *Education/Self Improvement*: If you plan to attend post-secondary classes, find out the monthly cost from the local community college and record it on your Budget Record.

- *Miscellaneous*: Use this category to record any expected expenses that don't fit into other categories.

File your completed worksheets (Forms 3-2 and 3-3) and Budget Record (Form 3-4) in the Financial file labeled *Budget*.

Check Up

Having completed the Student Activities in this chapter, you should have mastered the skills listed below. Put a checkmark next to the skills you have mastered. If you aren't sure of a skill, review that section of the chapter.

- ☐ How to determine budget goals
- ☐ How to determine net worth
- ☐ How to determine total monthly income
- ☐ How to determine monthly expenditures
- ☐ How to prepare a budget
- ☐ How to make budget decisions
- ☐ How to make a budget work
- ☐ How to record income and expenditures
- ☐ How to form budget categories
- ☐ How to prepare a yearly budget
- ☐ How to improve your budget skills

Now that you know all about setting up a budget, move on to Chapter 4, *Opening a Savings Account and Comparing Bank Services*.

Chapter

OPENING A SAVINGS ACCOUNT AND COMPARING BANK SERVICES

PHOTO: © GETTY IMAGES/
PHOTODISC

How to Figure Simple Interest

Now that Mark had an estimated budget, he wanted to start a savings account right away. He didn't know much about savings accounts, but he knew who did.

"Before you choose a savings account and other banking services, you need to understand how interest works," Kim said. "Basically, if you deposit money in a savings account, the banking institution *pays you* interest. If you borrow money from the institution, *you pay* the institution interest. Essentially, the bank is borrowing from you when you deposit your money in a savings account," she said.

Kim gave an example. "Let's say you put $100 in savings at 3 percent interest and leave the money in savings for one year." Kim demonstrated the interest calculations on paper while defining savings account terms for Mark.

Interest—the amount of money the bank pays you for the use of your money

Principal—the amount of money deposited

Time—the number of years or months for which interest is paid

Interest Rate—the percentage of the principal paid for the use of your money

This is how you figure the interest paid on $100 at 3 percent interest for one year:

$$\textbf{Principal} \times \textbf{Rate} \times \textbf{Time} = \textbf{Interest}$$
$$\$100 \quad \times \quad .03 \quad \times \quad 1 \quad = \quad \$3$$

"How did you get .03 out of 3 percent?" Mark asked.

Kim told Mark, "When converting a percentage to a decimal, move the decimal point two places to the left and drop the percent sign." Kim showed Mark how it works on paper.

Example: 3% = 3.0%
3.0% = .03 (move decimal 2 places to left; add a zero to show place value)

If you have a fraction as part of your percentage (a mixed number), convert the fraction to a decimal first. Convert a fraction to a decimal by dividing the denominator (number below the line) of the fraction into the numerator (number above the line).

Example: $3\frac{1}{2}\%$
$\frac{1}{2} = .50$ (fraction converted to a decimal)

$$\begin{array}{r} .50 \\ 2\overline{)1.00} \\ \underline{1\ 0} \\ 0 \end{array}$$

$3\frac{1}{2}\% = 3.50\%$ or simply 3.5%
3.5% = .035 (move decimal 2 places to left; add a zero to show place value)

Most fractions related to interest are expressed in fourths or halves, so remember the following fraction conversions for convenience:

$^1/_4 = .25$
$^1/_2 = .50$
$^3/_4 = .75$

Student Activity

Convert the following percentages into decimals:

1. $3^1/_2\% = $ _____

2. $3^1/_4\% = $ _____

3. $4^1/_4\% = $ _____

4. $5\% = $ _____

5. $2^1/_2\% = $ _____

"So, you see how interest works," said Kim. "Now all you have to do is find a bank that offers you the best interest rate."

Mark figured if he left $100 in savings at 3 percent interest for one year, he would earn $3. Not much money, for sure, but he would have more money than he would if he had spent the $100.

"The big advantage to saving is just that," said Kim. "You've saved it, instead of spending it on something that you didn't really want that badly. The extra incentive is this: while you're saving it, your money is making money for you."

The idea was appealing to Mark for a lot of reasons. He really wanted an apartment of his own and a car. Also, he had been thinking about improving his prospects for a job by going to a community college in the fall.

Mark calculated what he would earn in interest if he put $200 in savings at 3 percent interest for one year:

Principal × **Rate** × **Time** = **Interest**
$200 × .03 × 1 = $6

Principal + **Interest** = **Balance in Savings**
$200 + $6 = $206

Mark was catching on. He could easily see that putting money in a savings account is far better than leaving it in a shoebox for a year. He would try to add to his savings on a regular basis—like every month—to increase the principal. The greater the principal, the more interest earned; thus, the greater the total savings.

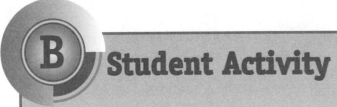

Student Activity

1. What is the formula for figuring simple interest? _____

2. In each of the following cases, find the simple interest and balance in savings.

	Interest	Balance in Savings
a. $300 for one year at 3¼% interest	_____	_____
b. $2,000 for one year at 5% interest	_____	_____
c. $400 for one year at 5½% interest	_____	_____

How to Calculate Compound Interest

If you leave the interest you earn in your saving account, you will earn interest on the interest. Interest earned on interest is called **compound interest**. For example, if Mark invests $100 in a savings account at the rate of 3 percent, by the end of one year his money will have earned $3. He can take the $3 out of savings and spend it if he wants, or he can leave it in his account. If he leaves it in his account, the principal will be increased to $103. Then he will earn interest on his total of $103.

Interest can be compounded in one of the following ways:

1. annually (every year)
2. semiannually (every six months)
3. quarterly (every three months)
4. monthly
5. daily

When interest is **compounded,** the interest is added to the principal, thus increasing the amount of the principal. The larger the principal and the more frequently interest is compounded, the greater the amount of interest earned.

For example, your principal will grow faster when interest is compounded daily rather than monthly, quarterly, semiannually, or annually. The difference between interest compounded annually and interest compounded semiannually is shown in the examples below.

Example: Interest compounded annually for two years at 3 percent annual interest rate.

First Year

Principal beginning of first year		Rate		Time		Interest first year
$100.00	×	.03	×	1	=	$3.00

Principal beginning of first year		Interest first year		Principal end of first year
$100.00	+	$3.00	=	$103.00

Second Year

Principal beginning of second year		Rate		Time		Interest second year
$103.00	×	.03	×	1	=	$3.09

Principal beginning of second year		Interest second year		Principal end of second year
$103.00	+	$3.09	=	$106.09

Example: Interest compounded semiannually for two years at 3 percent annual interest. When interest is compounded semiannually (every six months), the time is written as a fraction of twelve months (6/12) or ($^1\!/_2$). Converted to a decimal, $^1\!/_2 = .5$.

First Year—First Half

Principal beginning of first year		Rate		Time		Interest first half of first year
$100.00	×	.03	×	.5	=	$1.50

Principal beginning of first year		Interest first half of first year		Principal end of first half of first year
$100.00	+	$1.50	=	$101.50

First Year—Second Half

Principal beginning of second half of first year		Rate		Time		Interest second half of first year
$101.50	×	.03	×	.5	=	$1.52

Principal beginning of second half of first year		Interest second half of first year		Principal end of first year
$101.50	+	$1.52	=	$103.02

Second Year—First Half

Principal beginning of second year		Rate		Time		Interest first half of second year
$103.02	×	.03	×	.5	=	$1.55

Principal beginning of second year	+	Interest first half of second year	=	Principal end of first half of second year
$103.02	+	$1.55	=	$104.57

Second Year—Second Half

Principal beginning of second half of second year	×	Rate	×	Time	=	Interest second half second year
$104.57	×	.03	×	.5	=	$1.57

Principal beginning of second half of second year	+	Interest second half of second year	=	Principal end of second year
$104.57	+	$1.57	=	$106.14

 Student Activity

1. Figure the compound interest and the balance in savings at the end of each time period. *Remember*: When interest is compounded semiannually (every 6 months), time is written as a fraction of 12 months (6/12 or $^1/_2$). If interest is compounded quarterly (every three months), time is written as a fraction of 12 months (3/12 or $^1/_4$). Convert the fractions to decimals to do your calculations.

	Interest	Balance in Savings
a. $500 for three years at 3% interest compounded annually	_____	_____
b. $1,000 for one year at 4% interest compounded semiannually	_____	_____
c. $600 for two years at 5% interest compounded annually	_____	_____
d. $2,000 for one year at 3% interest compounded quarterly	_____	_____

2. Kim has a savings account that pays $5^1/_4$ percent interest, compounded annually. If her balance on January 1, 2003, is $800, and she makes no additional deposits or withdrawals, what will be her balance on January 1, 2005, assuming the interest rate stays the same? _____

_____

When Mark went to National Bank to check out savings accounts, he discovered the bank had interest tables already prepared. He didn't have to figure anything. He simply had to check the chart. However, he was glad Kim showed him how to calculate interest for himself. He would never have known how the bank came up with those figures. He certainly wouldn't have understood how compound interest could benefit him.

As he studied the interest chart, he realized that before deciding where to deposit his money, he should always check two things: the interest rate and how often interest is compounded. The interest chart Mark was studying is shown in Figure 4-1. Note that if you leave $50 in your savings account for two years, you will have a balance of $55.54 at the end of two years. The chart is based on a fixed amount in savings. If you add to your principal regularly, your savings will increase considerably each year.

Figure 4-1

Compound Interest Chart

How Savings Grow*	$50	$100	$500	$1,000	$5,000	$10,000
6 mos	51.34	102.69	513.47	1026.95	5134.75	10289.50
1 year	52.70	105.39	526.95	1053.90	5269.50	10538.00
2 years	55.54	111.07	555.35	1110.71	5553.53	11107.06
3 years	58.53	117.06	585.29	1170.57	5852.86	11705.72
4 years	61.68	123.37	616.83	1233.67	6168.33	12336.66
5 years	65.01	130.02	650.08	1300.16	6500.80	13001.81
10 years	84.52	169.04	845.21	1690.42	8452.09	16904.18
20 years	142.88	285.75	1428.76	2857.51	14287.56	28575.12

*This chart shows how given amounts grow when left in your savings account for various periods of time. Figures are projected at $5\frac{1}{4}$ percent a year, compounded daily.

Student Activity

Answer the following questions by referring to the compound interest chart in Figure 4-1.

1. What is the rate of interest used on the chart?_____

2. How often is the interest compounded?_____

3. How much will you have if you leave $500 in your savings account for three years?_____

4. How much will you have if you leave $5,000 in your savings account for one year? _____

5. How much will you earn on $10,000 in a savings account for one year as opposed to having $10,000 hidden in a shoebox for one year? _____

How to Compare Savings Accounts

Mark spotted Ms. Reed at her desk. She had been helpful before with his checking account. He decided to ask her about savings accounts offered by National Bank.

Regular Savings Account

Ms. Reed said that most young people begin with a regular savings account that provides easy access to funds. The minimum opening balance at National Bank was $100. The bank would not require Mark to pay the $4 monthly service charge if he didn't let his balance fall below $500. He could make four free withdrawals per month. Each withdrawal over four per month would cost $2 (including ATM transactions). The interest rate was $5\frac{1}{4}$ percent, compounded daily. National Bank would provide a monthly statement on the account.

Mark was relieved that Kim had explained compound interest beforehand. He actually understood everything Ms. Reed was saying about the savings account.

A **savings account** is an account from which you can easily withdraw your money without paying a penalty. However, a regular account usually pays the lowest interest rate. Ms. Reed said a savings account has the following features:

1. *Liquidity*: **Liquid assets** are assets you can quickly and easily turn into cash. All you have to do is withdraw your asset (cash) from your passbook savings account.

2. *Low minimum balance*: A small deposit is required to open a savings account. However, you may be required to keep a stated minimum balance in the account to keep it open or to avoid a service charge. The minimum balance will vary from one banking institution to another.

3. *Safety of amount deposited*: Money in a savings account is safe if commercial banks, savings and loans, and credit unions have insurance to cover deposits up to $100,000 per account. As long as your balance is below $100,000, your savings are insured and safe.

Ms. Reed explained that when you open a savings account, you receive a savings account register. She told Mark that he should use a register to record deposits, withdrawals, and interest earned on the account. National Bank provided the savings account register shown in Figure 4-2.

When you deposit or withdraw money from your account, you might want to take your savings account register with you. Most banking institutions don't require you to present your register. Still, it's a good idea to take it with you so you have your savings account number handy and you can record transactions and update your balance for each transaction.

A bank teller will record your deposit or withdrawal in the bank's computer. You will have to make the entries in the savings account register yourself. As with checking accounts, you receive an account number when you open a savings account. In case you lose your savings account register, you should have a record of this number in your Financial (green) file under the name of the account.

The form you complete to open a savings account is similar to a checking account signature card. Like the checking account, a savings account requires special forms for depositing and for withdrawing money from the account. When depositing money, you fill out a **savings deposit slip**. Savings deposit slips vary, but most are similar to the one illustrated in Figure 4-3. When withdrawing cash from the savings account, you fill out a **savings withdrawal slip** like the one shown in Figure 4-4. Notice that you should write the amount of the withdrawal as a figure and in words, as on a check.

SAVINGS ACCOUNT REGISTER

Account No: ____________

DATE	WITHDRAWALS	DEPOSITS AND INTEREST	BALANCE	

Figure 4-2

Savings Account Register

You should always get a receipt for your deposits and withdrawals. Often the receipt is a copy of the deposit slip or withdrawal slip. Keep the receipt in a folder in your Financial file. As with your checking account, you should keep your own records of deposits and withdrawals. You should not depend on the bank's recordkeeping. Banks make mistakes, too.

Savings Deposit Slip

CENTRAL BANK
Atlanta, GA

ACCOUNT NUMBER: 889299

DATE Dec. 3, 20--

DEPOSIT TO THE ACCOUNT OF:

NAME Kim Nguyen

ADDRESS 105 Rose Boulevard

CITY Township STATE GA 67811-1113

ENDORSE CHECKS PROPERLY	DOLLARS	CENTS
CURRENCY		
COIN		
CHECKS	500	00
TOTAL DEPOSIT	500	00

Figure 4-3

Kim's Completed Savings Deposit Slip

Savings Withdrawal Slip

CENTRAL BANK
Atlanta, GA

ACCOUNT NUMBER: 889299

DATE Dec. 6, 20--

NAME Kim Nguyen $ 100.00

One hundred 00/100 DOLLARS

FOR CLASSROOM USE ONLY

Kim Nguyen
SIGNED

Figure 4-4

Kim's Completed Savings Withdrawal Slip

Money Market Deposit Accounts

Mark asked Ms. Reed to tell him about other types of savings accounts. She told him about several types that he might want in the future.

A **money market deposit account (MMDA)** is another type of savings plan. When offered at a federally insured bank, the deposit is insured. A money market account usually earns higher interest than a regular savings account and offers limited check-writing ability. However, the interest rate on an MMDA is **variable**—it changes, sometimes daily.

National Bank charged a $5 service fee for an MMDA that was waived if your balance stayed at $1,000 or above. As with regular savings accounts, you could withdraw your funds from an MMDA at any time. However, money market accounts may limit the number of transactions you can make each month on the account.

Most people just beginning a life on their own rely on a regular savings account for emergency funds. It has the least restrictions, and their money is available whenever they need it. Once you build a savings buffer for emergencies, you may want to put some of your savings in an MMDA.

Certificate of Deposit

Mark learned that a **certificate of deposit (CD)** is a special type of savings account. The interest rate is higher than the rate offered on a regular savings account or an MMDA. In exchange for the higher rate, account holders agree to certain restrictions that make a CD less liquid.

When you purchase a CD, you agree to leave your money in the CD for a required length of time. The time may be six months, one year, two years, or more. Usually, the longer the time period, the higher the **yield** (interest rate). That is, a two-year CD will probably pay a higher interest rate than a six-month CD. At the end of the stated time period, the CD **matures**. At that time, you can either receive the cash earned from your CD or you can renew the CD at the rate the bank currently offers. You can renew it for the same period of time or extend or reduce the time period. However, if you withdraw money from a CD before it matures, you will have to pay a large cash penalty. Because of the penalty, you should avoid taking your money out of a CD before it matures.

A CD can be a good investment choice if you can do without the money for the required period of time. A CD is not the place to keep money for emergencies. To provide for emergencies, you should keep some money in a regular savings account or MMDA, so that you can withdraw it at any time without penalty.

A CD requires a minimum deposit. The minimum may be as small as $500 or as large as $100,000. Usually, the smaller the deposit minimum, the lower the interest rate.

When interest rates are low, you may not want to lock your money into a CD for a long period of time. The interest rate on a CD is **fixed**. This means that it does not change over the time period. Instead, when rates are low, you may want to invest in a six- or twelve-month CD instead of a three-year CD. Then, if interest rates rise, you can switch to a higher-interest CD when the short-term CD matures.

Individual Retirement Account

"I'm sure it's the last thing on your mind now, Mark, but everyone should make provisions for retirement," Ms. Reed said. "Yes, even young people like yourself."

She pointed out that social security (to be discussed in Chapter 8) provides limited income for retired people. The income from social security is not enough to live on comfortably during retirement. Frequently, places of employment offer a pension plan or some type of retirement plan that supplements social security income.

Individual Retirement Accounts (IRAs) are savings plans that offer a way to save for retirement and enjoy tax benefits. Income tax on the interest earned on an IRA is **deferred** (put off) until you withdraw the money at age $59\frac{1}{2}$ or later. By retirement age, most people have lower incomes. Therefore, they pay less income taxes than they would while fully employed. In the end, you will pay less taxes on interest earned on an IRA than on a CD or regular savings account. The present law requires you to begin to withdraw your IRA funds by age $70\frac{1}{2}$.

If you withdraw money from an IRA before age $59\frac{1}{2}$, you would have to pay income tax on the amount withdrawn that year. In addition, the **Internal Revenue Service (IRS),** which collects annual income tax, places a 10 percent penalty tax on the amount withdrawn early. Because of the costly penalty, it's best to think of money in an IRA as money not to be touched for a long time. For this reason, many young people feel they can't afford to invest in an IRA. They must use the money for more immediate needs. Mark was certainly in that category.

However, he was glad to know about IRAs for the time when he would be able to put some money aside for retirement. Ms. Reed said that any financial institution would be happy to describe its IRA savings plans when he was ready. There are a variety of plans, and there are rules for the amount a person is allowed to invest in an IRA each year. Periodically, the rules change. Mark decided that he would ask about the current regulations from a bank officer when the time came for him to save for retirement through an IRA.

Ms. Reed made one other point about saving early for retirement. She said that most young people, like Mark, decide not to save for retirement until they are "old," or at least older. "That's a mistake," she said. "True, you do need to save for emergencies first, but once you have a safe cushion, you need to force yourself to put away money for retirement."

She added, "When it comes to savings, time is really money. Remember what you learned about compound interest: Interest (money) = principal × rate × time. The earlier you start saving, the more your money will grow."

Ms. Reed then showed Mark a chart that shocked him (Figure 4-5). The chart demonstrated the power of compound interest working for you at an early age. Person One started to save $1,000 a year at age 21, saved for eight years, and then completely stopped. Person Two started saving at age 29 and saved $1,000 a year for 37 years. Both earned 10 percent on their savings.

Figure 4-5

Ms. Reed's Investment Chart

	Person One			Person Two	
Age	Contribution	Year-end Value		Contribution	Year-end Value
21	1,000	1,100		0	0
22	1,000	2,310		0	0
23	1,000	3,641		0	0
24	1,000	5,105		0	0
25	1,000	6,716		0	0
26	1,000	8,487		0	0
27	1,000	10,436		0	0
28	1,000	12,579		0	0
29	0	13,837		1,000	1,100
30	0	15,221		1,000	2,310
31	0	16,743		1,000	3,641
32	0	18,417		1,000	5,105
33	0	20,259		1,000	6,716
34	0	22,284		1,000	8,487
35	0	24,513		1,000	10,436
36	0	26,964		1,000	12,579
37	0	29,661		1,000	14,937
38	0	32,627		1,000	17,531
39	0	35,889		1,000	20,384
40	0	39,478		1,000	23,523
41	0	43,426		1,000	26,975
42	0	47,769		1,000	30,772
43	0	52,546		1,000	34,950
44	0	57,800		1,000	39,545
45	0	63,580		1,000	44,599
46	0	69,938		1,000	50,159
47	0	76,932		1,000	56,275
48	0	84,625		1,000	63,003
49	0	93,088		1,000	70,403
50	0	103,397		1,000	78,543
51	0	112,636		1,000	87,497
52	0	123,898		1,000	97,347
53	0	136,290		1,000	108,182
54	0	149,919		1,000	120,100
55	0	164,911		1,000	133,210
56	0	181,402		1,000	147,631
57	0	199,542		1,000	163,494
58	0	219,496		1,000	180,943
59	0	241,496		1,000	200,138
60	0	265,590		1,000	221,252
61	0	292,149		1,000	244,477
62	0	321,364		1,000	270,024
63	0	353,501		1,000	298,127
64	0	388,851		1,000	329,039
65	0	427,736		1,000	363,043

Total Investment [$8,000]   Total Investment [$37,000]

Total Amount Accumulated [$427,736]   Total Amount Accumulated [$363,043]

Note: This chart is based on 10 percent interest.

Student Activity

1. Define the following terms:

   a. yield _____

   b. liquidity _____

   c. fixed interest rate _____

   d. variable interest rate _____

   e. regular savings account _____

   f. certificate of deposit _____

   g. IRA _____

2. On January 3, Mark went to the bank to deposit his $325.01 weekly paycheck. While he was there, he decided to open a savings account. He deducted $100 from his paycheck to open a regular savings account. Since the minimum opening balance is $100 for this account, Mark decided to keep his savings for his emergency fund and college fund together for the present time. After studying Ms. Reed's chart in Figure 4-5, he understood the power of compound interest over a period of time. He wanted to start a savings account for retirement as soon as possible. In the near future, he planned to open an IRA account. Complete the following activities for Mark:

   a. From his $325.01 net pay, Mark deducted $100 for his savings account and $85 for his cash envelope. He then deposited the remaining $140.01 in his checking account. Record the $140.01 deposit in the check register. (*Note:* You will no longer be endorsing Mark's paychecks or completing his checking account deposit slips.)

   b. Remove a savings account deposit slip (Form 4-1) from the Source Documents section of this *Instructions and Source Documents Booklet*, and complete the form for Mark. The date is January 3, 20--. His savings account number is 5556299. Write Mark's full name: Mark L. Smith. Since he deposited cash, record $100.00 on the line labeled *Currency*. Also, write $100.00 on the Total Deposit line. File the savings account deposit slip in the Outgoing File.

   c. Mark received a savings account register when he opened his account. Remove the savings account register

Continued

Student Activity Continued

(Form 4-2) from the *Instructions and Source Documents Booklet* and complete the form for Mark. Record his savings account number, 5556299, at the top of the form. Record the date, 20-- 1/3, in the Date column. Record the amount of the deposit, $100.00, in the Deposits and Interest column and in the Balance column. File the savings account register in the Financial file labeled *Savings Account*.

3. When Mark got home, he recorded the transactions in his *Financial Management Records Booklet*. Complete these activities for Mark:

   a. Mark begins a new page in his *Records Booklet* each month. Turn to pages 4 and 5 of the *Records Booklet* and write *January* on the top line after the words *Month of*.

   b. Record the amount of Mark's take-home pay from his paycheck, $325.01, in the First Week Box.

   c. Record Mark's expenditures for January 3. Record $100.00 in savings; $10.00 for food; $10.00 for transportation; and $40.00 for entertainment. Add the expenditures for the day and record the total amount in Total Expenditures, line 23, for the day.

4. Study the chart in Figure 4-5 and answer these questions:

   a. Who accumulated more money by age 65?_____

   b. Who invested the most money in savings?_____

   c. Explain why one person accumulated a larger amount than the other while investing so much less over a 45-year period of time. _____

   _____

   _____

How to Use Electronic Banking

Mark had always known that his boss, Antwan, was a computer nut. Antwan could talk for hours about the wonders of the computer. He was always demonstrating how he used a computer to keep the financial records for Antwan's Auto Parts. He talked about how fast and accurately a computer can calculate amounts. Now, fresh from his own banking experiences, Mark was interested to learn all he could.

Electronic Funds Transfer

"Computer technology and the **electronic funds transfer (EFT) system** are gradually replacing paper-based banking procedures," Antwan said. He explained that electronic funds transfer eliminates the costly and time-consuming process of handling and processing checks, completing deposit slips, and dealing with related pieces of paper. EFT also cuts down on the time consumers spend writing checks, paying monthly bills through the mail, and waiting in line at the bank to deposit a paycheck or to withdraw cash.

Mark was suddenly upset. He had just spent the last month learning how to do all those things the electronic funds transfer system was supposed to eliminate!

As Antwan rambled on, Mark recalled Ms. Reed mentioning something about electronic banking when he opened his checking account. She said that National Bank was one of the first banks to introduce automatic transfer of funds. Bank customers give their approval for the bank to automatically pay certain bills on a regular basis for them.

Now he remembered. Instead of a customer writing a check to make a payment (such as for utilities or a car loan), the bank can automatically transfer the amount of the payment directly to the payee's account. The **payee** is the person or business to whom the payment is made. The person paying the bill and the payee sign an agreement ahead of time to approve such transactions. Ms. Reed had told Mark to keep an accurate record of the amounts deducted for these transactions. The monthly bank statement lists all automatic transactions, and he should check the list carefully.

Ms. Reed had mentioned that another popular feature of EFT is **direct deposit** of payroll checks. Some employers offer employees an option. Employees can receive a paycheck and deposit it in their bank account themselves. Or, they can have the employer deposit the money directly into their bank account for them. Direct deposit prevents the check from being lost or misplaced before being deposited, she said. It also eliminates the time between the date a check is issued and the date the employee deposits the check. Ms. Reed told Mark that if his employer deposited his check for him, then he would receive a receipt for the transaction from his employer instead of a paycheck.

Automated Teller Machine

Antwan said his favorite form of EFT (and the most common form) was the **automated teller machine (ATM).** An ATM is a computer terminal where bank customers can perform financial transactions. Ms. Reed had shown Mark the automated teller machine outside National Bank.

"The ATM may be located at the banking institution or at another location, such as a shopping center. National Bank has an ATM at the airport. Some can be used with automated teller cards from different banking institutions," said Ms. Reed.

Mark did like the convenience of the automated teller. The ATM provides services 24 hours a day, seven days a week, and every day of the year. When banks are closed, you can perform most financial transactions at an ATM that you can perform with a human teller. You can use the ATM to make deposits, withdraw cash, transfer funds between your checking and savings accounts, make loan payments, receive cash advances, pay bills, and obtain a statement of your current checking account balance. An ATM is shown in Figure 4-6.

Figure 4-6

Automated Teller Machine (ATM)

PHOTO: © GETTY IMAGES/PHOTODISC

Automated teller machines are activated by inserting a plastic ATM card that resembles a credit card. You punch your **personal identification number (PIN)** or **code (PIC)** into the computer terminal. You should choose a PIN that you can easily remember without writing it down. *Never write your PIN on your ATM card.* Do not use your birthday or social security number, since these numbers may be easily used by someone else if your wallet is lost or stolen.

When you complete a transaction using an automated teller, the machine issues a receipt verifying the transaction. Use the receipts to record the ATM transaction in your check register and to verify your monthly bank statement.

Online and Telephone Banking

Mark learned from Antwan that many financial institutions now offer banking services by phone or personal computer. Using a phone or the Internet, customers can transfer money from one account to another, check their account balances, and pay bills. Some banks even allow customers to apply for a loan online. In fact, customers can now do most of their banking without leaving home. Use of the Internet to perform banking activities is called **online banking**.

Antwan told Mark that he would need a password to access his account by phone or online. A password assures that only the account holder can make transactions on the account. Telephone and online banking would enable Mark to get the most up-to-date information on his account. Plus, he could do his banking at any time of the day or night.

Point-of-Sale Transfer

Kim told Mark about another type of EFT called **point-of-sale transfer** (**POS**). POS allows a customer to pay a retailer (seller) by using a debit card instead of a check or currency. A **debit card** activates the financial transaction in the store at the point of sale, usually the checkout counter.

"A debit card is similar to a credit card with one major difference," said Kim. "A credit card allows you to buy today and pay at the end of the month or even later. A debit card immediately transfers the amount of the payment from your checking account to the retailer's account."

Kim has a debit card and explained how it is used. In a completely automated system, the customer passes a debit card through a reader and punches a secret code into a computer terminal. The point-of-sale computer terminal operates like a cash register. The amount of the purchase is electronically withdrawn from the customer's checking account and transferred to the seller's checking account at the time of sale. You should receive a receipt from the POS transaction, showing the amount that has been transferred from your account to the retailer's account.

Today many grocery stores accept debit cards in place of checks or cash. Retailers, in general, like the POS system because no currency or checks change hands.

Guidelines for Using EFT

After talking with Antwan, Ms. Reed, and Kim, Mark decided the biggest problem with electronic banking is recordkeeping. He was just beginning to learn how to keep accurate records. He was afraid he would forget to record his withdrawals if he relied too heavily on electronic banking.

Kim agreed. "It's absolutely the biggest drawback to electronic banking. When you use your ATM card or a debit card, your money is automatically withdrawn. You had better be sure you have some in there!" she said.

Kim also warned that some people confuse debit cards with credit cards. You will learn about bank credit cards in Chapter 5.

Mark decided to apply for an ATM card. He went back to see Ms. Reed. She gave him an application form to complete. Ms. Reed also gave Mark a copy of the following *Guidelines for Using an ATM Card*.

Guidelines for Using an ATM Card

- Know where your ATM card is at all times.

- Memorize your PIN (Personal Identification Number). Do not write it on your ATM card or carry it in your wallet.

- At night, always use a well-lighted ATM. Take a friend with you so you won't be alone.

- Don't count your cash at the ATM, especially if strangers are around. When your transaction is complete, take your cash, card, and receipt, and then leave.

- Be alert before you get out of your car. If there are suspicious people around, go to another ATM.

- When using an ATM, don't let people stand close enough to see your PIN as you enter it into the machine. If someone does get too close to you or makes you feel uncomfortable while using an ATM, cancel your transaction, take your card, and leave immediately.

- When using drive-up ATMs, be sure to keep your doors locked and your engine running. At walk-up machines, turn your engine off and take your car keys with you to the ATM.

- Always retrieve your ATM receipts and examine them immediately. Promptly report all errors.

- Immediately report a lost or stolen ATM card.

- Keep your check stubs or check register accurate. Enter all ATM transactions in your check register or on the stubs immediately after the transaction, just as you would record each check written or deposit made.

- When you receive your bank statement, reconcile your ATM transactions, as well as your check transactions, with the bank statement.

- In general, protect debit cards, credit cards, and checkbooks as if they were cash.

Electronic Funds Transfer Act

Ms. Reed also told Mark about the Electronic Funds Transfer Act. This law provides some protection for consumers using EFT. She said that if he was going to use an ATM card, he should be familiar with the regulations. Some of the features of the act are explained below.

When you use an automated teller machine or point-of-sale terminal, you are entitled to get a written receipt. Each transaction must be recorded and appear on your bank statement. You have 60 days from the date a problem or error appears on your statement or terminal receipt to notify your financial institution.

After being notified, the financial institution has 10 business days to investigate and tell you the results. If the financial institution needs more time, it may take up to 45 days to complete the investigation—but only if the money in dispute is

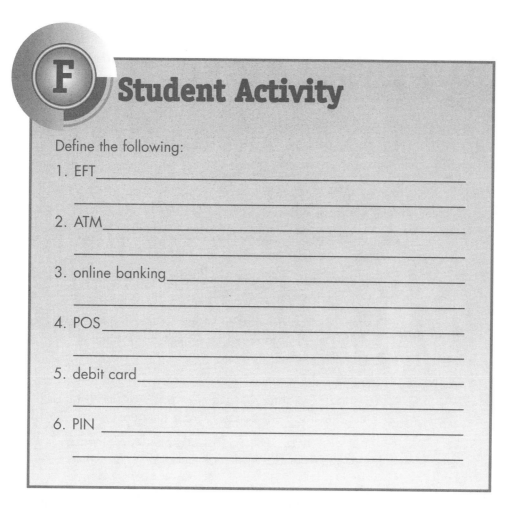

Student Activity

Define the following:

1. EFT _____
   _____

2. ATM _____
   _____

3. online banking _____
   _____

4. POS _____
   _____

5. debit card _____
   _____

6. PIN _____
   _____

returned to your account. If no error is found at the end of this investigation, the financial institution may take the money back, as long as it sends you a written explanation.

If you fail to notify the financial institution of the error within 60 days, you may lose the money. The financial institution has no obligation under the federal law to conduct an investigation if you have missed the 60-day deadline. So, you see the importance of always checking your EFT receipts and reconciling your bank statement with EFT transactions.

If your ATM card is lost or stolen, notify your financial institution within two business days after discovering the card is missing. You will then lose no more than $50 if someone else has used your card. If you do not notify the financial institution within two business days and your card is used, you can lose as much as $500.

After reporting the loss or theft of your ATM card, you cannot lose any more money if further unauthorized transactions are made The best way to protect yourself is to notify your financial institution by telephone and follow up with a letter, keeping a copy for yourself.

Again, it is also important to check your bank statement. If it shows transactions that you didn't make, tell the financial institution within 60 days after the statement was mailed. If you don't, the financial institution is not obligated to return any of the missing money.

Student Activity

1. What is the purpose of the Electronic Funds Transfer Act?

   _____

2. Answer true or false to the following statements about the Electronic Funds Transfer Act.

   _____ a. You are entitled to a written receipt when you use an automated teller machine.

   _____ b. You have 60 days from the date an error appears on your statement to notify your financial institution.

   _____ c. If your ATM card is lost or stolen, you can lose up to $500 even if you notify the financial institution within two business days.

   _____ d. If a financial institution needs more than 10 business days to investigate your claim of an error, it must return the disputed money to your account.

   _____ e. The best way to report a lost or stolen ATM card is to call the financial institution and then send a letter.

3. On Sunday morning, Mark received a phone call from Carlos reminding him that his share of January's rent had been due on January 1. Mark had thought he could wait and pay his $350 later in the month, when he actually moved in. He really wanted to share the apartment, so he offered to send Carlos a check on Monday. Carlos said that wasn't acceptable. Since the payment was overdue, he insisted on cash and he wanted it today. Mark was relieved he had his ATM card. He went to the nearest ATM and withdrew $350. Record the transaction.

   a. Remove the ATM receipt (Form 4-3) from the Source Documents section of the *Instructions and Source Documents Booklet.*

   b. Record the ATM transaction in Mark's check register. Write *AW* (automatic withdrawal) in the Number column. Enter the date: 1/5. As a description of the transaction, write (To) *ATM cash withdrawal* (For) *Apartment rent.* Record the amount of the payment, $350.00, and calculate the new balance.

   c. Record the ATM transaction in Mark's *Financial Management Records Booklet.* Record the payment for rent under the proper date.

How to Use Other Banking Services

Kim told Mark about other banking services that are available. She said that sometime Mark might need a bank money order, traveler's checks, an official bank check, or a safe-deposit box.

Bank Money Orders

People without a checking account sometimes buy a **bank money order** to make a small payment through the mail. The money order shows the name of the person to be paid and the name of the person sending the money. The buyer of the money order must pay the amount of the money order plus a service charge. See Figure 4-7 for an example of a bank money order.

```
NATIONAL BANK MONEY ORDER                          15-77
                                                   250

                                              No. 1966046

DATE _____ 20 _____

TO THE
ORDER OF_____

_____
SENDER'S NAME AND ADDRESS              FOR CLASSROOM USE ONLY

Payable at NATIONAL BANK, Atlanta, GA
                                       _____
⑆025000779⑆ ⑈4231126⑈            CHAIRMAN
```

Figure 4-7

Bank Money Order

Traveler's Checks

Kim explained that she would need to purchase traveler's checks before leaving for San Diego. She knew that it wouldn't be wise to carry a large amount of cash while traveling.

Traveler's checks can be purchased in amounts of $10, $20, $50, $100, or more. At the time of purchase, you sign each check in front of the bank teller. After the checks are issued, you can cash them wherever traveler's checks are accepted, which is almost anywhere in the world.

When cashing a traveler's check, you must sign it again in the presence of the person receiving the check. *Do not sign traveler's checks ahead of time.* If you do, anyone can cash them.

You may have to pay a fee when you purchase traveler's checks. However, some banks do not charge a fee for people who have certain accounts at their bank.

Always keep the slip of paper identifying the serial numbers of your traveler's checks. Be sure to keep the numbers separate from your traveler's checks in case your checks are lost or stolen. Report lost or stolen traveler's checks immediately to the financial institution that issued the checks. The financial institution will replace them immediately. Figure 4-8 shows an example of a traveler's check.

Figure 4-8

Traveler's Check

Official Bank Checks

A customer may buy an official bank check either with cash or through a bank account. The bank then issues a check to the person or business designated to receive it. You may need an official bank check when you are making a payment to someone who doesn't know you and won't accept your personal check. If for some reason the payee does not cash the check and it is returned to you, *do not tear it up.* Take it back to the bank so the amount can be added to your checking account or returned to you in cash.

Safe-Deposit Boxes

Another safety service offered by banks is the safe-deposit box. **Safe-deposit boxes** are rented containers inside the bank's vault. They provide protection for valuables such as jewelry and important documents that might be lost, stolen, or destroyed by fire.

When renting a safe-deposit box, the customer receives two personal keys. The bank has a master key. Both the customer key and the bank key are necessary to unlock the box. The financial institution cannot open a private safe-deposit box without an order from the court. If a customer loses the keys, the bank may, in the presence of witnesses and the customer's legal representatives, have a locksmith open the lock.

Kim reminded Mark that banks are always offering new services. She told him that it's a good idea to check out available services before using a bank and to periodically check around to compare services and fees.

Student Activity

Answer true or false to the following statements:

____ 1. If you buy a used car from someone who doesn't know you and won't accept your personal check, you can pay the person with an official bank check.

____ 2. You should sign a traveler's check for the first time when you are ready to cash it.

____ 3. When an unsigned traveler's check is lost or stolen, no one can cash it.

____ 4. The name of the sender appears on a bank money order.

____ 5. You should keep a record of the serial numbers of traveler's checks in a separate place from the checks.

____ 6. A bank has the right to open a private safe-deposit box without the customer's knowledge.

On Your Own For Life

1. Visit and compare two banking institutions in your community. Talk with a bank officer and obtain brochures on fees and services. You might use the following questions as guidelines:

   • What are the banking hours?

   • How convenient are the bank branches?

   • What services does the bank offer?

   • Does the bank offer online and telephone banking?

   • What are the fees and minimum balances for accounts?

   • What are the fees for other special services such as safe-deposit boxes?

   • How helpful does the bank staff appear to be?

   • Is the institution federally insured?

   • How do the two banking institutions compare with regard to services, fees, and convenience?

File the information in the Financial (green) file labeled *Banking*.

2. Talk with a bank officer and request sample copies of traveler's checks and money orders. Show and demonstrate their use to the other members of your class.

Check Up

Having completed the Student Activities in this chapter, you should have mastered the skills listed below. Put a checkmark next to the skills you have mastered. If you aren't sure of a skill, review that section of the chapter.

☐ How to figure simple interest

☐ How to calculate compound interest

☐ How to compare savings accounts

☐ How to use electronic banking

☐ How to use other banking services

Now that you know all about savings accounts and banking services, move on to Chapter 5, *Applying for Credit*.

5 Chapter

APPLYING FOR CREDIT

Mark was amazed at the changes that had taken place in his life in just six weeks. Not too long ago, he had had no idea of how to be "on his own." In a short period of time, he (and you) learned how to:

1. Set up a filing and record-keeping system.

2. Open and use a checking account.

3. Set up a budget and a budget-record system.

4. Open and benefit from a savings account.

He had to admit he was proud of himself. He had accomplished all this without an increase in salary. Yet, he felt richer and more financially independent. He was in control of his life.

Mark's parents were proud of him as well. In fact, they had learned a lot about record keeping and financial skills from Mark's research and experiences.

Kim had one more suggestion for Mark before he moved out of his parents' house and into the apartment with Carlos. She suggested that he establish his creditworthiness by applying for a bank credit card.

There are times when most of us have to **buy on credit** (borrow money) because we can't afford to pay a large sum of money at one time. Classic examples are buying a car or a house. Few people can come up with the total cost of either of these items all at once, but most can afford to pay a part of the total cost each month. In order to borrow money for major items, you need to establish a good credit rating. Your credit rating is a score that reflects your willingness and ability to repay borrowed money when it is due. Your rating is based largely on your past record for paying on time. You can establish a good credit rating by making small purchases with a credit card and paying off the debt on time, every time.

Mark was interested. For one thing, he had long wanted a stereo of his own, but he could never afford it. Kim suggested that he talk to his friend at National Bank, Ms. Reed. Kim said it isn't always necessary, but it's a good idea to apply for a bank credit card where you have your checking and savings accounts.

How to Establish Creditworthiness

Ms. Reed was happy to see Mark again. She seemed to take a personal interest in Mark's welfare. For his part, Mark realized how important it is to establish a trusting relationship with someone working in a banking institution.

"People must establish their creditworthiness before a bank will grant them the ability to buy on credit," said Ms. Reed. "**Creditworthiness** means that you're a good credit risk. The criteria used to determine a person's creditworthiness are character, capacity, and capital—the *three Cs of credit*. Let me explain."

Character refers to your sense of responsibility. Have you acted responsibly in financial and other life activities? Do you have a record of paying debts on time? Do you seem to take your obligations seriously? Have you lived at the same address for a long time, or have you changed residences frequently? How long have you worked for the same employer?

Capacity is your ability to earn enough income to repay a loan when it is due. How much do you earn? Do you have any debts (money owed)? How stable does your job seem to be? Does it seem likely that you will stay employed long enough to pay off the debt?

Capital is what you own—your assets. It includes money (checking and savings accounts) and property (car, house, and smaller items). The lender knows that your assets can be turned into cash, if necessary, to pay a debt. Lenders want to know what sources you can use to repay a debt other than your regular wages.

Ms. Reed suggested the following ways for a young person Mark's age to establish creditworthiness:

1. Find and keep a job that earns a steady income, either part-time or full-time. Ms. Reed said young people often don't realize the importance of establishing a good work record in their part-time jobs. Their job records and recommendations are an important factor in their creditworthiness. Mark was happy he could check off this one.

2. Establish checking and savings accounts at a local financial institution. Do not write a check if you have insufficient funds to cover it. The way you handle your account tells the lender something about your character and capacity to manage your personal finances. Once again, Mark could see the importance of keeping accurate financial records and an up-to-date balance in his checkbook. Happily, Mark could check off this requirement as well. So far, so good.

3. Apply for a credit card through a local bank, department store, or gas station. Ms. Reed recommended a major credit card, such as VISA or MasterCard. She said that banks are more willing to grant initial credit cards to customers who already have a checking or savings account with the bank. Young consumers may have to apply to a bank where their parents have an account. Some institutions offer special teenage accounts with low credit limits. The **credit limit** (also called a **line of credit**) is the maximum amount that the cardholder can buy on credit. Ms. Reed emphasized that once you have a credit card, you must use it wisely. You should charge only what you know you can pay off on time.

4. Apply for a small, short-term loan for something you need or want. Parents of young people may have to **co-sign** the loan. By co-signing, the parents become legally responsible for paying off the loan if their children fail to do so. However, young consumers in Mark's situation can usually obtain a small loan. If you successfully pay off the loan, you have increased your creditworthiness. Again, don't borrow what you can't repay.

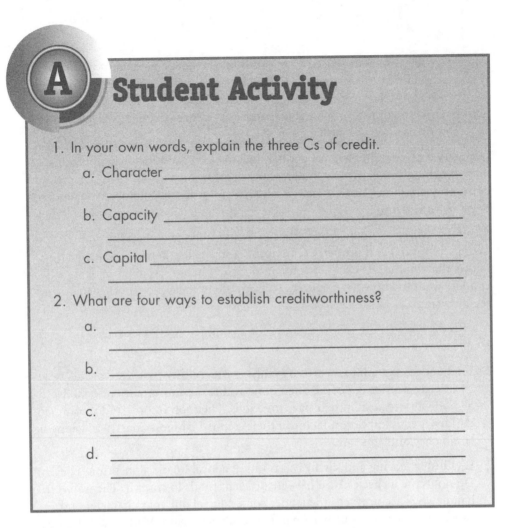

Student Activity

1. In your own words, explain the three Cs of credit.

   a. Character _____

   _____

   b. Capacity _____

   _____

   c. Capital _____

   _____

2. What are four ways to establish creditworthiness?

   a. _____

   _____

   b. _____

   _____

   c. _____

   _____

   d. _____

   _____

How to Establish a Good Credit Rating

Ms. Reed said that the bank would be taking a risk by issuing Mark a credit card since he hadn't yet established a good credit rating. However, he had a full-time job and had demonstrated character and a desire to act responsibly with his finances. The bank would probably take the risk. She did caution him to use his credit card responsibly. He should make small purchases that he was sure he could pay off quickly. If he couldn't pay his credit card bills, his credit rating would go down.

Your **credit rating** is a measure of your creditworthiness. It is based largely on your past record of borrowing and repayment, plus other aspects of the three Cs of credit. You establish a good credit rating over a period of time by borrowing and paying on time. Every time you make your payment on time, your credit rating is strengthened. Every time you miss a payment or pay late, your credit rating is weakened. Mark was learning the importance of a good credit rating.

Ms. Reed explained that credit rating is determined by a scoring system. A **credit scoring system** consists of a list of items that reflect how risky an applicant is as a debtor (borrower). Points are assigned to show how the applicant rates on each item. The points are added, and the total determines whether or not an applicant receives credit.

Ms. Reed said that **credit bureaus** collect credit information about you and sell it to lenders for use in establishing your credit rating. If you have ever borrowed money, had a check bounce, or been taken to court, you probably have a file in a credit bureau. The file contains your **credit history**—your record of borrowing and timely repayment. A missed or late payment will show on your record. Ms. Reed explained that the bureaus get information about you from banks, local newspapers, court records, and stores where you shop. This is perfectly legal. However, federal law protects you from the distribution of inaccurate or outdated information about your credit standing.

How to Understand Consumer Credit Laws

The federal government has passed several important consumer credit laws. Some of the most important are discussed below. Ms. Reed told Mark that before he buys on credit, he should know what these laws mean.

The **Truth-in-Lending Act** of 1969 requires that all contracts for credit clearly state the finance charge, which must be expressed as the annual percentage rate (APR). (You will learn more about finance charges later in this chapter.) The purpose of the Truth-in-Lending Act is to let consumers know exactly what they must pay for the use of credit. Also, by requiring all financial institutions to express the cost in the same way (as an APR), the law allows consumers to more easily compare the costs at different institutions.

The **Fair Credit Reporting Act** of 1971 states that credit bureaus cannot circulate inaccurate credit information about an individual. Anyone denied credit, insurance, or employment because of an unfavorable report by a credit bureau has the right to know why credit was not granted. Even if you have not been denied credit, you have the right to request a copy of your credit report.

This law was amended in 1996 when Congress passed the **Consumer Credit Reporting Reform Act**. This law makes it easier for consumers to correct mistakes in their credit report. If you disagree with an item on your report, the credit bureau must investigate the item within 30 days to make sure it is correct.

The **Equal Credit Opportunity Act** of 1975 banned discrimination because of gender or marital status in the granting of credit. For example, credit cannot be refused to a creditworthy single woman. An addition to the act in 1977 prevents discrimination against older people who apply for credit.

The **Fair Credit Billing Act** of 1975 guarantees the right of consumers to settle disputes with retail stores and credit card companies before any information about the dispute is reported to a credit bureau. If a consumer thinks that a billing error has been made, the consumer must notify the credit grantor in writing within 60 days after receiving the bill. A credit grantor must respond within 30 days and resolve the issue within 90 days.

The **Fair Debt Collections Practices Act** of 1977 forbids abusive practices by debt collectors. The law applies primarily to anyone in the business of collecting debts for others. It does not apply to banks, other lenders, or businesses that collect their own accounts. The law strictly prohibits harassing or abusive conduct in connection with the collection of a debt. For example, the law prohibits threatening phone calls, using false or deceptive means to obtain information, or suggesting that failure to pay will result in arrest or imprisonment.

B Student Activity

1. What is a credit rating? _____
_____
_____

2. What is the function of a credit bureau? _____
_____
_____

3. Kim's friend Tina wrote a check but did not have enough money in her checking account to cover it. The billing department of the store contacted her about the $300 she still owed. Tina said she would pay but never did. The store's bill collector sent Tina several notices about the debt. Six months after the check bounced, the billing department wrote to tell Tina that the matter would be taken to small claims court. Tina still did not pay. The store won a judgment against Tina for $300 plus court costs when she failed to appear in court.

a. Do you think Tina can get a credit card from a local retail store if she applies after the court judgment against her? Explain.
_____
_____

b. Which of the "three Cs" of credit has Tina harmed by her actions? Explain. _____
_____

4. Carlos applied for a loan at a local bank. He received a notice two weeks later saying he had not been approved for the loan. Carlos could not understand why, since he was making a regular salary. He knew he had taken much longer than expected to pay off his college loan, but he had paid it off.

a. Should Carlos question why his loan request was rejected? Explain. _____
_____

b. Does Carlos have a right to know the reason the bank refused to grant him a loan? _____

c. What law or laws apply in this situation? _____
_____

How to Apply for a Credit Card

Mark told Ms. Reed that he wanted to apply for a credit card and asked where he could get an application. "Banks usually have application forms for major credit cards, such as VISA and MasterCard," she said. "Gas stations have forms for their own gas credit cards. Retail stores have application forms for the credit cards they accept." Ms. Reed showed Mark the credit card application illustrated in Figure 5-1.

APPLICATION FOR CREDIT

This Application is for: (Check one or both)

☐ **MASTERCARD** ☐ **VISA**

Number of sets of above cards requested _____

Last Name	First	Initial	Age	Spouse	No. of Dependents

Home Address	City	State	Zip Code	Rent ☐ Own ☐ Live with Parents ☐

How Long	Phone	Previous address if at above less than three years	How Long Yrs. Mos.

Employer	Occupation	Salary Mo.	How Long Yrs. Mos.

Business Address	Business Phone	Social Security Number

Previous Employer	Business Address	Occupation	Salary Mo.	How Long Yrs. Mos.

Applicant is not required to provide the information requested in this section unless in applying for this account applicant is relying upon the additional creditworthiness (income and property) of co-applicant.

Full Name Co-Applicant	Age	Social Security No.

Home Address	City	State	Zip

Employer	Occupation	Salary Mo.	How Long Yrs. Mos.

Business Address	Business Phone

Name and Address of nearest relative not living with you	Phone	Relationship

Income from alimony, child support or maintenance payment need not be revealed if the applicant does not wish to rely on such income to qualify for credit.

OTHER SOURCES OF INCOME	Monthly Amount $	Source

CREDIT REFERENCES

COMPANY	ADDRESS	ACCOUNT NO.	BALANCE
1)			
2)			
3)			

Checking Account No. and Bank	Savings Account No. and Bank

THE ABOVE APPLICATION IS TRUE AND CORRECT AND APPLICANT ACKNOWLEDGES RECEIPT OF AND AGREES TO THE CONTRACT AND DISCLOSURES SET FORTH AND FURTHER AGREES TO PAY ALL INDEBTEDNESS INCURRED IN ACCORDANCE WITH SUCH CONTRACT.

Signature of Applicant Date

Signature of Co-Applicant Date

FILL OUT COMPLETELY, FOLD, SEAL WITH TAPE OR STAPLE BEFORE MAILING.

Figure 5-1

Credit Card Application

Having decided to apply for a credit card, Mark wanted to do some reading on the subject. He got some of his material from Ms. Reed. Kim pointed out that he could find information about buying on credit from the business section in the local newspaper and from magazines and books at the public library. "Also, the Internet is full of credit-related information and advice," she said. "Just don't fall for an Internet scam. If the credit offer looks too good to be true, it's probably a scam. For credit, stick with sources you know."

Mark surprised himself when he realized how interested he was in all things financial. "It affects you personally," Kim said. "A good way to get your attention is to tamper with your wallet. The more you know, the more you want to know, and that's good."

Mark learned that credit card holders establish a line of credit based on their credit rating. A credit card company may put a $500 limit on one cardholder, whereas another person, because of a better credit rating, may have a $5,000 limit.

If a credit card is lost or stolen, you should inform the issuer of the credit card immediately by telephone and later by mail. Federal law protects a cardholder from paying for unauthorized charges over $50 for each reported lost or stolen card. A cardholder should keep on file a record of each credit card account number in order to report a stolen or lost card quickly.

Credit card issuers must send regular statements to card users. You may question either the purchase or the price of an item that appears on the billing statement. As Mark learned earlier, the Fair Credit Billing Act of 1975 requires prompt corrections of billing mistakes. You should always *keep your charge card receipts* after a purchase on the card so you can verify the statement with your receipts.

Mark learned that a monthly finance charge is usually added to the unpaid balance of a credit card account. Some finance charges are as high as $1\frac{1}{2}$ percent of the unpaid balance of an account, which amounts to 18 percent annually ($1\frac{1}{2}\%$ per month $\times$ 12 months = 18%). For example, suppose you charge $200 worth of clothes and pay only $20. When you receive your statement, you will have a finance charge of $2.70 added to your next month's statement ($180 $\times$ .015 = $2.70). In other words, when you don't pay the full balance due on your credit card statement, you will have to pay interest on the remaining balance.

Worse, if you don't pay the full balance one month, you will also have to pay interest on new purchases for the next month. In other words, you are paying interest on the entire balance as long as you don't pay in full.

Worried, Mark called Ms. Reed to check on the annual percentage rate charged on National Bank's credit card. Sure enough, it was 18 percent. He was upset because he had seen credit card companies advertise lower annual percentage rates (APRs). However, Kim said that often the lower interest rates are initial rates that are effective for only the first six months. Then the rate is increased to 18 percent or more. She felt that Mark should still get his card from National Bank. Since he was just beginning to establish a credit rating, he should plan to pay the full balance each month anyway.

Student Activity

1. Record the following transactions for Mark:

   a. On January 7, Mark received his credit card in the mail and decided to use it to purchase slacks for a total of $63.57 at Britches Department Store. Remove his charge card receipt (Form 5-1) from the Source Documents section of this *Instructions and Source Documents Booklet*. Record the transaction on the appropriate line of the *Financial Management Records Booklet*. File the credit card receipt in the Financial file labeled *Credit—Bank Card*. (*Note*: Although the charges on Mark's credit card will not be paid until the following month, he will record and file the purchases as they occur.)

   b. On January 9, Mark wrote Check 109 for $18.00 to Fay's Drugstore to purchase some personal goods. Record the check in the check register; write the check; and record the transaction in the *Financial Management Records Booklet*. File the check in the Outgoing File.

   c. On January 10, Mark received and deposited his paycheck. He deposited $240.01, keeping out $85 for his cash envelope. Record the deposit in the check register. On the same day, he spent the following cash amounts: eating out, $15.00; transportation, $12.00; evening out, $30.00. In the *Financial Management Records Booklet,* record Mark's $325.01 weekly income in the Second Week box. Record Mark's January 10th cash expenditures under the appropriate date.

   d. On January 13, Mark charged a bottle of cologne for $15.90 at Lacy's Department Store for Kim's birthday and a shirt for himself for $31.79. Remove the charge card receipts (Forms 5-2 and 5-3) from the *Instructions and Source Documents Booklet*. Record the transactions in the proper category in the *Financial Management Records Booklet*. File the receipts.

   e. On January 17, Mark received and deposited his paycheck. He deposited $240.01 and kept $85.00 in cash. Record his deposit in the check register. That same day, Mark spent the following amounts: eating out, $10.00; transportation, $10.00; personal, $15.00; fun, $25.00. In the *Financial Management Records Booklet*, record Mark's expenditures. Record his third-week income of $325.01.

2. On January 20, Mark received his first credit card statement (Form 5-4). Remove the statement and answer the following questions:

   a. How much does Mark owe? _____

Continued

b. What is the minimum amount he can pay on the statement? _____

c. By what date must he pay the amount due?_____

d. Does he have any finance charge on this statement? Explain._____

e. What was the balance last month? _____

f. What is his credit limit? _____

g. What is the APR charged by the credit card company?_____

3. Remove Mark's receipts from the *Credit—Bank Card* file and verify the accuracy of the statement. If you have determined that the charges are accurate, return the receipts to the *Credit—Bank Card* file.

4. Since Mark's credit card balance was not due until February 20, he decided to wait until the first week of February to mail his check. File the bank card statement in the Financial file labeled *Bill to Be Paid*.

How to Buy on an Installment Plan

Mark had always wanted a good stereo system but could never afford it. Now that he was moving into his own apartment, he really wanted to have one in his room. He told Kim about it. She suggested that if he had to have it, to buy it on an installment plan rather than put it on his credit card. Kim explained that such a large sum on his credit card would limit his ability to use his card for other purchases.

"Installment buying involves signing an installment sales contract and making regular monthly payments," Kim said. She explained that when you buy on installment, you usually have to make a **down payment**, which is part of the price of merchandise paid at the time of purchase. Also, a **finance charge** is added to the purchase price and becomes part of the total amount you owe. A finance charge is sometimes called a carrying charge.

Kim also warned Mark that installment contracts frequently include fine print that he should read carefully before signing the contract. An insurance agreement may be included on the installment contract. Credit insurance is purchased through the institution financing the loan. The insurance pays off the debt if the borrower dies. Credit insurance is seldom necessary, especially if the borrower is young and healthy or has adequate life insurance. Credit insurance is expensive when compared to regular life insurance. By law, the borrower must be told that credit insurance is voluntary.

Always ask if there are any penalties for early payment of a loan. Also be sure you understand any late payment charges or penalties. If you fail to make your payments, a creditor can repossess (take back) and resell the goods.

Some contracts allow a creditor to **garnish**, or collect a portion of, your wages to pay off your loan if you fail to pay (default). A court order is not necessary to garnish your wages if this was stated in the contract you signed.

When you sign an installment contract, you are agreeing to the terms stated in the contract. Therefore, you should always read the contract thoroughly and carefully. Ask questions about any requirements or legal language you don't understand. Ask to take the form home overnight, if necessary, to study the terms of the agreement. In other words, don't get so caught up in your new purchase that you ignore the *terms* on which you are making the purchase.

Mark shopped around and found the perfect stereo at Great Fi-Buys for $274.54. The installment contract Mark signed is shown in Figure 5-2.

Figure 5-2

Installment Contract

Seller's Name: Great Fi-Buys, Atlanta, Georgia   Contract # 1506

RETAIL INSTALLMENT CONTRACT AND SECURITY AGREEMENT

The undersigned (herein called Purchaser, whether one or more) purchases from Great Fi-Buys (seller) and grants to Them a security interest in, subject to the terms and conditions hereof, the following described property.

PURCHASER'S NAME: Mark L. Smith
PURCHASER'S ADDRESS: 1040 Peachtree Dr.
CITY Atlanta STATE GA ZIP 30319-1396

QUANTITY	DESCRIPTION	AMOUNT
1	Stereo	259.00
	Sales Tax	15.54
	Total	274.54

1. CASH PRICE $ 274.54
2. LESS: CASH DOWN PAYMENT $ 74.54
3. TRADE-IN
4. TOTAL DOWN PAYMENT $ 74.54
5. UNPAID BALANCE OF CASH PRICE $ 200.00
6. OTHER CHARGES:
   $
   $
7. AMOUNT FINANCED $ 200.00
8. FINANCE CHARGE $ 36.00
9. TOTAL OF PAYMENTS $ 236.00
10. DEFERRED PAYMENT PRICE (1+6+8) $ 310.54
11. ANNUAL PERCENTAGE RATE 18 %

Insurance Agreement

The purchase of insurance coverage is voluntary and not required for credit. _____ (Type of Ins.) insurance coverage is available at a cost of $ _____ for the term of credit.

☐ I desire insurance coverage

Signed _____ Date _____

☐ I do not desire insurance coverage

Signed Mark L. Smith Date 1/21/X1

Purchaser hereby agrees to pay to Great Fi-Buys at their offices shown above the "TOTAL OF PAYMENTS" shown above in 12 monthly installments of $ 19.67 _____ (final payment to be $ 19.63), the first installment being payable Feb. 21 20--, and all subsequent installments on the same day of each consecutive month until paid in full. The finance charge applies from 1/21/X1 to 1/21/X2.

Signed Mark L. Smith Date 1/21/X1

NOTICE TO BUYER: YOU ARE ENTITLED TO A COPY OF THE CONTRACT YOU SIGN. YOU HAVE THE RIGHT TO PAY IN ADVANCE THE UNPAID BALANCE OF THIS CONTRACT AND OBTAIN A PARTIAL REFUND OF THE FINANCE CHARGE.

Student Activity

Read Mark's installment contract carefully and answer the following questions:

1. What is the cash price of the stereo? _____

2. How much of the purchase price is Mark borrowing? _____

3. What is the finance charge? _____

4. Did Mark buy the credit insurance offered by the seller? _____

5. What is the amount of Mark's monthly installment payment?

_____

6. Are all figures on the contract correct? _____

7. On January 21, Mark wrote Check 110 to Great Fi-Buys for the $74.54 down payment on his stereo. Write and record the check for Mark. Refer to the budget categories at the front of the *Financial Management Records Booklet* to determine the correct category for the down payment. File the check.

When Mark came home with his stereo, his father was irritated. He was glad his son was learning all about credit, but he didn't think Mark was being realistic. "Credit isn't free," he reminded Mark. "By buying a stereo on an installment plan, you've added a fixed monthly expense. Did you check your budget?"

Mark had to admit that he hadn't. "I get a paycheck for $325.01 every week," Mark said. "I can afford a $20 monthly payment."

"Sure you can—while you're living off us!" Mark's father was angry. "You're not being realistic. You aren't paying utility and telephone bills yet, and you haven't had to spend much on food. Since I've driven you to work most days, you've paid very little for transportation this month. You bought a lot of clothes. You opened a savings account. You started using a credit card. Now you buy a stereo and tie yourself to installment payments for a year. I'm glad you're trying to be financially independent, but your spending has gotten out of control."

Mark stormed out of the room. His parents didn't appreciate all he had accomplished over the past months. He knew one person would understand. He went to see Kim.

"I know you don't want to hear this, Mark, but your dad has a point," Kim said. "You started financial planning because you wanted to be independent. Buying on credit seems so easy, and it is. But if you're not careful, credit will eat up your earnings before you know what's happening! Let's take a look at your budget again."

Student Activity

Look back at Mark's final budget (Figure 3-8, page 44). Open the *Financial Management Records Booklet* to the January transactions you have recorded. Refer to the budget and the January transactions as you answer the questions below.

1. What is the budgeted amount of Mark's total expenditures?
   _____

2. How much did Mark budget in the clothing category? _____

3. How much has he spent for clothing in January? _____

4. For the month of January, is Mark over budget for clothing?
   _____

   If so, by how much? _____

5. By what method did Mark buy the clothes? _____

6. Under what category will Mark record his monthly installment payment for his stereo? _____

7. How much did Mark budget for this category? _____

8. How much has Mark spent in January for this category?
   _____

9. Do you think Mark will have to adjust this category to cover the $19.67 monthly installment payment for the stereo? Explain. _____
   _____

10. What should Mark have done before he bought the stereo on credit? _____
    _____
    _____

11. Do you think Mark can afford the stereo? Explain. _____
    _____
    _____

12. What will happen to Mark's credit rating if he is unable to make payments on the stereo? _____
    _____
    _____

13. If you had been Mark, would you have bought the stereo? Explain. _____
    _____
    _____

How to Obtain a Loan

One of Mark's long-range goals is to buy a used car one day. He decided to ask Kim how she had done it.

Kim said she investigated the different sources of credit. First, she checked with some banking institutions that grant loans. She learned that **personal loans** are loans that are relatively small. They are also referred to as **short-term** or **intermediate-term loans**. People generally apply for personal loans for financial emergencies, household appliances, or educational expenses. Loans for larger purchases, such as a home or car, are usually classified as **long-term loans**.

Where to Get a Loan

Kim told Mark that there are several institutions that lend money. Among them are banks, savings and loan associations, life insurance companies, consumer finance companies, and credit unions.

Banks handle a lot of the loans. Many people borrow from the bank where they have checking and saving accounts. By having accounts at the bank, they have established a credit rating at the bank.

Savings and loan associations specialize in loans for the purchase of real estate (land or home), but they also make personal loans.

Life insurance companies sometimes allow policyholders to borrow against some types of insurance policies. Usually, life insurance companies charge a lower interest rate than banks or other lending institutions, and the loan is fairly easy to get. If the policyholder dies before paying the loan, the company deducts the amount owed from the proceeds of the policy. You will learn more about this topic in Chapter 8.

Consumer finance companies often lend to consumers who don't have an established credit rating. Finance companies generally charge a higher rate of interest than other lending institutions do, for two reasons. First, they grant loans to people who are greater credit risks. Second, small loans, which consumer finance companies deal in most often, are costly to make. Loans at finance companies are processed more quickly and are usually easier to obtain.

Credit unions grant small loans to their members. Loans from credit unions usually carry a lower interest rate than do loans from banks, savings and loan associations, and certainly from consumer finance companies.

Pawnbrokers make loans to people who turn over personal property, such as a ring or watch, as security or pawn. Pawnbrokers charge an extremely high interest rate on loans. Such loans must be paid in full before the personal property is returned. Therefore, consumers run the risk of losing valuable property as well as paying high interest rates. Also, dealing with a pawnbroker usually does not improve your credit rating.

Licensed lending institutions should not be confused with unlicensed lenders, commonly known as loan sharks. Loan sharks operate openly in states without usury laws. **Usury laws** limit the interest rate a lender may charge. Loan sharks frequently swindle consumers who cannot get a loan from any other source by charging them extremely high interest rates. In addition to outrageous interest rates, loan sharks are known for underhanded practices, such as controlling circumstances to keep the borrower in constant debt or illegally reclaiming property. Loan sharks even operate in states where there are strict usury laws. They usually function under the cover of some legal business. Unfortunately, they are easily discovered by those who should avoid them most—people with poor credit ratings.

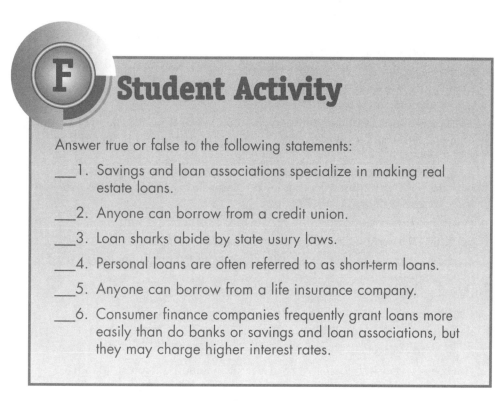

F Student Activity

Answer true or false to the following statements:

___1. Savings and loan associations specialize in making real estate loans.

___2. Anyone can borrow from a credit union.

___3. Loan sharks abide by state usury laws.

___4. Personal loans are often referred to as short-term loans.

___5. Anyone can borrow from a life insurance company.

___6. Consumer finance companies frequently grant loans more easily than do banks or savings and loan associations, but they may charge higher interest rates.

Terms Used on Loan Applications

Kim told Mark how she had applied for a loan. She had a friend at a bank, much like Ms. Reed, who showed her a typical loan application. Completing a loan application is the first step when applying for a loan. Kim said she could hardly fill out the application because she wasn't familiar with the terms used on the form.

Kim showed Mark a list of terms the banker gave her. "It's a list of terms often used on loan applications, credit applications; and contracts," Kim said. She said anyone about to borrow money should be familiar with these terms.

Mark understood some of the terms, but not all. Read through the list shown in Figure 5-3 to see how many you know.

Mark asked Kim to explain the Rule of 78. "The Rule of 78 works like this," she said. "The first month of a one-year loan, you pay 12/78 of the interest; the second month, 11/78; the third, 10/78; and so on until the last month, when you pay 1/78 of the interest. You are paying more interest the first month (12/78) than the last month (1/78). If you pay off the loan at the end of six months, you will save about 27 percent in interest, not 50 percent. In other words, you have paid 12/78, 11/78, 10/78, 9/78, 8/78, and 7/78 in interest, which equals 57 when you add the numerators (numbers above the line). Subtract 57 from 78. You have saved yourself only 21/78 (27 percent) in interest (21/78 = 27 or 27 percent). This is the total amount of interest owed after six months if the one-year payment schedule had been continued as planned. However, early

Figure 5-3

Terms Used When
Borrowing Money

TERMS USED WHEN BORROWING MONEY

alimony—a financial amount paid to one's former spouse for support after a legal separation or divorce

assets—any items of value that a person owns

bankrupt—financial situation in which a court declares one's debts to be greater than the total value of one's assets

cash value—amount that an insurance policy is worth if canceled before maturity. An insurance company will lend to a policyholder based on his or her policy

co-applicant, joint applicant, co-signer—someone who signs a loan with the borrower, thus accepting legal responsibility for paying the debt if the borrower defaults (does not pay)

co-ownership—joint ownership between two or more persons

creditor—lender; one to whom money is owed

credit references—people who will recommend the credit applicant as a good credit risk

debt—money owed

debt balance—amount still owed on a debt at a given time

default—failure to fulfill the terms of the loan agreement

dependents—those who rely on a person for support

finance charge—the total cost to use credit, including interest, loan fees, and credit insurance

interest—the amount paid for the use of borrowed money

interest rate—the percentage of the principal that a borrower pays for the use of the borrowed money

liabilities—financial obligations

mortgage—a loan for purchasing real estate. If the borrower does not repay the loan according to the terms of the contract, the lender can legally force the sale of the property to pay off the loan.

mortgage holder—person or institution that made the mortgage loan

proceeds—the amount of money a borrower receives from the loan

real estate—land and property attached to the land

repossess, reclaim—to take back what was sold on an installment plan or loan if payments are not made as agreed

Rule of 78—a method of calculating interest by which the borrower pays more interest during the early months of a loan and less at the end of the loan period

securities—stocks and bonds

---

payment always saves the borrower some money since the amount of time for which the loan is borrowed has been reduced. If you plan to pay off the loan early, try not to take out a loan that uses the Rule of 78 to calculate interest. You will pay less total interest with a simple-interest loan instead."

Types of Loans

Kim said that her banker also told her about different types of loans. She shared what she knew with Mark.

A **single-payment loan** is a loan to be repaid with interest in one lump sum at the end of the stated time period. For example, a year's loan of $500 at 8 percent interest would be repaid in one lump sum of $540 ($500 plus $40 interest) at the end of one year.

An **installment loan** is repaid with interest in a series of payments. For example, the same $500 borrowed on a one-year installment loan at 8 percent interest would amount to monthly payments of $45 for one full year ($540/12).

A **promissory note** is a written contract to repay borrowed money under agreed-upon terms. Loans made on the basis of a promissory note are called **signature loans** or **unsecured loans**. The promissory note Kim signed when she borrowed money for her pre-owned car is shown in Figure 5-4.

A **secured loan** is backed by property pledged to insure payment of the loan. If you own a car or other property of value, usually real estate, you may be able to offer the property as security for the loan. This means that if you fail to repay the loan, the creditor can claim the pledged property as repayment. The property pledged as security for a loan is called **collateral**.

PROMISSORY NOTE

Atlanta , Georgia
(City) (State)

April 1 20--

For value received, undersigned maker(s), jointly and severally, promise to pay to the order of _Central Bank_ at the above place _Five hundred 00/100_ dollars ($ _500_) in _12_ consecutive monthly payments of $ _46.67_ each beginning one month from the date hereof and thereafter on the same date of each subsequent month until paid in full. Any unpaid balance may be paid at any time without penalty, and any unearned finance charge will be refunded based on the "Rule of 78's." In the event that maker(s) default(s) on any payment, a charge of _$3.00_ may be assessed.

1. Proceeds $ _500.00_
2. _____ $ _____
   (Other charges, itemized)
3. Amount financed (1 + 2) $ _500.00_
4. FINANCE CHARGE $ _60.00_
5. Total of payments $ _560.00_
   ANNUAL PERCENTAGE RATE   _12_ %

Signed _Kim Nguyen_

Figure 5-4

Kim's Promissory Note

An **unsecured loan** is a written promise to pay a debt. This type of loan is usually granted only to borrowers with a good credit rating. This loan is granted on the borrower's reputation. No property is pledged to secure the loan.

Under the Truth-in-Lending Act, lenders must provide the borrower with a written statement explaining the cost of borrowing. The borrower should check for the following terms:

1. Bottom-line dollar amount of the finance charge

2. Annual percentage rate (APR)

3. Date when the finance charge begins

4. Number, date, due date of payments, and the total amount of the payments

5. Penalty for failure to meet the repayment of terms of the loan agreement

6. Penalty for early payments of the amount due (Rule of 78)

7. Collateral held by the lender, if any

Student Activity

The following terms should be part of your vocabulary before applying for a loan. Use these terms to complete the sentences below: **single-payment loan; debt balance; secured loan; interest rate; installment loan; finance charge; co-signer; mortgage; creditor; interest.**

1. _____ is a loan in which something of value has been pledged to insure repayment of the loan.

2. _____ is a loan for purchase real estate.

3. _____ is a person who accepts legal responsibility for repaying a debt if the borrower fails to do so.

4. _____ is a loan repaid with interest in one lump sum at the end of the stated time period.

5. _____ is a loan repaid with interest in a series of payments.

6. _____ is the amount still owed at a given time.

7. _____ is the total cost of borrowed money, including loan fees, credit insurance, and interest.

8. _____ is one to whom money is owed.

9. _____ is the amount paid for the use of borrowed money.

10. _____ is the percentage of the principal that a borrower pays for the use of borrowed money.

How to Use Credit Wisely

After talking with Ms. Reed and Kim, Mark realized that credit is a wonderful opportunity to get what you want or need before you're able to pay for it all at once. He also realized that if it's misused, credit can mean financial ruin. He hated to admit it, but his father was right about the stereo. Mark should not have bought it before looking at his budget. The deed was done. He would pay for it and make ends meet. But he knew that on his current budget, he couldn't buy anything else on installment with fixed monthly payments. Mark was not in credit trouble, but he could see what Kim meant. You can get into big trouble really fast by using credit irresponsibly.

Now was a good time for Mark to make a few rules for himself so he would use credit wisely in the future.

1. Pay for small purchases with cash—either by check or with currency. Cash is always cheaper than credit. When you buy on credit, you have to pay for the borrowed money. You are really spending future income. Avoid buying just because you can buy on credit. *Credit is not free.*

2. Buy only those things on credit that will last longer than the payment period. It isn't fun to continue payment on a used car that won't run.

3. Limit the total of installment debts to 15-20 percent of your take-home pay. Most borrowers have to use 80 percent of their income for food, housing, transportation, clothing, and emergencies.

4. Keep up-to-date records of anything bought on credit.

5. Shop for the least expensive credit, just as you shop for the least expensive merchandise.

On Your Own For Life

1. Remove the loan application (Form 5-5) from the Source Documents section of this *Instructions and Source Documents Booklet* and complete it for yourself. File the application in the *Credit* file.

2. Play investigative reporter. Check out the cost of credit in your own community. Give a specific amount to be borrowed. Check out car dealerships, banks, savings and loans, credit unions, finance companies, credit cards, and department stores. Prepare a chart for the class. Show the following: (a) total amount of the finance charge; (b) the annual percentage rate (APR); (c) total number of payments; (d) amount of each monthly payment; and (e) the amount of total payments. Rank the credit (loans) from the lowest to the highest cost for a consumer. File the chart in the *Credit* file.

Check Up

Having completed the Student Activities in this chapter, you should have mastered the skills listed below. Put a checkmark next to the skills you have mastered. If you aren't sure of a skill, review that section of the chapter.

☐ How to establish creditworthiness

☐ How to establish a good credit rating

☐ How to understand consumer credit laws

☐ How to apply for a credit card

☐ How to buy on an installment plan

☐ How to obtain a loan

☐ How to use credit wisely

Now that you know how to apply for credit, move on to Chapter 6, *Preparing Income Tax Records and Beginning a Job Search.*

6 Chapter

PREPARING INCOME TAX RECORDS AND BEGINNING A JOB SEARCH

On January 17, when Mark received his paycheck, he also received his Form W-2 showing what he earned in the previous year. Earlier in the month, he had received his booklet of tax forms. Since he had all the information and forms he needed, Mark decided to prepare his income tax return. The deadline for filing a tax return is April 15 of each year. However, Mark wanted to file as early as possible. Since he had worked for only part of the year, he thought he might receive a tax refund.

Anybody who receives income from wages, salaries, interest on savings, or dividends from stock must pay taxes on the income. These taxes are called **income taxes**. Employers withhold money from each employee's paychecks and send it to the government as payments on the employee's income tax. When the amount withheld is more than the tax owed, the government will return the difference as a **tax refund**.

How to File Income Tax Forms

The first time Mark had to prepare an income tax return, the form confused him. He learned that everyone with income must complete one of the forms provided by the **Internal Revenue Service (IRS)**, an agency of the federal government that collects income taxes.

The IRS mails a booklet of tax forms and instructions to those people who filed a tax return in the previous year. If this is your first year to file, or if you don't receive the forms you need, you can request copies from an IRS office. You can also get copies of most forms at the public library or off the Internet at www.irs.gov.

When filing a return, you have to fill out a short form (Form 1040A or Form 1040EZ) or the long form (Form 1040). Currently, Mark uses Form 1040EZ, a simplified form that can be used only by single taxpayers and married couples with no children to support. The 1040EZ tax return takes Mark very little time to complete, now that he knows how to do it. He can even file electronically through the IRS e-file program, if he wishes.

In addition to Mark's federal income taxes, he must file a return every year by the same deadline (April 15) for state (Georgia) income taxes. He must attach a copy of his Form W-2 to both the federal and state tax forms.

Taxpayers who need help in filling out their tax forms have four major sources of help: the IRS, professional tax preparation services, certified public accountants (CPAs), and tax lawyers. Service from the IRS is free. You should check with the IRS first to answer your questions. Don't be intimidated by all the information. A lot of it may not apply to you. The more you know before you ask for help, the better. If you still don't understand how to complete the form, contact an IRS tax center in your area or use the toll-free telephone number. The IRS Web site also offers a long list of frequently asked questions (FAQs), with answers. Remember, the IRS offers free service. The government wants you to complete the form correctly, so get all the help you can from the IRS.

For a fee, professional tax preparation services, certified public accountants, and tax lawyers will prepare your forms, but you have to provide all the records. The complexity of your tax return determines the fee. Most taxpayers don't need this kind of assistance until their finances become more complicated and they can no longer use the simple 1040EZ form.

If you choose to have someone prepare your tax forms for you, you must still understand and approve the information provided to the IRS because you are responsible for any errors or misinformation. If a penalty results from an error, *you* will have to pay the penalty.

For people who choose to complete their own tax returns, the tax form and booklet provide line-by-line instructions. Remember, the more accurate your record-keeping system, the less time you'll have to spend preparing your tax return once a year.

If you've had more than one employer in a year, you should receive a Form W-2 from each employer. Your employers must send you a W-2 in January after the tax year. In other words, if you are completing the tax form for the 2003 tax year, you will receive your W-2 in January, 2004. However, sometimes employers can't find their employees because they have changed addresses. It is your responsibility to report all employment during the tax year by attaching W-2 forms from every employer you had that year.

Student Activity

Help Mark fill out his tax return. Remove Form 1040EZ (Form 6-1), Mark's Form W-2 (Form 6-2), and the tax table (Form 6-3) from the Source Documents section of the *Instructions and Source Documents Booklet*. Complete his Form 1040EZ using the instructions on the form and the steps below:

1. Print Mark's name, address, and social security number in the appropriate spaces. You can get this information from his Form W-2. (*Note*: The IRS label is attached to the tax instruction booklet you receive from the IRS. You would normally place the label in this space after you complete the form. Using the IRS label speeds up the processing of your tax form. But sometimes—especially if you're a first-time filer—you don't receive a booklet with the label.)

2. *Line 1*: Record Mark's total wages from his Form W-2. Be sure to print your numbers on the correct line and space. Do not use dollar signs.

3. *Line 2*: Mark did not have taxable interest income. Enter 0.

Continued

4. *Line 3:* Mark received no income in these categories. Enter 0.

5. *Line 4:* Add lines 1, 2, and 3 to calculate Mark's adjusted gross income on line 4. Since Mark had no taxable interest income or other income, his adjusted gross income is the same as his total wages shown on line 1.

6. *Line 5:* Mark's parents cannot claim him on their tax return. Therefore, place an *X* in the *No* box and enter 7,450.00 on line 5.

7. *Line 6:* Subtract line 5 from line 4 to determine Mark's taxable income. Follow instructions on the form. Enter the amount on line 6.

8. *Line 7:* Rate reduction credit does not apply to Mark. Enter 0.

9. *Line 8:* Enter the amount of federal income tax withheld from Mark's wages from his Form W-2.

10. *Line 9:* Mark has no earned income credit. Enter 0.

11. *Line 10:* Add lines 7, 8, and 9a. Enter Mark's total credits and payments.

12. *Line 11:* Use the amount on line 6 (Mark's taxable income) and the tax table to figure Mark's income tax. The example at the top of the tax table shows how to use the table. Find the range where Mark's taxable income is located and follow across the line to determine his tax. Record this amount on line 11 of Form 1040EZ.

13. *Line 12a:* Determine whether or not Mark will receive a refund. If so, enter the amount here. If not, enter 0.

14. *Line 13:* Determine whether or not Mark owes the IRS. If so, enter the amount here. If not, enter 0.

15. Check all of your addition and subtraction. Sign the form for Mark. Use January 18 as the date. Mark's occupation is salesperson.

16. Make a copy of the completed tax form and file it and the tax table in the Financial file labeled *Tax Records.*

17. Attach Mark's Form W-2 to the original Form 1040EZ where indicated, and file the tax return in the Outgoing File. Mark would mail the tax form in the envelope provided in the tax instruction booklet he received from the IRS. (*Note:* If you don't receive an addressed envelope, you should mail your tax form to the appropriate IRS office for your state. The addresses for these centers are listed in the tax instruction booklet.)

You've just prepared a real tax return. You should now be ready to tackle your own with confidence. The tax forms and tables you used are the ones available when this text was written. The government can change the forms and tables for any given year. Therefore, be sure you're using the current tax booklet when you actually prepare your tax return.

Always remember to sign and date your income tax return. Attach your Form W-2 to the return and mail it to the IRS regional office designated for your state. Always make a copy of your completed tax form and file it in your *Tax Records* file.

How to Determine Your Career Values, Interests, and Abilities

Mark wasn't happy with his job at Antwan's Auto Parts. He appreciated his salary and he liked Antwan, but there was little opportunity to improve his position or salary there. Mark wanted a job with more potential, but he didn't know what that might be. He decided to visit the Career Center at City Community College, where he had previously taken a course. Counseling services offered by the Career Center were free.

Mr. Wang, a counselor at the Center, explained that a career choice is rarely permanent. Many people change careers three or four times in a lifetime. Sometimes their second and third choices are very different from their original choice.

"So, career choices and job choices are flexible," he said. "For a 19-year-old to view a career choice as a final decision is unrealistic. How many 19-year-olds, or even 30-year-olds, know what they want to do for the rest of their lives?"

"That's not to say career choices are unimportant," Mr. Wang added, "because frequently these choices can't be easily changed. Career changes become more difficult if years of experience and education have gone into them."

Mr. Wang suggested that before making a career choice, Mark should examine his interests, values, and abilities. Then he could choose a program of study focused on a career likely to suit him. "Exploration of different careers, as well as reevaluation of your personal reasons for choosing a career, should continue even after you make a career choice," Mr. Wang said. "The cycle of career choice should go on throughout your life."

Mr. Wang added that when a career matches a person's interests, values, and abilities, work can be fun. In the beginning, understanding your career needs may be difficult, especially with little or no job experience. But you will discover that you know more about yourself than you may realize.

Mr. Wang gave Mark a worksheet to complete on his values and interests. After finishing the worksheet, Mark was still confused about what type of job to look for. He knew something about his values and interests, but what about his abilities? What was he capable of doing?

Mr. Wang assured Mark that there were ways of discovering his abilities without actually working in every type job that interested him. Many careers are related to school subjects. Often that's the best place to start.

Maybe you always wanted to be a doctor or a nurse—for whatever reason: prestige, money, or service to others. Maybe you love animals and want to be a veterinarian. But maybe you hated biology and never did well in any science classes. Since success in those subjects is necessary for a career in medicine, your chances of getting a medical degree or even being happy in the required courses are slim.

As you can see, ability is as important in selecting a career as interests and values. One way to determine your abilities in school is to recall the subject areas in which you were most interested and achieved the greatest success. Mr. Wang gave Mark some worksheets to complete.

Student Activity

1. Remove the Values-Interests Worksheet (Form 6-4) from the *Instructions and Source Documents Booklet* and complete it for yourself. When finished, file the worksheet in the Self Improvement (yellow) file labeled *Careers*.

2. Remove the Abilities Worksheet (Form 6-5) from the *Instructions and Source Documents Booklet* and fill it out for yourself. File the worksheet in the Self Improvement file labeled *Careers*.

How to Learn About Careers and Locate Job Openings

Mr. Wang said that knowing your interests, values, and abilities is the first step in making a satisfactory career choice. The second step is learning how to carry out an effective job search. Mr. Wang noticed that Mark had a very limited picture of what was available in the job market. Mark had an even more limited idea of how he fit in the job market.

When Mr. Wang asked Mark to name some careers he knew about, Mark mentioned just the few he had been exposed to during his school years: teachers, counselors, principals, cafeteria workers, cooks, maintenance personnel, doctors, nurses, and—most recently—retail sales at Antwan's. Mr. Wang suggested that Mark take some time to observe other workers in his community and come back to the Career Center to talk about the jobs he saw. The list of jobs Mark identified is shown in Figure 6-1.

Mark was amazed at the different types of jobs available that he had never even considered and might enjoy as a career.

Figure 6-1

Jobs in Mark's Community

JOBS IN MARK'S COMMUNITY

administrative assistant	gardener
architect	insurance salesperson
bank teller	librarian
carpenter	mail carrier
chef	mechanic
computer analyst	medical technician
contractor	painter
dietician	paramedic
draftsman	police officer
electrician	restaurant personnel
engineer	telephone installer
firefighter	x-ray technician

Student Activity

Make a list of ten jobs you observe in your community. In the second column, indicate whether you think the job would satisfy your interests, values, and abilities.

	Jobs	Yes/No
1.	_____	_____
2.	_____	_____
3.	_____	_____
4.	_____	_____
5.	_____	_____
6.	_____	_____
7.	_____	_____
8.	_____	_____
9.	_____	_____
10.	_____	_____

School Resources

Mr. Wang pointed out that schools offer several valuable sources of information. School counselors have career information and can help students match careers with their interests, values, and abilities. Many school libraries (as well as public libraries) have copies of the *Dictionary of Occupational Titles (DOT)*, a publication in which many jobs are classified and coded. School and public libraries usually keep a copy of the *Occupational Outlook Handbook (OOH)*, which includes job descriptions.

Most schools and colleges also have career centers that provide information and services. Many offer work-study programs that allow a student to work and receive high school credit for the work experience. Internships in college offer on-the-job training, providing another opportunity to test your job interests, values, and abilities.

Community Resources

Your community offers sources of career information as well. Looking through the Yellow Pages can give you an idea of places and types of employment in the area. The want ads in the classified section of the local newspaper list jobs available in the community. Want ads often include the job requirements as well.

Many communities have a state employment office that provides information and services related to the job market, including free pre-employment testing.

Private employment agencies—often called job placement firms—are another way to find a job. Their function is to match people with jobs. Employers hire job placement firms to find needed employees. Private agencies charge a fee that is paid by either the employer or the person seeking the job. Be sure to ask about the fee before you sign up with a job placement firm. Sometimes the job may not be worth the fee you have to pay. There are hundreds of placement firms around the country. Find out about an agency's reputation before you sign an agreement.

People as a Resource

One of the best methods to learn about jobs is to ask people to describe what they do for a living. People usually like to talk about their work. You can find out what the person does on the job, the education and skills needed, personal and professional benefits, disadvantages of the job, and expected income. Also, this can be a good way to learn about openings for specific jobs that interest you.

Internet Resources

Mr. Wang walked Mark over to the computer. "The Internet has made learning about careers and finding a job easier than it has ever been," he said. He told Mark that he could find the *OOH* on the Internet at www.bls.gov/oco and the *DOT* at www.oalj.dol.gov/libdot.htm. He explained that the *DOT* is being replaced online by O*Net at http://online.onetcenter.org. O*Net is an online database of job information. It provides search tools for exploring careers.

Mr. Wang told Mark that he could also locate career information by entering keywords like "careers" or "jobs" into a search site, such as www.google.com. To narrow the search, he could enter a career field, such as "paralegal," as a keyword. If he was interested in working for a particular company, he could go to the company Web site. Many companies list their job openings and requirements on their sites.

Mr. Wang explained that some Web sites, such as www.monster.com and www.hotjobs.com, are devoted to helping employers and job-seekers find each other. He directed Mark to www.monster.com as an example.

"Monster.com is one of my favorite career online services," Mr. Wang said. " It offers tips on interview skills and on writing a resume and cover letter. Job-seekers can post their resumes on the site for employers to evaluate. It also maintains a database of job openings posted by employers for job-seekers to search." He helped Mark pull up the job profiles list on the site. "Click a job title to see its description," said Mr. Wang. Mark clicked "Paralegal" and found the profile shown in Figure 6-2.

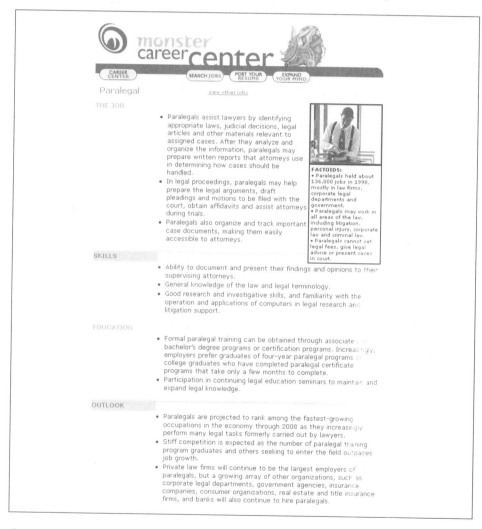

Figure 6-2

Paralegal Job Profile at the Monster.com Web Site

Source: Monster Career Center, http://jobprofiles.monster.com/App/Admin/ContentAdministration/Content/Vendors/HT/job_content/JC_LegalServices/JSC_LegalGeneral/JOB_291_paralegal/jobzilla_html?job profiles=1, accessed August 24, 2002. Courtesy of Monster.com.

Student Activity

1. Check the want ads in the classified section of your newspaper and list specific jobs that interest you. Note the education, skills, and previous work experience required. Item 0 is given as an example.

Job	Education Required	Skills Needed	Experience Required
0. teacher	college degree	teaching skills	student teaching
a.			
b.			
c.			
d.			
e.			

2. Check the Yellow Pages for the types of businesses operating in your community. List the businesses and jobs that interest you. If you know, indicate the education and skills needed for the jobs. Item 0 is given as an example.

Business	Job	Education/Skills Required
0. Speedy Copy	Work copy machines	High school diploma Technology skills
a.		
b.		
c.		
d.		
e.		

3. If you have Internet access, go online to one of the Web sites mentioned in this section, or search for another career information site. Read the descriptions of various jobs. Name three jobs that interest you and explain why.

a. _____

b. _____

c. _____

How to Apply Knowledge from Part-Time Jobs and Skills-Training Classes

Mark felt that his part-time jobs had helped him understand a lot about his interests, values, and abilities. Before working at Antwan's Auto Parts, he had worked part-time as a cashier at a convenience store. He had also made pizzas at a pizza parlor. Now he was a salesperson at Antwan's.

Thinking back, he tried to analyze what he had discovered about himself. He realized he liked working with people. He thought pizza-making was boring. He liked sales. He liked working as a cashier. He had been good in math in school, especially practical math. He liked figuring money. He was fascinated with what computers could do. He was ambitious. So, Mark felt lucky to have had experience as a part-time employee.

Mark also knew that part-time jobs aren't easy to find, especially if you're looking for a particular type of job. Here are some ways to find a part-time job:

1. Locate companies that offer summer or part-time jobs for students.

2. Ask friends or relatives to keep you in mind if they hear about job openings.

3. Read the want ads in the classified section of your local newspaper.

4. Check for Help Wanted signs in store windows.

5. Ask for assistance from your school counselor.

6. Check with temporary-help employment agencies listed in the phone book.

7. Check federal and state-funded jobs offered for young people in your community. The state employment office usually has information about such jobs.

E Student Activity

1. Give two reasons why part-time jobs can be helpful to you in choosing a career.

   a. _____
   _____

   b. _____
   _____

2. Have you ever had a part-time job? _____

Continued

If yes, what did you do? _____

What did you learn about your likes and dislikes? List them in the spaces provided below.

Likes   **Dislikes**

a. _____   f. _____

b. _____   g. _____

c. _____   h. _____

d. _____   i. _____

e. _____   j. _____

Skills training and associate degree programs in community colleges can be another helpful way to understand your career interests and abilities. Mark thought he would like to take some computer training courses at City Community College to improve his chances of getting a job more to his liking. He was fascinated with technology, and he liked business. If he decided to complete a four-year college program in the future, he would be able to transfer his courses at the community college toward a four-year college degree.

Most high schools offer some skills-training classes. Mark took keyboarding and an introductory computer course in school. If you have an interest in a particular career, high school might be a good time to find out about your abilities.

Inexpensive skills-training courses may be offered through public education after high school in your community. Some programs are government-sponsored. Some are offered as adult-education programs, and many are offered at community colleges. A school counselor or career counselor probably knows about the public skills-training programs in your community.

Some private schools offer specialized programs. One of the major advantages of a private vocational school or college is that you can usually complete the training in less time than at a publicly sponsored school. However, you will be paying much more money for a private school program than you will for the publicly supported program.

Before enrolling in a private vocational school, make sure it is accredited. An official review board grants **accreditation**, or approval, to schools that meet specific standards. Course credits earned at an unaccredited school may not transfer to other schools. Obtain information from several schools that offer the training you desire. Then compare the cost and benefits. It's a good idea to visit the schools you are considering. Make sure the advertised programs are what they say they are. If possible, sit in on the class before you register.

Talk to some of the current students about their classes and experiences at the school. Get a list of some graduates and their phone numbers. The school should willingly provide these for you. Contact a few to ask about job opportunities upon graduating from the school. Ask if the training at the school helped them get a job. If the school has a placement program, ask how helpful it was for them.

Before registering at any private school, check to see if the Better Business Bureau (BBB) has received any complaints about the school. The BBB can be found in the telephone book and online. If you decide to enroll, make sure you read the contract carefully and understand all the terms. You might have your parents or a career counselor look over the contract with you before you sign.

F Student Activity

1. List at least four steps to take before enrolling at a private vocational school.

   a. _____

   b. _____

   c. _____

   d. _____

2. Look under *Schools* or *Colleges* in the Yellow Pages. Find and list several vocational schools in your community or within commuting distance. _____

   _____

   _____

3. If you have Internet access, choose a vocational school that interests you and find its Web site. Look around the site to learn about the school. List five facts you learned from the site that will help you decide whether this school is right for you.

   a. _____

   b. _____

   c. _____

   d. _____

   e. _____

Continued

4. Look under *Vocational Guidance, Career Counseling,* or *Guidance* in the Yellow Pages. List several vocational guidance agencies, if any, listed in your area. _____

_____

_____

_____

5. Record the following transactions for Mark:

   a. On January 22, Mark used his credit card to buy new towels for his apartment. Remove the credit card receipt (Form 6-6) from the Source Documents section of this *Instructions and Source Documents Booklet* and record the transaction in the *Financial Management Records Booklet.* File the receipt in the Financial file labeled *Credit—Bank Card.*

   b. On January 24, Mark received and deposited his pay-check. He deposited $240.01 and kept $85.00 cash. Record the deposit in the check register. Record Mark's weekly income of $325.01 in the Fourth Week box in the *Financial Management Records Booklet.* Also record Mark's expenditures in the *Records Booklet.* Mark spent the following cash amounts on January 24: eating out, $15.00; transportation, $12.00; evening out, $30.00.

   c. On January 25, Mark got the flu and had to go to the doctor. The doctor prescribed antibiotics. Mark wrote Check 111 to Dr. Carl Jones for $48.00 for the office visit. He wrote Check 112 to Thrift Drugs for $52.57 for the antibiotics. Record the checks in the check register and *Financial Management Records Booklet.* File the checks in the Outgoing File.

How to Apply for a Job

Mark remembered how nervous he was when he was looking for his first full-time job. He was proud to be holding a high school diploma in his hand, but like so many high school or college graduates, he had little idea where to begin. His friend Troy had dropped out in 10th grade. Mark tried to imagine how difficult it must have been for Troy to find a job.

When Mark applied for his first full-time job, he walked into Southern Body Shop and announced he would do anything. He meant to sound like a friendly and willing worker. The manager interpreted Mark's statement to mean he had no particular skills. Mark wasn't hired. Even though Mark was willing to do almost anything, he should have specified his skills and how they fit the job he was applying for.

Preparing a Resume

Before Mark applied for his first full-time job, he should have prepared a resume. A **resume** is a history of the person's education and job experience. A resume tells a lot about you in a brief space. It will also provide you with the information you need to complete a job application form.

When compiling a resume, you want to emphasize your experience, skills, and abilities that relate to the job for which you're applying. If you're applying for a job as an administrative assistant, you want to mention any past experience in that role, even if it was volunteer work or clerical work done at school. If this is your first job, mention high school classes that relate (keyboarding, office technology, business communications, word processing, or other computer-related classes). Mention any special honors that relate to the job or offer evidence of your character. Never lie or overstate your accomplishments. What you are like as a person has everything to do with whether or not you are seriously considered as a potential employee. As you gain work experience, you need to update your resume.

You may want to include **references**, names of people who will testify to your abilities, character, and experience. Before naming someone as a reference, ask the person's permission. A negative response from someone whom you have given as a reference can certainly hurt your chances of getting a job.

List personal information only when it is to your benefit. It's not necessary to give your age, sex, marital status, weight, or height. Furthermore, it is against the law for an employer to discriminate because of any of these factors. Also, a job application cannot contain questions of this nature.

Resumes for most young people with little work experience should be limited to one page. You will not impress an employer by adding information that is unrelated to the job. You can add relevant information and drop irrelevant information as you apply for different types of jobs. However, as you gain more work experience, skills, and education, your resume will expand to another page or more to include these.

The appearance of a resume is extremely important. A resume that is sloppy and contains misspelled words and typing errors suggests that you will be a sloppy, error-prone employee. This is not the kind of worker an employer wants to hire.

Prepare your resume on a word processor. If you don't have a computer, you may be able to use one at school or rent time on one at a copy center. A word processor offers many options for type styles, type sizes, and layout, but don't get fancy. Keep it simple and professional. Arrange the categories in a way that is clear, easy to read, and uncluttered. The employer should be able to see at a glance your skills, education, and experience. Use the spell-checker to look for errors, but don't depend on it as your only check. Always proofread your resume several times and have someone else read it as well. When you are sure it is error-free and gives a good picture of your strengths, print it on good-quality paper. Use the best resolution setting on the printer.

- Do not enclose anything, including transcripts or other documents, with your resume. Take those documents with you to the interview.

Mark revised his resume three times before using it to apply for a job at Antwan's Auto Parts. The final version that got him an interview with Antwan is shown in Figure 6-3. Notice how the categories are arranged. List work experience and education from the most recent to the least recent. The style Mark used represents only one approach to preparing a resume. At a library or bookstore, you can find many good books about writing resumes. They include examples of styles that fit particular circumstances. Also, resume-writing software and many word-processing programs offer resume templates. A **template** is a ready-made framework for a document that already includes formatting. You would simply insert your own information into the resume template.

Figure 6-3

Mark's Resume

	MARK L. SMITH
	1040 Peachtree Drive
	Atlanta, GA 30319-1396
	(404) 555-1254

Education	
September, 20--, to June, 20--	Presidents High School, Atlanta, GA Diploma, June, 20--
Work Experience	
(part-time) September, 20--, to December, 20--	*Cook* Pizza Place, Atlanta, GA Mr. George Young, Manager: "Mark is prompt, efficient, and friendly. He keeps his composure during fast-paced, hectic situations."
June, 20--, to September, 20--	*Cashier* Food Bags Grocery, Atlanta, GA Ms. Joan Mills, Supervisor: "Our repeat customers would seek out Mark because of his friendly and efficient manner."
January, 20--, to May, 20--	*Cashier* Quick Stop, Atlanta, GA Mrs. Gloria Velez, Manager: "Mark is friendly and mature for his age. He is a quick learner."
August, 20--, to January, 20--	*Cashier in Campus Bookstore* Presidents High School, Atlanta, GA Ms. Ai-Ling Yan, Faculty Sponsor: "Mark is one of the fastest, most reliable cashiers in the store."
Special Skills	• Successfully completed classes in Keyboarding and Introduction to Computers • Excelled in Math • Skilled in handling money and working with cash-register scanning technology
Awards	Voted "Friendliest in the Senior Class"
References	Will be provided upon request

Mark's resume is contained on one page, but it says a lot about his character, skills, and work experience. A potential employer can easily perceive the following information about Mark: He had the initiative and responsibility to help out his family financially by working part-time jobs. He received good reviews from his supervisors, whose comments suggest that he is friendly, efficient, and reliable. His ability and competence as a cashier carried over to two other part-time jobs. The special skills he listed would be useful in many jobs. His being voted friendliest in his class supported his supervisors' assessment that he is good with people. He was smart to add that to his resume. Antwan hired him.

Notice Mark did not list references. However, he did name his supervisors for each job, so he is not hiding anything. By not listing references, he has the option of finding out more about his potential employer's contacts and may list those if he has a mutual contact and reference.

Kim used a similar style for her resume, but she decided to include references. Kim's resume is shown in Figure 6-4.

Figure 6-4

Kim's Resume

KIM NGUYEN
105 Rose Boulevard
Township, GA 67811-1113
(404) 555-4325   knguyen@skynet.com

Education
September, 20--, to
June, 20--

Presidents High School, Atlanta, GA
Diploma with Honors, June, 20--

Work Experience
July, 20--, to
present

Retail Salesperson
Mayapple Antiques, Atlanta, GA
Ms. Margaret Russell, Owner
• Acquired extensive knowledge of each antique in stock
• Responsible for closing the store on weekends
• Supervised three sales associates

January, 20--, to
July, 20--

Administrative Assistant
Jefferson Hospital, Atlanta, GA
Mrs. Ana Torres, Manager
• Keyed patient information into hospital's database
• Helped solve problems concerning insurance reimbursement

May, 20--, to
Present

Volunteer
Shelter Soup Kitchens, Atlanta, GA
Mr. Richard Klein, Volunteer Coordinator
• Prepared and served meals

Special Skills

• Skilled with database and inventory-tracking software
• Successfully completed training course in salesmanship
• Received A's in Keyboarding and Internet Basics

Awards

• National Honor Society all four years in high school
• Elected captain of the soccer team

References

Mrs. Ana Torres
Jefferson Hospital
2781 Main Street
Atlanta, GA 39411-1111
(404) 555-0800

Ms. Margaret Russell
Mayapple Antiques
2222 Running Way
Atlanta, GA 30312-4760
(404) 555-7819

Miss Sarah Ryder, Counselor
Presidents High School
5656 Reading Road
Atlanta, GA 39411-1232
(404) 555-8811

G Student Activity

1. In paragraph form, write what you know about Kim from her resume.

2. Prepare a resume for yourself. Make it realistic by giving the name of your school and the anticipated date of your graduation. If you have no information for a particular resume category, do not list that category. Some suggested categories in addition to education and work experience are special job skills, extracurricular activities, academic honors, community and school service, and volunteer work. Prepare your resume on a computer's word processor. Check it carefully. Then print it on a plain sheet of paper. File your paper resume and an electronic copy on a floppy disk in the Personal file labeled *Resume*.

Preparing a Cover Letter

Sometimes you will mail or e-mail your resume rather than hand-deliver it. When you mail your resume, you should send a **cover letter** that explains your interest in the job and the reason you are particularly qualified for it. If you're attaching your resume to an e-mail message, the body of the message is your cover letter. Do not repeat everything on your resume. Keep the letter concise and to the point. You want to get the employer to pay attention to your resume, so emphasize information that will interest the employer. Be sure to enclose your resume with the cover letter, or attach it to your e-mail cover letter.

A cover letter should always contain the following information:

1. The position for which you are applying and how you found out about it

2. Your qualifications that best fit the job

3. Your request for an interview

Figure 6-5 is a copy of the letter that Mark sent with his resume. Every cover letter will vary, according to the nature of the job to which you are applying. Think about the skills required for that particular job. Then select for your cover letter the two or three skills you have that best fit that job. The goal of your cover letter is to interest the employer in reading your resume and granting you an interview.

Never send a resume without a cover letter. The cover letter is your introduction. It is your first impression. It teaches the employer a lot about you:

- Your ability to get to the point

- Your ability to summarize

- Your ability to organize your thoughts

- Your ability to make a sales pitch—to sell yourself

- Your ability to express yourself clearly and appropriately

- Your attention to detail (grammar, spelling, clean paper)

- Your sincerity

- Your personality

Figure 6-5

Mark's Cover Letter

1040 Peachtree Drive
Atlanta, GA 30319-1396
July 15, 20--

Mr. Antwan Jackson
Antwan's Auto Parts
7890 Makeshift Drive
Atlanta, GA 30317-6247

Dear Mr. Jackson:

I would like to apply for the sales position you advertised in *The Atlanta Constitution*. I have experience as a cashier and enjoy working with people.

While a sophomore at Presidents High School, I participated in the work-study program and gained valuable business experience working as a cashier in the bookstore. As you can see from my resume, that experience prepared me for other jobs in the business world. My supervisors have all been pleased with my personal and professional skills. I get along well with people and was voted "Friendliest in the Senior Class" by my classmates.

I am available for an immediate interview. Please call me at 555-1254 after 4:30 p.m. to set up a time convenient for you.

Sincerely,

Mark L. Smith

Mark L. Smith

Enclosure

Completing an Application Form

When applying for a job in person, make sure you have all the needed information with you. Be sure to take several copies of your resume. It should contain most of the information asked for on an application form. Also have a list of references, including addresses and phone numbers, that you can supply if asked.

When filling out an application form, you should do the following:

1. Follow directions carefully.

2. Complete the form in blue or black ink.

3. Print answers neatly.

4. Answer all questions.

5. Give complete answers.

6. Never lie or try to deceive!

Sometimes the completed job application is the first impression an employer has of you. If you don't understand a question on the form, ask for an explanation. The receptionist is usually very willing to help you. Take a pocket dictionary with you to check for misspelled words.

Whenever possible, pick up the application form and take it home. Make a copy of the form and complete the copy at home. Have someone look it over for you. Then, type or print in ink on the original form.

Student Activity

1. You are applying for your first full-time job after graduation. Remove the Job Application Form (Form 6-7) from the *Instructions and Source Documents Booklet*. Remove your resume from the *Resume* file. Using the information from your resume, complete the form as if it were the real thing.

2. Rate yourself on your ability to fill out an application by answering yes or no to the following questions:

   _____ a. Did you read the application through before you filled it out, so you knew what was coming? (If you filled in your first name where they wanted your last, the employer might assume you can't follow directions on the job.)

Continued

_____ b. Did you fill it out in ink?

_____ c. Did you fill in every space, even if you had to put _no, none,_ or _not applicable?_ (The person reviewing the application may assume you overlooked the questions or just didn't care to answer.)

_____ d. Were you neat? (Some businesses use forms merely to test how careful you are.)

_____ e. Did you give exact dates of education and experience, and not vague answers? (Don't pretend to have knowledge or experience that you lack.)

_____ f. Where it said _Date,_ did you put today's date, and not when you want the job? Did you spell out the month and include the year?

_____ g. Did you give your full legal name, as you would like it on the permanent record of the company? (Don't use a nickname on official documents.)

_____ h. Did you give the complete company name and address of your previous employment? Usually you are asked to list your most recent job first.

_____ i. Did you answer yes to all the questions above?

3. File your job application in the Personal file labeled _Job Search_ for future reference. Return your resume to the _Resume_ file.

4. Find a job advertised in the want ads of your newspaper (or elsewhere), and write a letter of application for the job. Place the letter in the _Job Search_ file.

How to Prepare for a Job Interview

Consider yourself lucky if you are granted an interview for a job. A large majority of job applicants never get past the application or resume. If an employer offers an interview, he or she is interested in your qualifications. It is your opportunity to sell yourself, so make the best of it. Remember, always go to the interview. Even if you don't think you want the job, you'll gain valuable interviewing experience. Going to an interview does not necessarily mean you are going to take the job, even if it is offered. While the employer is interviewing you, you are interviewing the employer.

Some interviews are more formal than others. The formality of the interview usually depends upon the type of job. Whether formal or informal, the interview is very important.

Wear appropriate clothes for the interview. If you apply to a fast food restaurant, you don't need to wear a suit unless you're applying as a manager. On the other hand, you shouldn't wear your worst pair of jeans. As a general rule, dress neatly, modestly, and conservatively. Much of an employer's opinion of you will be based on that first impression—the way you look and act during the interview.

Interview Guidelines

Mark knew how important an interview can be. It may last only 10 or 15 minutes, but within that short time, an employer is making decisions about the possibility of hiring you. Mark's school counselor had given him a set of interview guidelines when Mark scheduled his first job interview outside school. For the first time, Mark realized nobody knew him outside the school. When he had applied for the job in the bookstore, his teachers (who knew his qualifications) put in a good word for him, and he got the job. But to apply for a job in the community was a different story. He remembered being very nervous. The counselor's guidelines are shown in Figure 6-6 on page 123.

Questions Commonly Asked in an Interview

The following questions are frequently asked by the interviewer. Before you go to your interview, think about how you will answer them.

1. Why do you want to work for this company?

2. What jobs have you had, and why did you leave them?

3. What do you have to offer us if you work here?

4. What are your weaknesses?

5. What special qualities and abilities do you have that qualify you for this job?

6. Why should we hire you, rather than someone else, for this job?

7. What kind of salary expectations do you have for this job? (You should find out the general pay range before the interview.)

Figure 6-6

Interview Guidelines

INTERVIEW GUIDELINES

Before the Interview

1. Make sure you know the time and place of the interview. Be sure you know how to get there and how long it will take. Don't be late! Arrive 15 minutes early.
2. Know the full name and position of the interviewer.
3. Get adequate rest the night before your interview so you'll be at your best mentally and physically.
4. Take the necessary tools with you: pen, pencil, social security card, your resume, and your list of references.
5. Gather as much information as you can about the company's background, products, and services. Know something about the position you are applying for, what you will be expected to do, and what skills will be required. Be prepared to give reasons for wanting the job.
6. Show your independence by going to the interview alone. Do not go with a friend or your parents.
7. Dress appropriately. Take care of personal hygiene: brush your teeth, wear deodorant, comb your hair. Do not chew gum.

Selling Yourself at the Interview

1. Enter the room confident and poised, but not overconfident. Greet the interviewer and use his or her name with title (Mr., Ms., Dr.). Introduce yourself, giving your name distinctly. If a hand is offered to shake, do so with a firm handshake as you look the person directly in the eyes. Remain standing until invited to sit down.
2. Maintain good posture during the interview. Do not touch articles on the interviewer's desk, bite your nails, chew gum, or smoke. Occasionally look directly at the interviewer.
3. Let the interviewer direct the conversation but don't hesitate to focus attention on your strengths. Answer questions sincerely. Do not exaggerate or mislead by telling half-truths. Admit any limitations you may have and explain what you are willing to do to eliminate shortcomings. For instance, if you don't have the education or experience that you feel your employer may desire, emphasize other skills such as "hard worker" and "fast learner." Give examples. Do not interrupt the interviewer.
4. Listen carefully to the questions and comments of the interviewer so you don't miss the point or overlook valuable information.
5. Do not discuss your personal problems, air your prejudices, or criticize others.
6. If the interviewer has not offered information about salary by the end of the interview, ask what the pay will be for a person with your education and experience.
7. If you haven't been offered the job at the conclusion of the interview, ask when you can expect to hear the company's decision.
8. When the interview is over, don't hang around. Thank the interviewer for the consideration, reemphasize your interest in the job, and politely leave.

After the Interview

1. Write the interviewer a short follow-up letter. Again, thank the interviewer and indicate your continuing interest in the job. You would be surprised how few job candidates write a follow-up letter after an interview. For those who do, it often means a job offer.
2. If the job is offered to you, make sure you understand all the requirements for acceptance (completing a health exam, for example) and fulfill them as soon as possible.
3. Don't be discouraged if you fail to get the first few jobs for which you apply. Think about the interviews and try to determine how you can improve them. If you feel comfortable enough with the person who interviewed you, call and ask his or her opinion of the interview. Ask how you might improve on future interviews.

Student Activity

1. List five preparations you should make before going to a job interview.

   a. _____

   b. _____

   c. _____

   d. _____

   e. _____

2. Choose a job advertised in the want ads of a local newspaper or choose any job you might be interested in applying for after graduation. Answer the following questions as if you are really being interviewed for that job.

   a. What job are you applying for? _____

   b. Why do you want to work for this company? _____
   _____

   c. What do you know about this company? _____
   _____

   d. What jobs have you had, and why did you leave them?
   _____
   _____

   e. How does your work experience match this job? _____
   _____
   _____

   f. What are your weaknesses? _____
   _____

   g. Why should we hire you, rather then someone else, for this job? _____
   _____

   h. What kind of salary expectation do you have for this job?
   _____

Questions an Interviewer Cannot Ask

Title VII of the Civil Rights Act of 1964, as amended by the Equal Employment Opportunity Act of 1972, prohibits job discrimination because of race, color, religion, sex, or national origin. This is enforced by the U.S. Equal Employment Opportunity Commission. Because of these laws, it is illegal for an interviewer to ask certain questions about the birthplace of the applicant, dependents, plans for pregnancy, religious background, or history of arrests (history of convictions can be asked). A photograph of the applicant cannot be required. The applicant may offer any personal information he or she wishes but should dwell only on information that will increase the chances of getting the job.

Questions You Should Ask

Near the end of the interview, the interviewer may ask if you have questions. Take full advantage of this opportunity. You may want to ask about benefits, such as health insurance and vacation time. You may want to know more about the specifics of the job or about the promotional opportunities within the company. Write down your list of questions before you go to the interview. If these questions have not been answered during the interview, ask them at the end.

Preparing a Follow-Up Letter

Within a day or two after the interview, you should send a follow-up letter. The purpose of the letter is to prompt the interviewer to remember you and to remind him or her of your key qualifications. Thank the interviewer for his or her time. Again express your interest in the job. If several people interviewed you, mention each of them. You never know who has the most influence in making the hiring decision.

If the interview left you with the impression that you were lacking in some way, you might offer a solution in your follow-up letter. For example, you might offer to enroll in an enrichment or skills course in the area in which you are considered weak. However, if nothing was said about a weakness, don't mention it. As a general rule, keep the letter positive and upbeat. Figure 6-7 on page 127 is an example of a typical follow-up letter.

J Student Activity

1. List three questions that an interviewer cannot legally ask.

   a. _____

   b. _____

   c. _____

2. Record the following transactions for Mark:

   a. On January 31, Mark received and deposited his paycheck. He deposited $240.01 and kept $85.00 in cash.

   Continued

Record the deposit in the check register. Record Mark's $325.01 income and cash expenditures for the week in the *Financial Management Records Booklet*. Mark had become careless about writing down his cash expenditures this week, so he had to estimate. Worse, he didn't know what he spent when. All he knew was he had spent every nickel in his cash envelope. He decided to record all cash expenditures on January 30 in his *Records Booklet*. Mark estimated he spent the following cash amounts: food, $50.00; transportation; $10.00; personal, $25.00; entertainment, $30.00.

b. While recording his cash expenditures, Mark remembered he had run out of cash mid-week and withdrew $50.00 using his ATM card. He misplaced his ATM receipt before filing it, so he was not sure when he withdrew the money. He thought it was January 29. He recorded the $50.00 withdrawal in his check register. He entered the $50.00 in his *Records Booklet* as an expenditure on January 29 under Miscellaneous.

c. On January 31, Mark received his bank statement dated January 27, 20--. Remove the bank statement (Form 6-8) and canceled checks (Form 6-9) from the *Instructions and Source Documents Booklet*. Verify Mark's bank statement against his check register and complete the reconciliation form on the back of the bank statement. Record the bank service charge in Mark's check register and *Financial Management Records Booklet*. If you need to review the procedures for reconciling a bank statement, refer to Chapter 2. File the canceled checks in the *Checking Account—Canceled Checks* file.

d. Total Mark's *Financial Management Records Booklet*. If you need to review the procedures for these activities, refer to Chapter 3. Use Mark's monthly budget figures from Figure 3-8, page 44.

Figure 6-7

Kim's Follow-Up Letter

105 Rose Boulevard
Township, GA 67811-1113
June 23, 20 --

Ms. Stephanie Hermann
Downtown Chic
109 Park Lane
Atlanta, GA 30312-2691

Dear Ms. Hermann:

Thank you for the opportunity to meet with you Wednesday to discuss the position of retail sales
associate at Downtown Chic. The job is most attractive to me and offers the kind of opportunity I
am looking for. I especially appreciated your view of sales in light of the present competition. I
feel that my previous sales experience and knowledge of inventory practices will be a great asset
to your store.

Please express my appreciation to Mrs. King for showing me the inventory process. I look
forward to hearing from you soon.

Sincerely,

Kim Nguyen

Kim Nguyen

On Your Own *For Life*

In Student Activity I, you answered questions as if you were really being interviewed. Now you feel you have had a successful interview for the job. Write a follow-up letter to the interviewer. File the letter in the Personal file labeled *Job Search*.

Check Up

Having completed the Student Activities in this chapter, you should have mastered the skills listed below. Put a checkmark next to the skills you have mastered. If you aren't sure of a skill, review that section of the chapter.

☐ How to file income tax forms

☐ How to determine your career values, interests, and abilities

☐ How to learn about careers and locate job openings

☐ How to apply knowledge from part-time jobs and skills-training classes

☐ How to apply for a job

☐ How to prepare for a job interview

Now that you know how to prepare income tax records and conduct a job search, move on to Chapter 7, *Looking for Housing*.

Chapter 7

LOOKING FOR HOUSING

PHOTO: © GETTY IMAGES/
PHOTODISC

As he was finishing his record keeping for January, Mark received another unpleasant call from Carlos. Carlos wanted to know why Mark had not yet moved into the apartment. Mark explained that he had been sick with the flu. Carlos told Mark he had budgeted for only half the rent in February, so he needed Mark's check for $350 immediately. Carlos also said that Mark should pay for his part of the utilities in February since that was the arrangement. Carlos had paid for all the utilities in January. Mark was also expected to pay for the first week's groceries since they had agreed to alternate grocery shopping by the week.

How to Prepare for Independent Living

Mark didn't remember making these specific arrangements with Carlos. In fact, he knew he hadn't. Mark called Kim and complained.

"Well, you did agree to share expenses," Kim said. "And if I remember correctly, Carlos wasn't too wild about your moving in with him in the first place."

"I can't help getting the flu," Mark said. "He acts like he's doing me a favor."

"Well, I guess he thinks he is. You know, Mark, you don't have many options," she said. "You can't live at home too much longer, and you can't afford to live in an apartment by yourself. You're not in college so you can't use campus housing. It goes without saying you can't buy a house. Those are about the only options anybody has when it comes to housing."

Mark was beginning to feel resentful—not the best way to begin a shared housing situation.

Discuss Living Arrangements

Although Mark had two months to prepare for the move to apartment living, he felt he needed a longer planning period before moving into an apartment with anybody. Now he knew that he should have discussed major living arrangements with Carlos before agreeing to share an apartment with him. Because he felt pressured, he had allowed Carlos to make all the living arrangements. Here are some points to consider if you plan to share an apartment:

1. *Discuss your responsibilities and living habits.* Discuss how you will divide household responsibilities and expenses, including rent, utilities, groceries, and any other bills you will share. Agree ahead of time about all financial arrangements if either partner moves out before the lease is up and how damages to the apartment will be shared. Discuss living habits such as neatness, apartment guests, entertainment rules, and quiet time.

2. *Put everything in writing* to avoid misunderstandings later.

3. *Look for and decide on an apartment together* so that, later on, one partner can't blame the other for a poor choice of housing.

Mark thought he had made arrangements with Carlos about procedures for paying apartment costs, but the agreement wasn't in writing. Evidently, they didn't agree on the manner of sharing expenses. Also, Mark was moving into Carlos's apartment, which put Mark at a disadvantage, at least in this case. They didn't choose the apartment together. It was Carlos's apartment, and he seemed to be setting all the rules.

Mark forgot to tell Kim something else. Carlos said Mark had to bring his own household items, including furniture. Mark was required to provide lamps, pillows, bedroom furniture, a TV for his bedroom, and cooking utensils. Mark couldn't believe what he was hearing. He had been gradually purchasing sheets and some household items in preparation for the move, but to buy them all at once would be impossible according to his monthly budget. Mark was sure he had seen a bed in the second bedroom of the apartment and assumed he could use it.

Plan for Initial Apartment Expenses

Obviously, Mark had not planned for the initial expenses of renting. In addition to monthly rent, the following expenses should be included in the first month's budget:

1. *First and last month's rent.* Some rental contracts require that the first and last month's rent be paid up front. These payments protect owners from loss if renters leave without notice or payment of rent due.

2. *Security or damage deposit.* Find out to what extent you are held responsible for possible damage to the apartment. If you leave the apartment in the same condition as when you rented it, the deposit must be returned.

3. *Gas and/or electric utility service.* A fee is often charged for initial hookups.

4. *Telephone installation.* The amount of the fee varies according to your specifications: number of wall jacks, call-forwarding, call-waiting, caller ID, or cellular service.

5. *Cable installation.* A fee is often charged for initial hookups.

6. *Water and garbage services.* Arrangements may have to be made for water usage and garbage pick-up. Sometimes the owner pays for these services. You need to ask.

How to Look for an Apartment

Before now, Mark really hadn't thought about how to look for an apartment. He had been lucky to run into Carlos and find a place so quickly. You can find out about apartments for rent from the following sources:

1. *Family and friends.* Family and friends often know about a place to rent before the apartment is advertised in the newspaper. Owners frequently like to rent to people they know or to those referred by trustworthy acquaintances.

2. *Classified section of your local newspaper.* Ads in the newspaper will give you a good idea of the cost of various types of apartments in different sections of the city or community. The ads also provide information such as the number of rooms, whether pets are allowed, and if utilities are furnished. Often, newspapers post their classified ads on their Web sites as well.

3. *Real estate agencies.* Some agencies have apartment listings. Usually the agent's fee is paid by the owner of the building, so the assistance is free for you. Real estate agencies are a big help when you are moving to an unfamiliar place.

4. *Apartment managers.* Call or visit the apartment manager's office and ask if there are any apartments for rent.

5. *The Internet.* Some Web sites, such as www.homestore.com and www.forrent.com, allow you to search for apartments in many cities across the country. You can enter specifications, such as price range and number of bedrooms, to narrow your search. These sites usually offer other useful resources, such as links to moving services and tips about packing and moving yourself.

When you have selected several apartments that you like and can afford, take a careful look at each apartment. Ask the apartment manager the following questions:

1. What is the monthly rent? Initial deposit?

2. What expenses does the rent include? Water? Garbage? Utilities?

3. Is a lease required?

4. What type of security is provided?

5. What are the parking provisions?

6. What are the rules and regulations? Are pets allowed?

Before deciding on an apartment, talk to the tenants. Ask what they like and don't like about the living conditions. If they are willing to give you some time, ask the following questions:

1. How good is security?

2. Is the place noisy?

3. How often is the rent increased? By how much?

4. Are repairs made quickly?

5. Is the building kept in good repair?

6. How long have they lived there?

7. Would they recommend living there to their friends?

Student Activity

1. What three points did Mark fail to consider when he agreed to share an apartment with Carlos?

   a. _____

   b. _____

   c. _____

2. What initial expenses should you plan for during the first month of renting?

   a. _____

   b. _____

   c. _____

   d. _____

   e. _____

3. Name five sources for locating apartments for rent.

   a. _____

   b. _____

   c. _____

   d. _____

   e. _____

4. If you were Mark, what would you do? Check one.

   _____ Move in with Carlos February 1.

   _____ Look for another living arrangement.

   Give reasons for your answers.

   _____

   _____

   _____

   _____

5. If you move into an unfurnished apartment after graduation, you will need to plan for the costs of household items and initial apartment expenses. First, list the household items you think you will need. Then, research prices by looking for ads in the newspaper or by visiting stores in your area. Enter a typical price for each item and calculate the total costs. Finally,

Continued

enter the cost of each initial apartment expense and calculate the total costs.

Household Items   **Costs**

_____   _____

_____   _____

_____   _____

_____   _____

_____   _____

_____   _____

_____   _____

_____   _____

                                        Total _____

**Initial Apartment Expenses
(Use averages for your area.)**   **Costs**

First and last month's rent   _____
Security deposit   _____
Gas/electric utilities   _____
Telephone installation   _____
Cable installation   _____
Water and garbage services   _____

                                        Total _____

6. Answer the following questions:

   a. If you are earning $6 an hour for a 40-hour week, what is your weekly gross pay?_____

   b. If approximately 20% of your gross pay is withheld for taxes, what is your weekly net income? _____

   c. What is your yearly net income?_____

   d. What is your monthly net income? _____

   e. With the help of your banker, you determine that you can afford no more than 50 percent of your net income for housing. How much can you afford to pay each month for an apartment?_____

Kim offered to drive Mark around just to see what they could find as an alternative to living with Carlos. When they stopped for gas, Mark's high school football buddy, Roberto Gonzalez, was working the cash register. Roberto was glad to see them. He said he was taking classes at City College and had a part-time job working at the gas station.

When he heard Mark was looking for an apartment, he was full of good news. Roberto was renting at a place called College Park. The complex was not connected with City College but housed mostly college students and young people.

Roberto described the housing arrangement at College Park. Each apartment housed four people in separate bedrooms but had a common living area and kitchen. Each of the **tenants** (people renting the apartment) had a separate lease, so Roberto was not responsible for the others' bedrooms and rental payments. The complex had a swimming pool, tennis courts, and exercise room. Roberto saved the best part until last. One of the four in his complex was moving out February 1 because he got a job out of town.

Mark couldn't believe his change of luck. "So, how much?" he asked.

"The apartment rents for $1,200. Each of us pays $300 a month," Roberto said. "We share the cost of utilities and water."

"Where do I sign?" Mark was excited about the prospect of sharing living space with Roberto.

"Let's go take a look," Kim said more cautiously.

Roberto and Mark had similar personality types, and Roberto clearly indicated that Mark was welcome to share the apartment. Roberto was sure the other two roommates would like Mark. Still, Kim reminded Mark of his quick decision to move in with Carlos. Also, he had already paid a month's rent as a deposit for Carlos's apartment. In Carlos's present mood, Mark did not expect to get it back.

How to Interpret a Lease

On the way to the College Park complex, Kim and Mark talked about leases. A **lease** is a written contract allowing the use of the owner's property for a designated period of time. A common period of time is one year. Mark and Kim discussed various features of a lease.

It is possible to rent property without a lease for an indefinite period of time. However, if there is no lease, the owner, called the **landlord**, can raise the rent at any time or ask you to leave with little notice. (State law may require 30 days' notice.) On the other hand, if there is no lease, you—the **renter** or **tenant**—have the right to move out of the apartment whenever you want. Again, this depends on state law, since you are not under contract for a specified period of time.

It's a good idea to sign a lease, unless you definitely plan to stay in the apartment for just a few months. Before you sign a lease, you should read it carefully and inspect the apartment that you intend to rent. Don't ever rent after seeing only a model (showroom) apartment.

You will probably be required to pay a security deposit for possible damage to the apartment. Therefore, you should note the condition of everything in the place so you will not be held financially responsible for someone else's damage. One way to avoid disagreement when the time comes for you to get back your deposit is to complete a condition report (checklist) before signing a lease. Be sure both you and the owner sign it so there will be no misunderstanding later. There is no substitute for a written agreement.

Figure 7-1 is a copy of the lease Mark eventually signed at College Park. When signing a lease, know that the landlord (**lessor**) and the tenant (**lessee**) are bound by all the terms agreed upon in the lease. Do not rely on any "agreement" that is not in writing. The lessor is legally responsible only to written agreements. All agreements should be contained in the lease.

In general, take note of the following in the apartment lease before signing:

1. Requirements for the return of the security deposit

2. Responsibilities placed on both parties by the lease

3. Legal rights of both the lessor and the lessee if any violations of the lease occur

4. Party responsible for repairs and maintenance

5. Oral agreements that should be added to the lease

Now that Mark had signed a lease on the apartment at College Park, he had to call Carlos. Mark explained that he would not be moving into Carlos's apartment. At first Carlos was very upset. He had counted on Mark to share the rent and other expenses. However, as they continued to talk, they both agreed that sharing an apartment probably would not have worked for them since they had gotten off to such a bad start. They had made one big mistake: they had not discussed living arrangements before agreeing to share housing. Carlos said he would return Mark's $350 rent deposit as soon as he had a little extra cash. Mark knew he was lucky to have the matter end on a friendly note.

After Mark signed the lease, Kim explained to him that he should notify the bank of his new address. Mark went to the bank and completed the paperwork to have his new address at College Park printed on his checks and deposit slips. He was told that his new checks would arrive in a couple of weeks. In the meantime, he could continue to use the checks he already had. The bank also needed to have his address in order to send him his bank statement. Mark then filled out a form at the post office to have his mail forwarded to his new address.

Figure 7-1

Mark's Apartment
Lease

APARTMENT LEASE

Date *February 1, 20--*

Parties

College Park (hereafter referred to as Lessor)
hereby leases to *Mark L. Smith* (hereafter referred to as
Lessee) the following described property:

Premises

Apartment No. *3* at *333 College Drive*
in *Atlanta, GA* for use by resident as a private residence only.

Term

This lease is for a term commencing on the *1* day of *February*
20 *--*, and ending on the last calendar day *February*, 20 *--*.

Automatic Renewal

If Lessee, or Lessor, desires that this lease terminate at the expiration of its term, he or she must give to the other party written notice at least 30 days prior to that date. Failure of either party to give this required notice will automatically renew this lease and all the terms thereof except that the term of the lease will be for one month. This provision is a continuing one and will apply at the expiration of the original term and at the expiration of each subsequent term.

Rent

This lease is made for and in consideration of a monthly rental of *($300)*
Three hundred Dollars per month payable in advance on or before the
1st day of each month at *333 College Drive*
. Any monthly rental payment not received by the 5th of the month shall be considered delinquent. If Lessee pays by check and said check is not honored on presentation for any reason whatsoever, Lessee agrees to pay an additional sum of $25.00 as a penalty.

In the event that the rent is not paid by the 10th of the month, Lessee shall be deemed to be in default; and Lessor shall have the option to cancel this lease effective at midnight of the 14th of the month. On or before the termination date, Lessor shall deliver written notice of Lessor's election to cancel this lease to Lessee's premises.

Lessor acknowledges receipt from Lessee of the sum of *($300) Three hundred*
Dollars which is pro-rated rental for *30* days from the date of commencement of this lease to the first day of the following month.

Security Deposit

Upon execution of this lease contract, Lessee agrees to deposit with Lessor, the receipt of which is hereby acknowledged, the sum of *($100) One hundred* Dollars. This deposit, which is non-interest bearing, is to be held by Lessor as security for the full and faithful performance of all the terms and conditions of this lease. This security deposit is not an advance rental, and Lessee may not deduct any portion of the deposit from rent due to Lessor. This security deposit is not to be considered liquidated damages. In the event of forfeiture of the security deposit due to Lessee's failure to fully and faithfully perform all the terms and conditions of the lease, Lessor retains all of his or her other rights and remedies. Lessee does not have the right to cancel this lease and avoid his or her obligations thereunder by forfeiting the said security deposit. Deposit refund will be mailed.

Lessee shall be entitled to return of the said security deposit within 30 days after the premises have been vacated and inspected by Lessor, provided said lease premises are returned to Lessor in as good condition as they were at the time Lessee first occupied same, subject only to normal wear and tear and after all keys are surrendered to Lessor. Lessor

(continued)

Figure 7-1 (continued)

Mark's Apartment Lease

agrees to deliver the premises broom clean and free of trash at the beginning of this lease, and Lessee agrees to return same in like condition at the termination of the lease.

Notwithstanding any other provisions expressed or implied herein, it is specifically understood and agreed that the entire security deposit aforesaid shall be automatically forfeited as liquidated damages should Lessee vacate or abandon the premises before the expiration of this lease, except where such abandonment occurs during the last month of the term of the lease, Lessee has paid all rent covering the entire term and either party has given the other timely written notice that his or her lease will not be renewed under its renewal provisions.

Occupants

The leased premises shall be occupied by the following persons only:

Mark L. Smith

Pets

No pets allowed to live on the premises at any time. However, this provision shall not preclude Lessor for modifying any lease to allow pets by mutual written agreement between Lessor and Lessee.

Sublease

Lessee is not permitted to post any "For Rent" signs, rent, sublet or grant use or possession of the leased premises without the written consent of Lessor and then only in accordance with this lease.

Default or Abandonment

Should the Lessee fail to pay the rent or any other charges arising under this lease promptly as stipulated, should the premises be abandoned by Lessee or should Lessee begin to remove furniture or any substantial portion of Lessee's personal property to the detriment of Lessor's lien, or should voluntary or involuntary bankruptcy proceedings be commenced by or against Lessee, or should Lessee make an assignment for the benefit of creditors, then in any of said events Lessee shall be *ipso facto* in default and the rent for the whole of the expired term of the lease together with the attorney's fees shall immediately become due. In the event of such cancellation and eviction, Lessee is obligated to pay any and all rent due and owing through the last day said premises are occupied.

In the event that during the term of this lease, or any renewal hereof, either the real estate taxes or the utility costs, or both, should increase above the amount being paid on the leased premises at the inception of this lease, the Lessee agrees to pay his or her proportionate share of such increase and any successive increases. Such payment or payments by Lessee shall be due monthly as increased rent throughout the remainder of Lessee's occupancy; and all such sums may be withheld from Lessee's security deposit if not fully paid at the time lessee vacates the premises. A 30-day notice will be given to Lessee before any increase is made.

Other Conditions

A temporary visitor is one who inhabits the property for no more than ten (10) days.

Executed in duplicate at:

333 College Drive   *College Park*
                                        Lessor

this __*1*__ day of __*February*__   *John Murret*
                                        Manager

20__-- __   *Mark L. Smith*
                                        Lessee

 **Student Activity**

1. Read the lease in Figure 7-1 and answer the following questions:

   a. Who is the lessor? _____

   b. Who is the lessee? _____

   c. What must Mark do if he wishes to move out of the apartment at the expiration date on the lease? _____
   _____
   _____

   d. How much rent does Mark owe if he pays before the 5th of the month? _____

   e. What is the penalty if Mark writes a check not honored by his bank (a "bad" check)? _____

   f. What right does the lessor have if the lessee does not pay the rent by the 10th of the month? _____
   _____

   g. What was the amount of Mark's security deposit? _____

   h. Is Mark entitled to the return of his security deposit? ____
   When? _____
   Under what provisions? _____

   i. Can Mark keep a cat in the apartment? _____

   j. Is Mark permitted to rent (sublet) the apartment to anyone if he temporarily moves out of his apartment for the summer? _____

   k. Can Mark move out during the term of the lease without notifying the lessor? _____

   l. Can the lessor raise the rent during the designated term of the lease? Explain. _____

2. Record the following transactions for Mark:

   a. On February 1, 20--, Mark signed his apartment lease. At that time, he wrote Check 113 to College Park for $400.00, which included the $100.00 security deposit and the $300.00 rent for February. Record the check in the check register and write the check. Record the amount in Mark's *Financial Management Records Booklet*. Remember that Mark starts a new page in the *Records Booklet* each month. File the check in the Outgoing File.

   Continued

b. College Park provides the furniture in the living area of each four-bedroom apartment and the appliances in the kitchen. However, the tenants are expected to provide the furniture for the bedrooms. Since the former tenant of Mark's bedroom is moving to California, he offered to sell all his bedroom furniture, including a TV, to Mark for $300.00 cash. This was a deal Mark couldn't refuse. He went to the nearest automated teller machine and used his ATM card to withdraw the cash from his checking account. Remove the ATM receipt (Form 7-1) from the Source Documents section of this *Instructions and Source Documents Booklet.* Record the ATM transaction in Mark's check register and the *Financial Management Records Booklet.* File the ATM receipt in the *Checking Account— ATM Receipts* file.

c. On February 1, Mark realized he had not deducted $100.00 for his savings account when he deposited his last paycheck on January 31. He went to the bank and transferred $100.00 from his checking account to his savings account. Record the transfer in the check register and record the deposit in Mark's *Financial Management Records Booklet.*

How to Buy a Home

Mark's parents were happy with the outcome of his apartment search. The bad luck of having to move out of the house had actually turned out to be an exciting opportunity for Mark in many ways. He had learned so much in a brief period of time. Mark and his parents agreed that experience is a great teacher.

When Mark arrived home that evening, his parents had some exciting news of their own. They had learned of low-income housing that might become available soon. Mark's parents were really excited. They had never owned their own home.

Mark's parents had papers and information spread out before them on the kitchen table. Mark thought renting an apartment was complicated, but he was amazed at all that was involved in buying a home.

Owning your own home is still part of the American dream, and most of us have such a goal in our financial picture. Financial experts estimate that people can afford to pay no more than 40 percent of their gross monthly income for all debts *combined.* For example, if your gross income is $2,000 a month, you could afford to pay 40 percent of that ($800) monthly for housing *if you have no other monthly payments.* However, if payments on your credit card, car loan, and other debts add up to $300 a month, then you could afford only $500 a month for housing ($800 - $300).

The Internet offers a wealth of information about home buying. A couple of popular sites are http://quickenloans.quicken.com and www.fool.com/homecenter, though you can find many more with search words such as "mortgage" or "home buying."

Advantages of Buying a Home

There are advantages and disadvantages to buying a home. First, let's look at the advantages.

Without question, one of the biggest advantages of owning your own home is the privacy and freedom it gives you. Apartments are often noisy, and you aren't free to make improvements without the owner's permission. Even then, if you make improvements, they become the property of the owner. Improvements on your own home increase the value of your property.

If you own your home, your payments on the **mortgage** (home loan) add to your equity. **Equity** is the difference between the value of your home and the amount you owe. So, if you own a $100,000 home and owe $30,000 on the mortgage, you have equity of $70,000. To put it another way, if you sell the property for $100,000, you will have $70,000 after paying off your $30,000 debt. Financial institutions often lend money to borrowers who want to use their home equity as collateral (property pledged as security) when borrowing more money for some purpose.

Also, houses tend to **appreciate**, or increase in value over time. If you have owned the home for more than a couple of years, you can probably sell it for more than you paid for it.

Owning a home can result in tax savings. You can deduct the interest paid on your home loan from your federal income tax. Because most lending institutions use the Rule of 78, you pay more interest during the early years of your loan. (You learned about the Rule of 78 in Chapter 5.) The more interest you can deduct, the less income tax you have to pay. Therefore, you are saving on taxes while gradually increasing your equity.

Disadvantages of Buying a Home

After learning about the advantages of buying a home, you may be wondering why anyone would rent. Well, there are also a number of disadvantages to buying a home. Let's take a look at some of them.

When you buy a home, you automatically reduce your mobility. You can't give a 30-day notice and take off for California. You have to sell your house first, and that can take a long time. Few people can afford two monthly housing payments, which is what you're stuck with if you move before selling the house. So if you don't intend to live in the house for a few years, you probably shouldn't buy.

Once you own a home, you are responsible for maintaining it. You must mow the lawn, clean out the gutters, and paint. When something breaks, you have to fix it, or pay the cost of a repairperson. Some maintenance expenses, such as a new roof or furnace, can be quite high.

When you buy a home, you incur a lot of costs. These costs include a down payment, interest, and closing costs. A **down payment** is a percentage of the purchase price, usually 5 to 10 percent. For a $100,000 home, you might be required to pay a 10 percent down payment of $10,000. The larger your down payment, the less you have to borrow and the smaller your monthly house payments. With a larger down payment, you can also get a better interest rate.

On the other hand, you don't want to use all of your savings for a down payment. You will have to pay additional costs as part of the purchase process. Also, a general rule is to keep about six month's salary in savings in case of an emergency, such as illness or unemployment.

When you sign a mortgage agreement, you agree to repay the principal (amount borrowed) plus interest. Mortgage payments are usually made monthly over a 15- to 30-year period of time. For example, a $60,000 loan at 10 percent amounts to $6,000 in average yearly interest. Multiply $6,000 by 30 years (the length of the loan) and you get $180,000. This amount is the total interest you will pay over the length of the loan.

Many people don't realize that they are paying so much more than the purchase price of the house. However, most people can't buy a house without borrowing the money. To reduce the cost, it is important to shop for and take advantage of the lowest interest rates. If you can make a large down payment, you will reduce the amount you have to borrow. This will also reduce the amount of interest you must pay.

At the completion of the sale, commonly referred to as the **closing**, the buyer must pay closing costs. **Closing costs** include fees for services required to transfer ownership of the property from one person to another. Closing costs usually include a **title search**, which is an investigation to see if the **title** (legal right to ownership of property) is clear. A title search should reveal whether or not the property to be sold has any **liens** (claims against property for a debt) against it. A person who buys property with a lien against it must pay the **creditors** (those who are owed money). It is extremely important to have a title search and be assured of a clear title to the property before the closing takes place.

Closing costs may also include the attorney's fees, the recording fee, the loan origination fee, and the appraisal fee. These additional fees are explained below. In all, closing costs may range from $1,000 to $5,000.

Things to Consider Before Buying

To begin a house search, figure out on paper the amount you can afford to spend on a house of your own. This will prevent you from being tempted by houses out of your range. Here are some questions you might answer before looking for a home:

1. What are my needs now and later? Do I plan to own a home for at least 2 to 3 years?

2. What can I afford to pay as a down payment? What amount can I afford for monthly mortgage payments?

3. How important to me are each of the following?

   a. Neighborhood
   b. Shopping nearby
   c. Distance to my job
   d. Probable resale value
   e. Construction of the house; charm

4. What are the sources of mortgage loans for a home purchase?

   a. Savings and loan associations
   b. Commercial banks
   c. The company with whom you have a life insurance policy
   d. Mortgage companies
   e. Private lenders, such as relatives or the seller of the property

5. What are the initial costs of buying a home?

   a. Down payment
   b. Closing costs:
      - Property taxes—the seller may be entitled to a refund for a portion of the year for which property taxes were already paid.
      - Attorney's fees—for preparing and checking legal documents covering the sale and the mortgage.
      - Loan origination fee—fee for processing the loan application, often called **points**. The fee is expressed as a percentage of the amount borrowed.
      - Title search—an investigation of ownership to make certain there are no claims to the property by others.
      - Recording fee for the deed to the property. A **deed** is a written document used to transfer ownership of property (title) from one person to another.
      - Appraisal fee—for determining the value of the property. Usually the lender will request an appraisal of the property.
      - Title insurance—a policy that protects the lender's interest in the property against the claims of others when the claims were not disclosed by the title search.
      - Termite inspection—to check for termites and/or damage.

   c. Moving expenses.
   d. Other initial expenses:
- Repair, especially on an old home
- Initial utility installations
- Appliances (replacement of old or needed new ones)

6. What are the ongoing costs of owning a home?

   a. Mortgage payments
   b. Property taxes
   c. Homeowner's insurance
   d. Maintenance and repair
   e. Utilities

Making an Offer and Agreeing to Buy

Once you decide you can afford a home and like a particular house, you make an offer. Generally, the offer you make is below the asking price. The owner may accept your offer or make a counteroffer—that is, agree to sell the property for a price above what you offered.

Once you and the owner come to an agreement on the price and other terms relating to the sale, you sign an agreement to buy the house at a stated price. You offer **earnest money** (usually $1,000 or so) to indicate that you are serious about buying the house. The earnest money is deducted from the selling price at the closing. If you fail to meet the terms of the agreement, or back out of the sale, you may lose the earnest money. You should always include a clause in the agreement saying the sale is not definite until you are approved for the loan.

Most of these transactions take place through a real estate agent, who is selling the house for the owner. Even though the real estate agent usually explains all the above agreements to you, read everything for yourself. Take it home if necessary and discuss it with an attorney. You need to understand what you are signing. Sometimes the house is being sold *By Owner,* which means there is no real estate agent involved. You should know what you are doing and decline signing any documents you don't understand.

After you and the seller reach an agreement, a neutral third party called an **escrow agent** arranges for the closing. The escrow agent is often an officer of a bank or a savings and loan association. The closing date is usually 30 to 60 days after you sign the agreement to buy. At the closing, the buyer, seller, real estate brokers, lender, and lawyers meet to sign and deliver all legal papers. The seller is paid for the home at this time. If there is a mortgage loan, the lender and the buyer together pay the seller, and the mortgage goes into effect.

Student Activity

Mark was amazed at the terms involved in buying a home. See how many you remember. Match each of the following terms with the appropriate definition.

Terms

_____ 1. Mortgage

_____ 2. Down payment

_____ 3. Closing costs

_____ 4. Appraisal fee

_____ 5. Title

_____ 6. Points

_____ 7. Deed

_____ 8. Equity

_____ 9. Earnest money

_____ 10. Escrow agent

Definitions

a. Fee for processing the loan application, expressed as a percentage of the amount borrowed

b. Part of the purchase price the buyer pays at the time of purchase

c. Legal right to ownership of property

d. Home loan

e. Neutral third party who handles the closing

f. Payment to indicate interest in buying a home

g. Difference between the value of a home and the amount still owed on a mortgage

h. Fees for services required to transfer ownership of property from one person to another

i. Charge for determining property value

j. Written document used to transfer property ownership from one person to another

On Your Own *For Life*

1. Remove the condition report (checklist) for an apartment (Form 7-2) from the Source Documents section of the *Instructions and Source Documents Booklet.* This condition report is for an unfurnished apartment. If the landlord does not supply such a report, complete this form before signing a lease. If the apartment is furnished, include all furnishings in the report. File the condition report in the Personal file labeled *Housing.*

2. Look for newspaper ads that list apartments for rent and require a lease. Choose two apartments in a neighborhood where you would like to live. Remove the Renters' Checklist (Form 7-3) from the *Instructions and Source Documents Booklet* and use the checklist to help you examine the two apartments you selected. Also, request a copy of the rental agreement or lease from the landlord. Write a summary about the similarities and differences in the apartments. File the checklist, lease, and summary in the Personal file labeled *Housing.*

3. Look in the Business/Real Estate section of your local newspaper or online for information about rates currently charged for mortgage loans in your area. Make a chart listing the financial institutions, the length of the loan (15 or 30 years), and the rate. File your chart in the Personal File labeled *Housing.*

4. Look at advertisements for houses for sale to become familiar with how houses are listed and the kinds of information provided to interest buyers. If you have Internet access, look online for house listings in your area. Select one or two houses that would interest you if you were in the market for a home. Make a list of the things you like about the houses you selected. File the list in the Personal file labeled *Housing.*

Check Up

Having completed the Students Activities in this chapter, you should have mastered the skills listed below. Put a checkmark next to the skills you have mastered. If you aren't sure of a skill, review that section of the chapter.

☐ How to prepare for independent living
☐ How to look for an apartment
☐ How to interpret a lease
☐ How to buy a home

Now that you know how to look for housing, move on to Chapter 8, *Looking at Insurance: Health and Life.*

8 Chapter

LOOKING AT INSURANCE: HEALTH AND LIFE

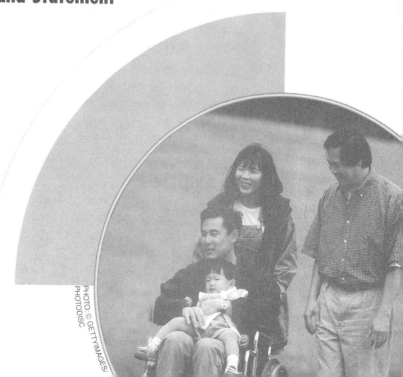

PHOTO: © GETTYIMAGES/PHOTODISC

Mark was packing for his move to College Park when he felt so weak he had to lie down. When he took his temperature, it registered 103 degrees. He called the doctor, who advised him to take aspirin and to come in as soon as possible.

To Mark's surprise, he was diagnosed with bronchial pneumonia, or walking pneumonia. Mark had a second surprise waiting for him when he saw the cost of the office visit. As part of the examination, the doctor had taken x-rays. The doctor's office manager said that if Mark had his health insurance policy number, the office staff would file a claim for him. A **claim** is a policyholder's formal request to the insurance company for payment of losses. His insurance company would then pay some of the costs.

Mark did not have health insurance through his job; and since he had already graduated from high school, he was no longer covered by his parents' policy. He would have to be a full-time college student to be covered by the school's policy. The office manager told Mark that he would have to write a check for the amount then and there.

How to Evaluate Health Insurance Policies

Until now, Mark had given little thought to any kind of insurance, including health insurance. Like most young people, he felt healthy and didn't consider the possibility of getting sick. Besides, health insurance was always something taken care of by his parents.

When he talked with his parents that night, he learned how dangerous the situation could have been. Fortunately, the doctor did not put him in the hospital. A stay in the hospital would wipe him out financially. According to the doctor, Mark would probably get well if he took his antibiotics and rested for two weeks. Mark was glad he had ten days' sick leave at Antwan's. But Antwan offered no health insurance to his employees.

Mark's parents explained that health insurance is based on the concept of sharing risks. No matter how careful or young you are, there is always the risk of accident or serious illness. Since you can't eliminate risk, you pay an insurance company to cover a portion of the costs of personal injury or illness.

Mark learned that there are numerous health insurance companies, policies, and types of coverage from which to choose. A **policy** is an insurance contract. The **policyholder** is the person who owns the insurance policy. He knew he needed to buy health insurance, but what company to choose and the amount and type of coverage was a different matter. His parents said comparison shopping is as important when looking at insurance as when shopping for clothes, furniture, or anything else.

When you buy an insurance policy, you pay premiums for the policy. A **premium** is a regular payment required to buy insurance. Policyholders usually pay health insurance premiums monthly. In return for the premiums, the policy provides **benefits**, or payments for covered losses. Different companies may charge different premiums for the same coverage. **Coverage** is the specific losses for which the policy pays. Mark needed to shop around for the most thorough coverage for the lowest premiums. He also had to be sure the insurance company was reliable. He needed to compare at least two or three companies regarding premiums, coverage, and reliability before purchasing an insurance policy.

Compare Reliability of Insurance Companies

The reliability of the company is an important consideration when shopping for insurance. Mark learned about *Best's Insurance Reports,* which can be found in most libraries. A.M. Best Company rates insurance companies on financial strength and stability. Your policy has value only if the insurance company is financially able to pay your claims. If the company is not financially strong enough to cover claims from many policyholders at once, it could go out of business, making your policy worthless.

Few experts would advise buying the cheapest insurance policy. Look for a reasonably priced health plan with a financially stable company. Choose a company that is rated at least in an *A* category by the A. M. Best Company. This rating means the company ranks near the top for financial stability.

If you have Internet access, go to www.ambest.com for information on the financial ratings of insurance companies, though you would have to pay for a complete report for a particular company. You can obtain free ratings from www.moodys.com or www.standardandpoors.com.

If you don't have Internet access, go to the library and check an issue of *Money* magazine or *Smart Money.* Check the ads for insurance quotation telephone services. Most companies provide an 800 number. While you are in the library, go to the Internet and look at insurance quotes on the company's Web site. If you don't understand the information provided or if you feel unsure of yourself, print the information. Ask a friend or someone who understands health insurance policies to help you.

When investigating the reliability of an insurance company, *always* make sure the company is licensed by your state. If not, your state department of insurance may not be able to help you if the company does not pay your valid claims.

Compare Coverage

Mark was starting to feel really sick. He had been proud of himself for the healthy surplus in his checking account last month. Now he was hit with these medical bills. But Mark knew it could be worse. He had to get some kind of health insurance. He went to his parents.

Mark's parents emphasized that one of the most important factors related to health insurance is coverage. Health insurance coverage essentially falls into three areas: (1) basic hospital/surgical/physician coverage, (2) major medical, and (3) disability income insurance.

Student Activity

1. Fill in the blank with the term that matches the definitions given below. Select terms from the following list: **benefits; claims; coverage; policy; premiums.**

   a. _____ The specific losses for which an insurance policy pays

   b. _____ An insurance contract

   c. _____ Policyholders' formal requests to their insurance companies for payment of losses

   d. _____ Regular payments required to buy insurance

   e. _____ Payments for covered losses

2. Complete the following transactions for Mark:

   a. On February 3, 20––, Mark wrote Check 114 to Dr. Aruna Nazami for $160.00 for the office visit and x-rays. Record the check in Mark's check register and *Financial Management Records Booklet*. File the check in the Outgoing File.

   b. On his way home from the doctor's office, Mark stopped at Thrift Drugs to have his prescription filled for the antibiotics. He wrote Check 115 for $67.00. Record and file the check for Mark.

Basic hospital/surgical/physician coverage includes payment for a hospital room, doctor's visits to your room, surgeon's fees, and operating room costs. Some policies pay almost the full amount; others pay only a portion of the cost.

Major medical covers services not provided by the basic plan. It is additional protection for hospital/surgical/physician coverage, usually picking up where basic coverage ends. Major medical covers serious and costly accidents and extended illnesses. It often covers blood tests, physical therapy, and partial cost for treating mental illness. Since the risk of serious illness is slight, the extra cost for major medical coverage is less then basic coverage and well worth the added cost of the premium.

Disability income insurance pays a portion of your salary if you are unable to work because of illness or injury. Policies vary in several respects, such as the percentage of income paid; the time period the policy is in effect (one year, two years, to age 65, lifetime); the waiting period before payments begin; and the definition of disability. Most people don't think to buy disability coverage until it's too late or a relative or friend suffers terrible losses as the result of not having disability insurance. You should clearly understand the policy's terms before buying disability insurance.

Understand the Policy's Provisions

The more Mark learned about insurance, the more he realized how important it is to understand the insurance contract. However, an insurance policy is not easy to understand. If you don't understand it, do not sign anything. Take it home so you can read it carefully. Go over it with someone who has more experience with insurance policies. If you don't know anyone who understands such policies, check with the local legal aid society or a similar agency listed in the telephone book. Insurance policies are legal documents and, therefore, enforceable in a court of law.

Whether or not your losses are insurable (protected) depends on the provisions in the policy. **Provisions** are the specific agreements spelled out in the insurance contract. They may include maximum coverage, policy renewability, deductibles, co-insurance, exclusions, and special limits to the coverage.

Maximum coverage is the most money an insurance company will pay for a policyholder's covered expenses. The higher the maximum coverage, the better. Check to see if the coverage applies to individual illnesses. Does $50,000 maximum coverage apply to each illness or is it the total coverage over your lifetime? This should be spelled out in the policy. Some companies provide unlimited maximum coverage.

Renewability refers to the conditions under which the policy may be continued or canceled. Guaranteed renewability means that you can renew your policy as long as you want, with some exceptions. These exceptions may include giving false information on the application, failing to pay premiums, or the insurance company going out of business. Look out for **optional renewability**. This means the company can cancel your policy at a premium due date for reasons given in the policy.

The **deductible** is the amount of money policyholders must pay toward their own covered expenses before the insurance company pays any of the costs. The deductible varies from $100 to as much as $5,000 in a year. Usually, the higher the deductible, the lower the monthly premiums. Some people take a higher deductible in order to avoid paying very high premiums each month.

The **benefit period** is the time limit before you have to pay another deductible to receive payments for losses. Benefit periods usually extend over one year. For example, if you agree to a $200 yearly deductible, you will have to pay a total of $200 in medical costs that year (usually January 1 to December 31) before the insurance company pays any medical bills. At the end of the year, a new benefit period begins. Then you will have to meet the deductible again before the insurance company pays any of the costs.

Be sure you know how the deductible works. Depending on the policy, deductibles can apply to each illness or each individual covered by the policy before the company makes payment. If you have to pay $200 for each illness, you are worse off than if you have a yearly $200 deductible that covers everything.

Co-insurance is the portion of covered expenses that the policyholder must pay, after meeting the deductible. Most companies require a certain percentage of co-insurance, such as 20 percent. This means that the policyholder must pay 20 percent of the costs, after paying the deductible. Then the insurance company pays 80 percent. For example, suppose your hospital visit costs $1,000 and you have already paid your deductible. Your out-of-pocket expenses for the hospital stay will be 20 percent, or $200. The insurance company will pay 80 percent, or $800.

You may want to look for a policy that will cover the entire cost of the medical bills after you meet the deductible. Some companies require co-payment up to $1,000. After you have made co-payments totaling $1,000, the insurance company will pay the full 100 percent of the medical bill.

Exclusions are items or conditions for which the company will not provide coverage. Cosmetic surgery is an example of a typical exclusion, unless the damage is caused by an injury. Exclusions are stated in the insurance policy. Make sure you know all the exclusions. Ask the agent to identify them, and then read them carefully yourself before signing.

Limits, sometimes called *internal limits*, refer to a ceiling (limit) the company is willing to pay for hospital rooms, operations, and doctors' fees. In other words, the company agrees to pay a fixed amount for certain medical procedures.

The following is additional advice about health insurance policies:

1. Be entirely truthful on health application forms. If you lie about a previous illness or family history (heart disease, cancer, etc.), this is considered **concealment** (unlawful withholding of information). As a result, the insurance company can refuse payment on the claim and/or cancel your policy.

2. Be cautious about any riders in the policy. A **rider** is an amendment that changes some provision in the policy. A rider may be used to add or exclude something. For example, if you have a history of alcoholism or drug abuse, the company may add a rider excluding treatment of these medical problems. Sometimes the company will include coverage but increase your premiums. You would be considered high risk in these areas.

3. Be cautious about dropping a policy for another one. It is far better to do your homework before taking out a policy. However, there are times when you may be offered a better deal. Look at it carefully.

4. If a group health insurance policy is offered to you, take advantage of it. **Group insurance policies** are offered to employees working for the same company or to members of the same association. Group policies are usually cheaper and offer more coverage because the insurance company has the advantage of collecting premiums from the entire group. The disadvantage of the group policy is that your policy ends when you leave your job or the group.

   Investigate whether you can convert the group policy to an individual policy if you resign or retire. Conversion to an individual policy means you will pay the entire premium. When you were an employee, your employer probably paid part of the premium.

   COBRA, a federal law, allows employees who leave their jobs to continue coverage under their company's group health plan for up to 18 months. They must pay the entire premium, however. This law helps people stay insured until they become a member of their new employer's plan.

Compare Premiums

We have talked a lot about premiums. Premiums vary according to your age and state of health at the time you buy the policy, as well as with the area in which you live. Premiums also vary according to the amount of your deductible and co-insurance and the amount of coverage you buy. In addition, as hospital and medical costs rise, so do premiums.

Although the amount of the premium is important and you need to be concerned about what you can afford, you should consider other factors as well. Get the best coverage you can afford from a reliable company. Take the time to compare coverage, companies, policies, and premiums before you sign anything.

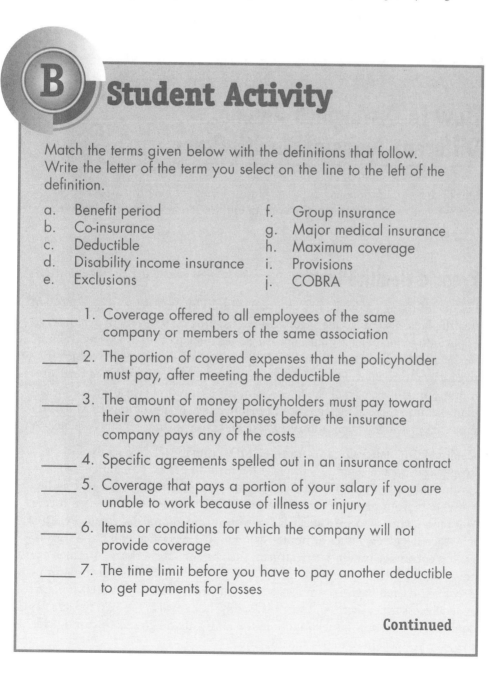

B Student Activity

Match the terms given below with the definitions that follow. Write the letter of the term you select on the line to the left of the definition.

a. Benefit period
b. Co-insurance
c. Deductible
d. Disability income insurance
e. Exclusions
f. Group insurance
g. Major medical insurance
h. Maximum coverage
i. Provisions
j. COBRA

_____ 1. Coverage offered to all employees of the same company or members of the same association

_____ 2. The portion of covered expenses that the policyholder must pay, after meeting the deductible

_____ 3. The amount of money policyholders must pay toward their own covered expenses before the insurance company pays any of the costs

_____ 4. Specific agreements spelled out in an insurance contract

_____ 5. Coverage that pays a portion of your salary if you are unable to work because of illness or injury

_____ 6. Items or conditions for which the company will not provide coverage

_____ 7. The time limit before you have to pay another deductible to get payments for losses

Continued

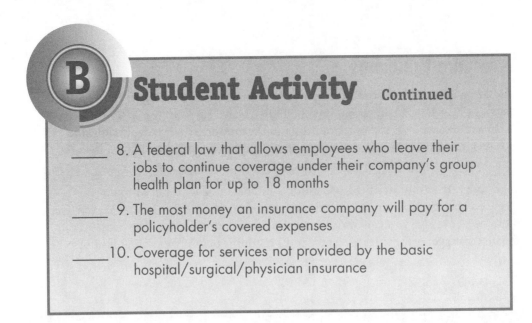

_____ 8. A federal law that allows employees who leave their jobs to continue coverage under their company's group health plan for up to 18 months

_____ 9. The most money an insurance company will pay for a policyholder's covered expenses

_____ 10. Coverage for services not provided by the basic hospital/surgical/physician insurance

How to Distinguish Among Different Types of Health Plans

Mark learned that there are different kinds of prepaid health plans. He also learned that the government sponsors an employer-paid plan to cover job-related illness and injury.

Prepaid Health Plans

Because of rising medical costs, alternative health plans have emerged. **Prepaid health plans**, also called **managed care plans**, provide a variety of health services, including doctors, hospitals, nurses, lab technicians, and other medical professionals. Members of a prepaid health plan pay a monthly fee, for which they receive health services. Often the fee is less than a private health insurance premium. Sometimes, part of the fee is paid by the employer. Most prepaid health plans fall into three categories: health maintenance organizations (HMOs), preferred provider organizations (PPOs), and point-of-service (POS) plans.

Health Maintenance Organizations (HMOs) provide all services except hospitalization at a central medical center, including x-rays, treatment, and routine checkups. As an HMO member, you must choose a doctor within the HMO to be your **primary care physician (PCP)**. Your PCP manages your care. You cannot choose to see a specialist on your own. You must see your PCP first, who then decides whether or not to refer you to a specialist within the HMO. HMOs encourage preventive treatment, such as annual checkups. Another advantage of the HMO is convenience. You go to one health center for all your needs and do not have to complete a lot of insurance claim forms. HMOs are generally less expensive than other plans, but they are also the least flexible. Your choice of doctors is limited to those in the HMO. If you go to a doctor outside the plan, you will have to pay the full cost.

Preferred provider organizations (PPOs) are networks of doctors and health facilities that have contracted with employers to offer health services to their employees. Unlike HMOs, a member of a PPO does not have to choose a primary care physician. You can see any doctor within the plan's network of providers. You can also choose to see a doctor outside the plan and still receive some reimbursement.

Point-of-service (POS) plans include aspects of both HMOs and PPOs. You would have more flexibility in your choice of doctors than in an HMO. You can go to a doctor outside the network, and your POS plan will pay part of the cost. However, the plan will pay more of the cost when you see a doctor within the network. Also, in some POS plans, you may have to choose a primary care physician within the network and get that doctor's permission (referral) to see a specialist or to see a doctor outside the network.

Dental Insurance

Some plans include **dental insurance**, though dental coverage is less common than it used to be. Most dental insurance covers regular dental examinations, x-rays, and major dental work. Many policies even include orthodontics. Read the provisions carefully. Most policies include a deductible and co-payment.

Medical Savings Account Plan

If you are young, healthy, and uninsured, a **medical savings account (MSA)** might be the health insurance plan for you. An MSA is a combination plan that includes a health insurance policy with a high deductible and a tax-deferred savings account. Here's how it works. With a deductible of about $2,500, you are insured for catastrophic illness or injury—that is, illness that requires major medical expenses. Because of the high deductible, the premiums are exceptionally low. The money you don't pay in high premiums goes into a tax-free savings account. When you have medical expenses, you draw on the MSA savings account until you meet your deductible.

The MSA works for uninsured young people in several ways:

1. The cost for an MSA is affordable while offering protection for catastrophic illness or injury.

2. The money in the savings account rolls over from year to year so, over time, you may accumulate a good bit of money in savings.

3. Eventually, you get the money in the MSA savings free of income tax.

The MSA is not helpful for the payment of small medical bills or prescriptions.

Workers' Compensation

Workers' compensation is employer-paid insurance that covers expenses for job-related injuries, illness, or death. Under the state workers' compensation laws, most employers are required to pay regular fees to the state to cover job-related accidents and illness. The employee does not pay any fee for this coverage.

The benefits differ from state to state, just as policies differ in coverage. In some states, workers' compensation insurance pays all the medical costs; in others, it pays a portion. There is usually a waiting period before the employee receives benefits, just as there is for private disability income insurance.

If the employee is unable to return to work, a portion of his/her salary (usually two-thirds) is paid to the worker as income, according to workers' compensation laws. If the employee is killed on the job, the spouse and children receive benefits. Benefits for death or injury are paid whether the employee was at fault or not.

C Student Activity

1. Answer true or false to the following statements:

   ___ a. If you belong to a POS plan, you would have less flexibility in choosing a doctor than in an HMO.

   ___ b. Workers' compensation benefits differ from state to state.

   ___ c. If you are a member of an HMO, you would receive no reimbursement if you went to a doctor outside the HMO.

   ___ d. Health maintenance organizations are usually less expensive than conventional health insurance.

   ___ e. An MSA is a good health plan for elderly people.

   ___ f. As an employee, you would have to pay premiums for workers' compensation insurance.

2. Read the following cases and answer the related questions:

   a. After 20 years of carrying health insurance with Risk Free Insurance Company, you have a heart attack. The company pays medical expenses of $100,000 and promptly cancels your policy. What provisions in the policy should you have checked? _____

   _____

   _____

   b. Your spine is seriously injured by a work-related accident. You are hospitalized for six weeks and return weekly for physical therapy. What type of insurance would pay for

Continued

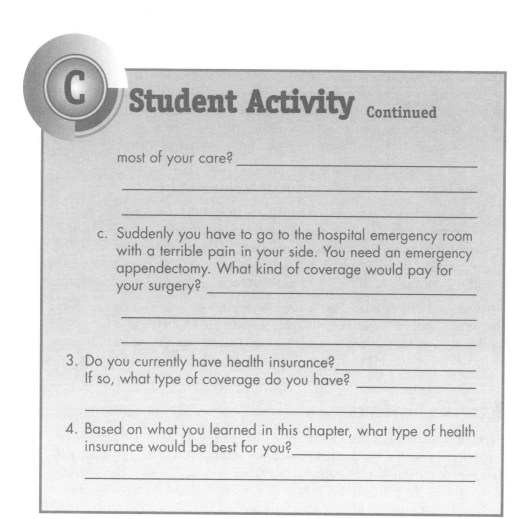

most of your care? _____

_____

_____

    c. Suddenly you have to go to the hospital emergency room with a terrible pain in your side. You need an emergency appendectomy. What kind of coverage would pay for your surgery? _____

_____

_____

3. Do you currently have health insurance?_____
   If so, what type of coverage do you have? _____

_____

4. Based on what you learned in this chapter, what type of health insurance would be best for you?_____

_____

How to Evaluate Differences Among Life Insurance Policies

While Mark was learning about insurance, he decided to ask his family about another type of insurance—life insurance. His parents told him he might not need life insurance at the present time because he had no dependents who would need financial help if he died. His parents had purchased policies several years ago because they wanted to be sure their children were cared for in case of their death.

Mark's parents said that before buying life insurance, you should identify your needs. Sometimes, after hearing a sales pitch, people think they need coverage when maybe they don't. His parents mentioned four factors he should consider when making decisions about life insurance:

1. What are your financial responsibilities regarding dependents, usually family? Do you have children who need support and an education? Will your spouse be able to support himself/herself if you die? Do you have financial obligations now that you will not have 25 years from now, when you can cancel the life insurance?

2. What are your present financial assets and responsibilities? Do you own a home that you are making payments on? If you die, will your spouse be able to make those payments with his/her salary alone? If not, will the home be repossessed by the lender? Are you making payments on a car? Do you have any other debts that will have to be paid off by your dependents?

3. As you look ahead, will the rate of *inflation* (rise in the cost of living) cause your dependents to go broke without your financial help?

4. What are your social security benefits? Are they sufficient to care for your dependents? Social security provides income for a spouse and children of a deceased person if the deceased contributes to social security as a wage earner. Most social security benefits are not adequate if not supplemented by other income. (You will learn more about social security later in this chapter.)

Mark learned that determining the need for life insurance is the first step. If you decide you need life insurance, you must then decide what type to buy. Essentially, the choice is between term life insurance, which provides protection only, and cash-value life insurance, which combines protection and savings.

Term Life Insurance

Term life insurance, as the name implies, insures you for a specified *term* (number of years). If the insured person dies within the stated term, the **beneficiary** (person named in the policy to receive the benefits) receives the amount designated by the policy. If the insured person lives beyond the term, the policy ends and must be renewed to receive further coverage. Term policies pay benefits only upon death. You cannot accumulate savings with a term policy.

There are several variations of term policies. A **convertible term policy** can be converted into a cash-value policy. Some companies allow conversion to a cash-value policy at any time without an additional medical examination.

Two other variations are level term and decreasing term policies. With a **level term policy**, your premiums and your dollar coverage remain the same (level) throughout the term. With a **decreasing term policy**, your premiums remain the same, but the dollar coverage decreases over the term. You might choose this kind of policy if you have young children. They would need a larger payout if you died while they were young than if you died later, when they were nearly old enough to support themselves.

Always study a term policy for the renewability options. Is renewability guaranteed, or is the option up to the company? If it is not guaranteed, you may be denied a policy after you develop a serious illness or after you reach a certain age.

The premiums for a term policy are lower than the premiums for an equivalent cash-value policy. The reason for this is that you are not accumulating savings with a term policy so it is not worth as much. Term policies are attractive to young people and young families because they need protection but may not be able to pay large premiums.

Cash-Value Life Insurance

In addition to paying benefits upon death, **cash-value life insurance** has a savings component. The insurance company invests part of each premium for you. As these investments grow, your policy gains cash value. **Cash value** is the amount paid to the policyholder if the policy is terminated. For example, if the cash value of your policy is $4,000 at the end of eight years, you will receive that amount if you cancel the policy at that time. In contrast, you receive nothing if you cancel a term policy after eight years. Because of the savings component, the premiums for cash-value policies are higher than for term policies.

There are different types of cash-value life insurance policies. A common type is **whole life**, sometimes called **ordinary life** or **permanent insurance**. Whole life insurance is designed to stay in force throughout the insured's lifetime. As long as you make your payments as required by the policy, the policy will cover you for life, regardless of any changes in your health.

There are also variations within the whole life policies. One example is **limited-payment life**, which is sometimes referred to as **paid-up whole life**. With limited-payment life, the insurance protection lasts for life, but the premiums stop at a certain age, such as 65. The shorter the payment period, the more expensive the premiums. Another variation is **modified whole life**. With modified whole life, premiums increase throughout the life of the policy, rather than remain level. Some people choose this type because premiums are less at the beginning, when most people are not able to make large payments.

Universal life policies are adjustable. As your needs change, you may change the amount of your premium and the amount of death benefits you want to buy. The insurance company deducts its stated expenses from your premium. It also deducts the amount needed to pay for the level of death benefits you choose. The remaining amount of your premium earns interest for you.

Another type of cash-value life insurance is the **endowment policy**. The endowment policy protects the policyholder for a stated number of years. At the end of the time period, the cash value of the policy is paid to the policyholder and the insurance ends. If the policyholder dies beforehand, the beneficiary receives the full face value of the policy. The endowment plan is the most expensive form of life insurance.

Cash-value policies offer the following advantages:

1. *Low-interest loans*. You can borrow from your insurance company an amount equal to the cash value of your policy. The interest rate will be lower than if you borrowed the same amount from a bank or other lending agency. However, the amount borrowed is subtracted from the total amount the beneficiary receives if you die.

2. If you fail to pay a premium, your policy is not canceled. The insurance company will probably pay the premium out of the cash value of your policy. This provision is called **automatic premium loan**. Interest is charged for the amount, as with any loan.

3. If you cancel the policy, you can collect the accumulated cash value of the policy.

Figure 8-1 summarizes the advantages and disadvantages of term and cash-value life insurance policies.

Figure 8-1

Term vs. Cash-Value Life Insurance Policies

TERM		CASH-VALUE	
Advantages	**Disadvantages**	**Advantages**	**Disadvantages**
1. Cheapest premiums	1. Offers protection only; no savings	1. Offers lifelong protection	1. Not until 2nd or 3rd year does policy acquire cash value
2. More affordable during years when protection is most needed and income is lowest	2. Sometimes not renewable without a medical examination	2. Low-interest loans	2. Interest is earned at low rate on cash value
3. Usually, option of renewability and conversion to whole life policy		3. Cash-value payment if policy is canceled	3. Face amount of policy cannot be increased in many cases

Basic Insurance Guidelines

Mark's parents stuck to these rules regarding life insurance and shared them with Mark:

1. Assess your need for life insurance at various stages of your life. For example, most single young people without property don't need life insurance. If you are married and have a child, you probably do. When you are older, and you and your spouse are guaranteed a good source of income if one of you should die, you may need little or no life insurance.

2. After determining your need for life insurance, decide on the amount needed. Buy about ten times your income. If you make $30,000 a year, buy $300,000 worth of life insurance in order for your dependents to live securely after your death. As your income increases, you might periodically raise your coverage.

3. Life insurance is primarily intended to be financial protection for the dependents you leave behind. If your income is limited, do not use life insurance as an investment. Instead, choose term insurance, which is cheaper.

4. Don't cancel a whole or universal policy. Once you've purchased it, keep it.

5. Avoid buying more than one life insurance policy per person. Life insurance policies have fees.

6. Always check the financial ratings of the insurance company. If the insurance company goes broke, you may not get your money back.

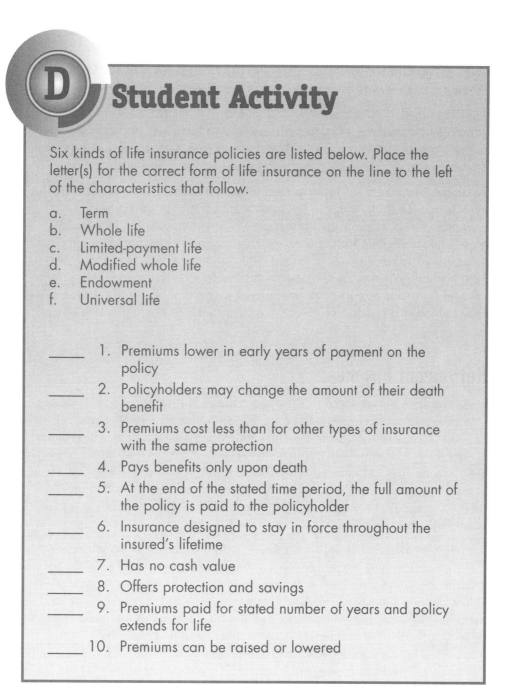

D Student Activity

Six kinds of life insurance policies are listed below. Place the letter(s) for the correct form of life insurance on the line to the left of the characteristics that follow.

a. Term
b. Whole life
c. Limited-payment life
d. Modified whole life
e. Endowment
f. Universal life

_____ 1. Premiums lower in early years of payment on the policy

_____ 2. Policyholders may change the amount of their death benefit

_____ 3. Premiums cost less than for other types of insurance with the same protection

_____ 4. Pays benefits only upon death

_____ 5. At the end of the stated time period, the full amount of the policy is paid to the policyholder

_____ 6. Insurance designed to stay in force throughout the insured's lifetime

_____ 7. Has no cash value

_____ 8. Offers protection and savings

_____ 9. Premiums paid for stated number of years and policy extends for life

_____ 10. Premiums can be raised or lowered

How to Benefit from Social Security

Antwan was the one who told Mark about the benefits of social security. Antwan felt bad when Mark told him he was having a hard time with his medical bills. He told Mark that he wished he could offer group health insurance, but he didn't have enough employees working for him. However, Antwan wanted Mark to know that he was paying a portion of social security for Mark.

Antwan told Mark about the benefits covered by social security. He reminded Mark that an amount was deducted for social security from his paycheck every week. In addition, Antwan was required to pay an equal amount for Mark. "You need to know what you're paying for," Antwan said.

Antwan gave Mark a little history of social security. In 1935, the United States government started the social security system as a relatively simple program for retired workers, their survivors, and the unemployed. Since then, the program has been expanded to include disability insurance and health insurance.

To support the program, employees pay a portion of their wages to social security with each paycheck. The employer has to match the amount paid by the employee. The U. S. government manages the fund and pays out benefits to those who are eligible. Today's wage earners pay for the benefits of those persons who have retired or are unable to work and who paid into the fund while they were working. When today's wage earners reach eligibility, they will receive benefits paid for by the next generation of wage earners. Only those who have worked and paid into the system for ten years or more (a minimum of 40 calendar quarters) are eligible for social security benefits.

Retirement Income

Most people recognize social security as a retirement program. The monthly payments retirees receive depend on their age at retirement and the amount they paid into the social security system during their working years. You may retire at 62 and receive benefits, but your benefits will be reduced. People born before 1960 may retire with full benefits at age 65. However, if you were born in 1960 or later, the age at which you can retire and receive full benefits will gradually increase to age 67. The social security program is under study, so changes may occur in the coming years.

Antwan said that most people don't understand the purpose of social security. It was never set up to be the sole source of income for retirement years. Social security should be considered a supplement to your own retirement savings. When you begin to work, you should start building alternative sources of retirement income as soon as you can, such as in a company-sponsored pension plan or an IRA (Individual Retirement Account). Ms. Reed had explained IRAs to Mark when he was asking about savings accounts at the bank. He had not given any further thought to retirement. It was all he could do to put away $100 a month in savings, but his savings were for medium-range goals. He could see the wisdom of preparing for retirement and planned to do so as soon as he was able.

Disability Insurance

Disability insurance was added to the social security program in 1954. If you have paid into the system long enough and can prove that you are physically or mentally unable to work, you can draw the same benefits as you would at age 65. Also, dependents (spouse and children under 18) may receive the same benefits they would receive if the disabled person were 65 years old. However, the social security definition of disability is very specific. Only about 1/3 of those who apply for disability under social security receive disability benefits. Therefore, it is a good idea to have additional disability insurance, especially before age 65.

Unemployment Insurance

Under the Social Security Act of 1935, each state must have an **unemployment insurance program**. This program is operated in cooperation with the federal government, although each state sets up its own eligibility rules and determines benefits. In most states, to qualify for unemployment benefits a worker must:

1. Be unemployed through no fault of his or her own.

2. Register at a public employment office for a job.

3. Make a claim for unemployment benefits.

4. Be able and available for work.

5. Be employed for the minimum length of time specified by state law.

6. Have been employed in occupations covered by the unemployment law.

Unemployment insurance is the only social security benefit not paid for in part by the employee. Unemployment taxes are paid by the employer. Nothing is deducted from the employee's paycheck.

Health Insurance

Health insurance was added to the social security system in 1965. There are two forms of social security health insurance: Medicare and Medicaid. **Medicare** pays medical expenses for people 65 and over. **Medicaid** pays medical expenses for people who are unable to pay because of their low income or disabilities, regardless of age. The federal and state governments share the cost of providing health care for the needy. For the elderly, the amount the government will pay changes from time to time. There are deductibles and time limits on hospital visits. Antwan said it may not be wise to depend totally on Medicare in old age. Some people feel that Medicare may not provide enough coverage and should be supplemented by private health insurance.

Life Insurance or Survivor's Insurance

If a wage earner covered by social security dies, two types of benefits are paid: (1) a small lump sum to the spouse for burial and (2) a monthly payment to the surviving spouse and/or children. In order to receive the lump-sum payment, you have to file within two years of the person's death. If there are no surviving children or spouse, no one is eligible for the benefit.

How to Apply for a Social Security Number and Statement

When you apply for a social security number, you receive a social security card. Mark's social security card is shown in Figure 8-2.

Notice that Mark's **social security number** has nine digits. You may have exactly the same name as someone else, but your social security number is always unique. It is yours for life. The Social Security Administration records all your earnings and the amount you paid into the system under your number. The benefits you receive depend on the amount of your contributions during your working life. The Internal Revenue Service (IRS) uses your social security number as your identification number for processing your tax returns. Therefore, it is a very important identification tool.

You get a social security number and card by applying to the social security Administration Office. When applying for a number, you will need a document showing your age and U.S. citizenship, such as your birth certificate. A copy of the application for a social security card is provided in the Source Documents section of your *Instructions and Source Documents Booklet* (Form 8-1).

Federal law now requires that taxpayers claiming a tax exemption for dependents one year old or older must list that dependent's social security number on their tax return. Therefore, parents must apply for social security numbers for their children who reach age one during the tax year.

You can keep a record of your contributions to the social security system through your W-2 forms issued by your employer each year. Contributions are listed for social security tax and Medicare on both your W-2 form and your paycheck stubs. It is also a good idea to request a Social Security Statement about every three years. This statement will give you an estimate of what your social security benefits will be when you retire.   You will find a copy of the request form in the Source Documents section in the *Instructions and Source Documents Booklet* (Form 8-2).

Figure 8-2

Mark's Social Security Card

Student Activity

1. List five ways in which social security provides benefits for the eligible wage earner.

   a. _____

   b. _____

   c. _____

   d. _____

   e. _____

2. Answer true or false to the following statements:

   _____ a. If your parents did not apply for a social security number for you, you are ineligible for one.

   _____ b. At age 62, anyone can retire and receive the full benefits of social security.

   _____ c. If you have paid into the system long enough and can prove that you are physically or mentally unable to work, you can receive full benefits before age 65.

   _____ d. You are 35 and cannot pay your medical expenses because of your very low income. You may be eligible for Medicare benefits.

   _____ e. In order to receive unemployment benefits, you have to have lost your job through no fault of your own.

On Your Own For Life

1. If you don't yet have a social security number, obtain an application for a social security card from a Social Security Administration office or from the Administration's Web site at www.ssa.gov. Remove the copy of the application (Form 8-1) from the Source Documents section in the *Instructions and Source Documents Booklet* and follow the instructions on the form. Complete Form 8-1 before copying the information onto the *official* application form you obtained.

2. If you have been paying social security taxes, you may want to obtain a Social Security Statement to get an idea of what your benefits will be when you retire. You can get a request form from a Social Security Administration office or online at www.ssa.gov. Remove the copy of the request form (Form 8-2) from the *Instructions and Source Documents Booklet*. Complete Form 8-2 before copying the information onto the *official* form you obtained. Then mail the official request form, or submit it online according to the instructions at the Web site.

3. Ask your parents or other adults if you may examine their health insurance or life insurance policies. Compare the terms of the policies with the types of coverage and special provisions discussed in this chapter. Give a report on your findings to the class.

Check Up

Having completed the Student Activities in this chapter, you should have mastered the skills listed below. Put a checkmark next to the skills you have mastered. If you aren't sure of a skill, review that section of the chapter.

☐ How to evaluate health insurance policies

☐ How to distinguish among different types of health plans

☐ How to evaluate differences among life insurance policies

☐ How to benefit from social security

☐ How to apply for a social security number and statement

Now that you know all about health and life insurance, move on to Chapter 9, *Looking at Insurance: Auto and Home*.

9 Chapter

LOOKING AT INSURANCE: AUTO AND HOME

PHOTO: © GETTYIMAGES/
PHOTODISC

Mr. Smith said he might sell Mark his old car since he and Mrs. Smith were considering buying another one. Mark was excited. He had not given a thought to buying a car on *his* budget! Now that Mark had moved in with Roberto, he was rather far from work. A car would be a help.

His father cautioned him about getting too excited before considering all expenses involved and how those extra costs worked with his budget. "You'll have to get your own auto insurance," his father said.

"I'll just get the basics," Mark said.

"Yes, well, the basics might include more than you think when it comes to auto insurance," his father replied.

Mr. Smith explained that the cost of auto insurance depends on several factors: a person's gender, age, marital status, past driving record, claims history, and school grades (if presently in school); the year, model, and make of the car insured; the type of protection; and the amount of deductibles.

Mark was staggered. "Why all the personal stuff?" he asked. "Isn't that discrimination?"

"Well, in a way it is," his father said. "Insurance companies make it their business to determine which drivers are low risks and which ones are high risks. Auto insurance rates, like health and life insurance rates, are based on risk. Drivers who are in a high-risk group are going to pay higher premiums than drivers in a low-risk group. Historically, men under age 25 have had more auto accidents than women in the same age group have had. Therefore, you're going to pay more for the same amount of protection."

How to Interpret Risk Factors in Auto Insurance Policies

Mr. Smith was right. There are many factors that determine the cost of auto premiums for the same coverage. These factors are rating territory; driver classification; personal driving record; use of car; age and make of car; claims history; assigned risk; and deductibles and limits.

Rating Territory

The community in which a person lives affects the price of premiums because each state is divided into rating territories. A **rating territory** is a city, county, or rural area.

Insurance companies monitor the number of claims connected with the registered drivers in each territory. The greater the number of claims from a territory, the higher the insurance rate or premium. If you move from Flora, Mississippi, to Los Angeles, California, chances are your insurance premiums will increase, simply because you have moved into a territory with higher rates. Even if your driving record remains the same, your premiums will be higher.

Driver Classification

A driver's age, gender, and marital status are used to determine the risk classification of the driver. Certain classifications (groups) of drivers tend to be involved in more auto accidents or commit more traffic violations than other groups of drivers. Therefore, if your classification is a high-risk group, your rate will be higher.

The highest rates are paid by unmarried young males who own or are the main drivers of an automobile. If you are a 24-year-old male, you will probably have to pay a relatively high rate, even if you have a good driving record. In some states, female drivers aged 30-65 pay a lower rate because they are in a group considered to be low-risk drivers. The lowest rates go to a family with no male driver under 25 years of age and with a car not used for business. However, a few states now prohibit insurance companies from considering gender, age, and marital status as factors in determining insurance rates.

Personal Driving Record

If you and all members of your household who drive your car have a clear driving record, your rates will be lower than if one family member has a poor driving record. If you have numerous traffic violations on your record, you are a greater risk.

Use of Car

The purpose for which you use the car and the number of miles you drive it each day affect insurance rates. Cars used for business are usually driven more miles in a year than cars driven for pleasure. People who drive more miles are more likely to be involved in an accident. For the same reason, if you drive 50 miles to work each day, you will pay a higher rate than a person who drives only 5 miles a day. Again, the longer you are on the road, the greater the risk of an accident and the higher your insurance rate.

Age and Kind of Car

The year, model, and make of a car affect insurance rates. Generally, the newer and more expensive your car, the more you will have to pay for insurance. The older the car, the lower the rate. Older cars cost insurance companies less money to replace if totally demolished in an accident. Also, the premium is determined by how costly it is to repair your car if it is damaged. If you own a sports car or a foreign car, parts are often expensive to replace. These cars also tend to be stolen more often. Therefore, sports cars and foreign cars usually cause your rates to be higher.

Claims History

The more claims you make for reimbursement for repairs, the higher your rates are likely to be. Sometimes insurance companies drop the insured altogether because of what they consider excessive claims. If you get dropped, it is difficult to get another company to insure you.

Assigned Risk

If you are dropped by an insurance company because of a poor driving record, you may end up in your state's Automobile Insurance Plan as an **assigned risk**. This means you won't be able to choose your own auto insurance company. You will be assigned a company and charged very high rates.

You don't have to remain an assigned risk forever. If you establish a good driving record over a period of time, you will be able to choose your own insurance company again. If you feel that you've been unjustly categorized as an assigned risk, contact your state insurance department and request a reevaluation of your case.

Deductibles and Limits

The higher the deductible, the lower the premium, because the policyholder pays a greater portion of the damages before the company has to pay. Limits of protection (amount of coverage) also affect the cost of the premium. The more coverage the policyholder has, the higher the potential claims the insurance company will have to pay. As a result, the company charges higher premiums for more coverage.

A Student Activity

1. List six factors that affect the cost of auto premiums:

   a. _____

   b. _____

   c. _____

   d. _____

   e. _____

   f. _____

2. Your friend is furious because she moved to another state and her insurance premiums increased considerably. She has a good driving record and doesn't think this is fair. What explanation can you give her? _____

   _____

3. Record the following transactions for Mark:

   a. On February 7, Mark received and deposited his paycheck. He deposited $240.01 in his

   Continued

checking account and kept $85.00 in cash.

(1) Record the $240.01 deposit in his check register.

(2) Record Mark's $325.01 income and the following cash expenditures in his *Financial Management Records Booklet.* On February 8, Mark recorded the following cash amounts for the week: eating out, $30; transportation, $10.00; personal, $25.00; entertainment, $45.00.

(3) a. On February 9, Mark realized he needed more cash for the upcoming week so he withdrew $50.00,using his ATM card.

b. Roberto told Mark it was his week to buy groceries and prepare meals. On his way home from the ATM machine, Mark stopped at Thrifty Grocery and wrote Check 116 for $120.00 for groceries. Record the transaction in the check register and the *Financial Management Records Booklet* and file the check in the Outgoing File.

c. Mark wanted to be sure he made his installment payment on time for his stereo so he could establish a good credit rating. Therefore, on February 9 he wrote Check 117 to Great Fi-Buys for $19.67 for the first installment payment on his new stereo. He recorded the installment contract number, 1506, on the check. Record the transaction and write and file the check. Record the transaction in the *Financial Management Records Booklet.*

d. Mark also wanted to be sure he paid his credit card statement on time so he would not have to pay a finance charge. On February 9, he wrote Check 118 to National Bank for the total amount due, $111.26. Remove Mark's credit card statement from his *Bills to Be Paid* file. Record the transaction in his check register, and write the check. Record Mark's credit card account number, 00011222, on the check. (*Caution:* Do not record this transaction in the *Financial Management Records Booklet.* Mark recorded his credit card purchases at the time he made them. Therefore, if he were to record this payment in the *Records Booklet*, he would be recording the expenditure twice.) Detach the part of the statement that is to be mailed with the check. File that part and the check in the Outgoing File. On the part of the statement that Mark keeps, write the following record of payment: *Pd. 2/9/-- Check 118.* File this part of the statement in the Financial file labeled *Credit—Bank Card.*

How to Determine the Amount of Auto Protection Needed

How much protection should you buy? Most automobile policies offer six types of coverage: bodily injury liability, property damage liability, collision, comprehensive physical damage, medical payments, and uninsured motorist. You can buy one or more of these types of coverage.

Liability Coverage

Mr. Smith told his son that before buying insurance or even buying a car, he should understand the concept of liability. **Liability** means that a person may be held legally responsible for any damage that occurs as a result of an accident in which that person is at fault. If you run a red light and cause $3,000 damage to another car, you are responsible for paying for the damages—whether you have insurance or not. If you have **property damage liability** coverage, the insurance company will pay the cost of the damage to the other person's car or property up to the amount of coverage you have.

If you injure someone in that same accident, you are liable (or responsible) for the costs resulting from the injuries. If you have **bodily injury liability** coverage, the insurance company will pay the claims of injury or death up to the amount of coverage you have. If you are sued because of bodily injury or death caused by an accident in which you are at fault, the liability coverage may pay some or all of the costs.

Liability insurance on a car also covers those who drive the insured car with permission of the insured. Most states require that you carry auto liability insurance in order to get car license tags.

Automobile policies are written in different ways, and you need to know what you are buying. The amount of money an insurance company will pay to cover the costs of injury and damage depends on the **limits in the policy**. Some policies are written on a **single-limit basis**, which means there is one amount the company will pay for any one accident. Other policies are written on a **split-limit basis**, which means that separate limits are set for different categories. If the coverage limit reads 25/50/10, up to $25,000 will be paid for bodily injury for one person; up to $50,000 will be paid for bodily injury for more than one person; and up to $10,000 will be paid for property damage. The insurance company will pay no more than the limit set for each category.

Let's look at how a 25/50/10 split-limit policy works in the case of your running the red light. Let's say you caused $30,000 damage to a Porsche and caused bodily injury to the driver that amounted to $100,000. What does this mean? It means you're in big trouble. You'll have to come up with a lot of the money out of your own pocket. Your insurance company will pay only $10,000 for damage to the Porsche. You will have to pay $20,000 ($30,000 − $10,000 = $20,000). The company will pay $25,000 in medical expenses for the driver's injuries. You will have to pay the remaining $75,000 ($100,000 − $25,000 = $75,000). In all, you will have to come up with $95,000 ($20,000 + $75,000 = $95,000)!

You can see how quickly you can be wiped out if you aren't sufficiently covered by auto insurance. Considering today's cost of auto repairs and medical bills, you should think about how much increased insurance limits will cost. In general, $50,000 of coverage can be increased to $100,000 for very little more a year for the premium. The added coverage is well worth the slight increase in your premium.

The usual recommendation is a minimum of 100/300/25 under a split-limit plan, and $300,000 minimum under a single-limit plan. It's far better to make sure you are covered for the big one than to conserve on your premium.

Collision Coverage

Collision coverage pays for repairs of damages to your car only. The insurance company will pay for repairs to your car when you collide with any object, turn your car over, or are hit by an uninsured motorist. It is the most expensive coverage because the risks of damaging a car through an accident are great. Most buyers reduce the cost of this coverage by buying a policy with a deductible (often $250 to $500). Policyholders pay the amount of the deductible out of their own pockets before making a claim for additional costs for damages. Again, the higher the deductible, the smaller the premiums.

As the car gets older and its value decreases, you might consider dropping the collision insurance all together. Collision insurance pays only for the estimated value of the car at the time of loss. If your car isn't worth much, the cost of your collision insurance can exceed the amount you'll be paid if your car is totaled.

Comprehensive Physical Damage Coverage

Comprehensive physical damage coverage pays for damage to your car caused by something other than collision. This coverage will pay if the car is stolen or damaged by fire, storms, flood, vandalism, or other causes listed in the policy, though you will probably have to pay a deductible. If your car is stolen or totally destroyed, the company will pay the actual cash value of the car at the time of loss. The **actual cash value** of a property is its worth on the market at the moment before the accident. A good estimate of the actual cash value of a car is the amount buyers are currently paying for cars of that model and age. For example, if you could sell your old car now for no more than $500, then the insurance company would pay you no more than that amount if your car were destroyed today.

Medical Payments Coverage

Medical payments coverage pays medical expenses for the driver, all members of the driver's family, and any guests riding in the car at the time of the accident. Limits on medical payments are listed in the policy.

Uninsured Motorists Coverage

Uninsured motorists coverage protects you against hit-and-run drivers and motorists who have no insurance or are underinsured. Considering how many motorists today are not insured, this additional coverage is well worth the small amount added to your premium. This protection covers you whether you are injured while in your car or even while crossing the street. In most states, uninsured motorists protection covers only bodily injury. You must carry collision insurance to cover damage to your car caused by an uninsured motorist.

B Student Activity

1. Read the following auto insurance cases and answer the questions about each case:

   a. Your friend's new car was stolen only six months after she purchased it. It was never recovered. Since the car was insured with comprehensive coverage, she filed for the purchase price of the car. However, the insurance company was willing to pay only the actual cash value of the car, which was considerably less than what your friend expected.

   Who is legally correct? _____

   Explain. _____

   _____

   _____

   b. You lose control of your car and crash into your neighbor's parked car. No one is hurt, but there is considerable damage done to your neighbor's car. What type of auto coverage will pay the cost of the damage? _____

   _____

   c. You discontinued your liability coverage when you dropped your collision coverage on your old car. While on vacation, you violated a yield sign and permanently disabled the driver in the other car. Are you in trouble? Explain. _____

   _____

   _____

   Continued

d. While crossing an intersection, a woman was struck by a hit-and-run driver. The woman has auto insurance on her own car. What type of coverage, if any, would pay for her medical expenses? _____

_____

e. You have all six types of insurance on your 10-year-old car. Should you drop all or any part of the coverage? If so, which ones? _____

Explain. _____

_____

_____

f. Your family is sued because a motorist was injured in an accident in which you were speeding. Your family has liability coverage for 25/50/10. What does the coverage mean? _____

_____

_____

2. Mark's dad showed him a copy of the Smiths' auto policy renewal notice. This renewal notice is shown in Figure 9-1. Refer to Figure 9-1 as you answer the following questions:

a. What model car is covered? _____

b. The car is covered by insurance from (date) _____ to _____

c. How many cars are covered by this policy? _____

d. What is the deductible for collision? _____

e. What is the deductible for loss other than collision? ____

_____

f. The rates are based on how many drivers in the household? _____

g. What is the amount of the Smiths' total premium? _____

h. What is the limit of liability for liability coverage for Auto No. 1? _____

i. How much are the Smiths paying for their liability coverage? _____

j. How much are the Smiths paying for their medical payments coverage? _____

Figure 9-1

Auto Policy Renewal Notice

Figure 9-1 Auto Policy Renewal Notice

RENEWAL NOTICE-RETURN PROMPTLY IF YOU WISH TO MAKE ANY CHANGES

THE INSURANCE COMPANY

Atlanta, Georgia

Your insurance covering the automobile(s) listed below expires on December 31, 20--.
This notice contains information about your renewal policy. Any changes you have noted will be
made on the effective date of the renewal policy unless an earlier date is requested. Your renewal policy
will be prepared as shown below if this notice is not returned.

NAMED INSURED AND ADDRESS (No., St., Apt., Town or City, State, Zip Code)

Helen and Michael Smith
1040 Peachtree Dr.
Atlanta, GA 30319-1396

Previous Policy No.   930717-2014

County   Fulton

*The auto(s) or trailer(s) described in this policy is principally garaged at the above address unless otherwise stated.
Occupation of the named insured is   MECHANIC
LOSS PAYEE: (Name and Address)

Final Due Date

POLICY PERIOD: 12:01 A. M., STANDARD TIME From JANUARY 1, 20--   to JANUARY 1, 20--

DESCRIPTION OF AUTO(S) OR TRAILER(S)	YEAR 1999	TRADE NAME—MODEL CHEVROLET MONTE CARLO S COUPE			YEAR	TRADE NAME—MODEL		
	VIN 1H57V6R447431				VIN			
	PURCHASED 12/00 USED	FOB	COST 10,247	SYM	AGE	PURCHASED	FOB	COST	SYM	AGE

THE PREMIUMS SHOWN ARE RENEWAL RATES AND ARE QUOTED SUBJECT TO ANY CHANGE IN THE RATE SCHEDULE.

COVERAGES	LIMIT OF LIABILITY AUTO NO. 1	LIMIT OF LIABILITY AUTO NO. 2	PREMIUM AUTO NO. 1	PREMIUM AUTO NO. 2
A. LIABILITY	$ 100,000 Each Accident	$ Each Accident	$ 318.00	
B. MEDICAL PAYMENTS	$ 10,000 Each Person	$ Each Person	$ 27.00	
C. UNINSURED MOTORISTS	$ 50,000 Each Accident	$ Each Accident	$ 32.00	
D. DAMAGE TO YOUR AUTO	ACV means Actual Cash Value			
1. Collision Loss	ACV Minus $ 200 Deductible	ACV Minus $ Deductible	$ 130.00	
2. Other than Collision Loss	ACV Minus $ 50 Deductible	ACV Minus $ Deductible	$ 50.00	
TOWING AND LABOR COSTS	$ Each Disablement	$ Each Disablement		

TOTAL PREMIUM $ 557.00

ENDORSEMENTS

RATES ARE BASED ON FOLLOWING DRIVERS IN HOUSEHOLD

SAFE DRIVER PLAN
CHARGEABLE POINTS -- NONE

Driver	Date of Birth Mo.	Day	Year	Male or Female	Married or Single	Operator under 21 with Driver Training	Owner or principal operator is male under 30 or single female under	Student away at school over 100 miles and auto not at school
1	01	04	58	M	M			
2	01	13	60	F	M			
3								
4								
5								

AUTO	USE OF AUTO
1	PLEASURE
2	

IF THE DATA ABOUT DRIVERS IN HOUSEHOLD OR USE OF AUTO SHOULD BE CHANGED IN ANY WAY, KINDLY ADVISE:
*If garage location has changed, please give details—is the auto garaged indoors at night at the new location? ....

Please Sign Here ....

PLEASE DO NOT FORWARD CHECK UNTIL YOU RECEIVE POLICY AND BILL.

Unless advised to the contrary we shall renew and forward your policy.

How to Keep Auto Insurance Premiums to a Minimum for Adequate Coverage

Auto insurance is not cheap, but it is especially expensive for someone in Mark's classification of driver. However, there are ways to reduce your premiums and still have adequate coverage. Here are five ways to lower your auto insurance premiums:

1. *Take a higher deductible.* Collision and comprehensive coverage costs much less if you pay a higher deductible.

2. *Avoid sports cars.* If you've fallen hopelessly in love with a sports car, at least check with your insurance agent before purchasing the car. Compare the insurance premiums with premiums for other models.

3. *Take advantage of discounts.* Insurance companies often offer discounts, but to get them, you must know what you need in order to qualify. Also, you must tell the company when you are qualified. For example, companies often offer reduced rates to drivers who have taken a driver's education course, to students with good grades, and to drivers with a safe-driver record. Ask your insurance company what you need in order to qualify for a discount.

4. *Eliminate duplication of coverage.* Your homeowner's or renter's insurance may cover loss of personal property. Your health insurance may cover personal injury for you and your passengers. However, before dropping any coverage, check out the other policy to make sure you are covered by one or the other.

5. *Shop around for the best insurance for you.* As with everything else, insurance premiums vary greatly. You may be able to get the same coverage for a lot less. Comparison shopping is essential for getting the best coverage for the least amount. This doesn't mean that the cheapest company is always the best. Before signing anything, check the company's reputation in *Best's Insurance Reports,* an annual publication that evaluates the financial strength and stability of insurance companies. *Best's Insurance Reports* can be found in most public libraries.

Another good source of information about service and costs is *Consumer Reports* magazine. (You will learn more about this helpful consumer magazine in Chapter 11.) The articles in *Consumer Reports* often include customer surveys about their satisfaction with auto insurance companies. You can get some information free at the Web site (www.consumerreports.org), but you will need a subscription for full access.

How to Interpret No-Fault Insurance Laws

To reduce the costs of determining who is at fault in an auto accident, some states have passed no-fault insurance laws. **No-fault insurance** means that your insurance company pays for bodily injuries to you and your passengers no matter who caused the accident.

However, to date no state has adopted a pure no-fault law. There are variations on the theme for each state. Before buying an insurance policy, you should find out whether or not you live in a no-fault state and just what the law entails.

If you do live in a no-fault-state, you must buy what is called wage-loss coverage. **Wage-loss coverage** reimburses the insured for income lost because of an auto injury. In states without no-fault insurance, wage-loss coverage is optional.

Many no-fault states require **substitute-service coverage,** which pays for services that you cannot perform for yourself because of an auto-related injury. For example, your insurance company would pay for a cook or sitter for the time needed. Substitute-service coverage is not required in all no-fault states.

You can still be sued for big claims if you live in a no-fault state. However, no-fault does eliminate court costs by eliminating the need to go to court for small claims. The biggest advantage of good no-fault insurance is that the injured are usually paid immediately, without waiting for the courts to settle a case.

The important point is that whether you live in a no-fault state or not, you must have adequate auto insurance to protect you in case you are sued. An auto injury lawsuit could mean financial disaster. Therefore, you still need adequate liability coverage.

What to Do if You Have an Auto Accident

No matter how careful a driver you are, you will probably be involved in an accident at some point. It is important to know what to do. What you do at the time of the accident may affect your insurance claim. Here are some suggestions:

1. Never just drive away. Contact a police officer, even if it is just a fender-bender. Someone may make a bodily injury claim against you later.

2. Exchange insurance and phone information with the other driver. If the other driver is not insured, you will have to file a claim with your insurance company.

3. If possible, get names and phone numbers of several witnesses to the accident. Witnesses can be very helpful if you are wrongfully blamed for the accident.

4. As soon as possible, report the accident to your insurance company, even if you are not at fault and don't plan to make a claim.

5. Document every phone call you make to the insurance company, to the other driver, and to witnesses.

If your car is totaled, you can get an idea of the actual cash value of your car by checking Kelley Blue Book online at www.kbb.com.

How to Interpret Home and Property Insurance Policies

While they were on the subject of insurance, Mark recalled the story of his Uncle Ray getting upset because his insurance company did not pay for damages caused by floodwaters from a hurricane.

"He had paid into that company for about 20 years, right?" Mark asked.

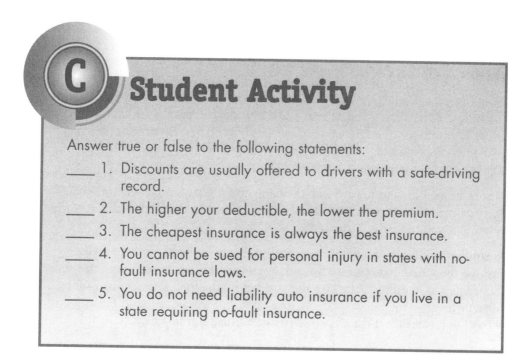

Student Activity

Answer true or false to the following statements:

_____ 1. Discounts are usually offered to drivers with a safe-driving record.

_____ 2. The higher your deductible, the lower the premium.

_____ 3. The cheapest insurance is always the best insurance.

_____ 4. You cannot be sued for personal injury in states with no-fault insurance laws.

_____ 5. You do not need liability auto insurance if you live in a state requiring no-fault insurance.

"He sure did," said Mrs. Smith, "but Ray never read his policy. It didn't cover damage by flood waters."

Kinds of Protection

Homeowner's insurance includes two basic kinds of protection: property protection and liability protection.

Property protection pays for losses to the home and other property. It may include everything from payments to cover the illegal use of lost credit cards to living expenses if your house burns down. The amount and kinds of protection you choose to buy will be listed in your policy. In general, property insurance covers damage caused by fire, windstorm, lightning, explosions, riots, aircraft, vehicles, vandalism, and theft. Usually, you have to pay extra for flood and earthquake insurance, a detail Uncle Ray didn't check.

Liability protection usually covers bodily injury to others, damage to property of others, and medical payments to a person injured on your property. With full liability coverage, you would be protected if someone fell and was injured on a damaged sidewalk in front of your home.

Most homeowner's policies cover the house itself and the contents in the house. Homeowner's policies distinguish between personal property and real property. **Personal property** includes furniture, clothing, appliances, and anything else contained in the house, unless specifically excluded in the policy. **Real property** includes physical structures that are attached to the land, such as the house, garage, and fences. Make sure you know what the policy covers before signing the contract.

Renter's insurance protects tenants in a house or apartment. It provides personal property and liability coverage. There's no coverage for the building since that's the landlord's responsibility.

Amount of Coverage

Most insurance companies agree that homeowners should insure their property for at least 80 percent of replacement cost in order to be fully paid at the time of a loss. If you have your $70,000 home insured for 80 percent of its replacement cost and a fire causes damages of $40,000, your insurance company will pay the full $40,000, minus your deductible.

If your home burns to the ground, the company will pay 80 percent, or $56,000. It is assumed that 20 percent of your home's value is in the land, which you will not lose if your house is destroyed.

Furniture, appliances, and other personal property in the home are usually insured for actual cash value. If your five-year-old TV burns, the insurance company will pay you its actual cash value just before the fire, not the price you paid for it or the price of a new TV. In other words, you will not be paid the amount it costs to replace the TV, unless otherwise specified in the policy.

Some companies do offer **replacement cost coverage** on personal property. In such a case, the company will pay the amount needed to replace property destroyed. The cost of replacing your belongings at today's prices can be quite a bit more than the actual cash value you receive from the insurance company for the loss. Compare the cost of insuring for replacement cost rather than for actual cash value. It might be worth the extra premium.

It is important to update the amount of coverage every few years. If your house has increased in value, you may not have enough coverage to pay for its replacement. Also, replacement costs may have increased.

Personal property of exceptional value, such as antiques, jewelry, and artwork, is not usually covered by a general policy. To cover the loss of these items, you will probably need to buy a separate policy or cover the items through a **floater policy**. This insurance names each item and its value and "floats" with the property wherever it goes. If your ring is stolen while you are on vacation, it is covered. Floaters are usually written as riders (additions) to a homeowner's policy. Floaters usually have no deductible and provide coverage for the full value of the property.

When you insure your personal property, you need to keep an inventory record of the property insured. Take photos or make a video of the contents of each room. Keep this picture record in a safe place, such as a safe deposit box or fireproof file cabinet. Even though you think you own very little, you will be surprised at how much you can forget you own if it is destroyed. You certainly will have difficulty remembering when you purchased the item and for how much. Since most personal property is insured at actual cash value, it is important to keep a record of when you purchased each item and the purchase price. If you do not have this information, settling claims can be a nightmare.

Now that Mark had moved into his first apartment, he began to think about a renter's policy. After all, he was the proud owner of a new stereo. Mark decided to find out what kind of coverage Roberto had.

Student Activity

1. Answer the following questions:

   a. Why did Uncle Ray's insurance company refuse to pay for damages caused by floodwaters to his home? _____

   _____

   _____

   b. What two kinds of protection does a homeowner's insurance policy include? _____

   _____

   c. List some reasons why a renter might need renter's insurance. _____

   _____

   d. What is a floater policy?_____

   _____

   _____

   e. How do insurance companies distinguish between personal property and real property?_____

   _____

   _____

2. Examine Roberto's Renter's Insurance Statement shown in Figure 9-2 on page 182 and answer the following questions:

   a. Name the coverages that Roberto included in his policy.

   _____

   b. How much does he pay for the policy? _____

   _____

   c. Does he pay a deductible? If so, what amount?_____

   _____

   d. What coverage would you buy if you had an apartment?

   _____

   Explain. _____

   _____

   _____

Figure 9-2

Roberto's Renter's
Statement

POLICY TERM: 12 MONTHS FROM	MO-DAY-YEAR 1/19/--	TO	MO-DAY-YEAR 1/19/--	PRODUCER'S CODE 072430	POLICY NUMBER 426960890 634 1

NAME OF
INSURED AND
MAILING ADDRESS
OF INSURED
PREMISES

ROBERTO GONZALEZ
333 COLLEGE DRIVE, APT. 3
ATLANTA, GA 30322-3315

ADDITIONAL COVERAGES	LIMITS OF LIABILITY	PREMIUMS
PERSONAL PROPERTY	$ 10,000	$ 101
ADDITIONAL EXPENSES	$ 2,000	INCLD IN C
PERSONAL LIABILITY	$ 24,000	INCLD IN C
MEDICAL PAYMENTS TO OTHERS	$ 500	INCLD IN C

TOTAL PREMIUM
$ 101

POLICY EDITION C2
POLICY FORM   634

Loss Deductible Amount
$ 100

Producer: Towne Insurance Agency

Declarations and any attached endorsements form a part of your "Policy Provisions" jacket bearing the policy edition and policy form number stated above. If a change number and effective date are entered at the top of this page, these declarations are made a part of your policy numbered above as of such date and all of the above entries supersede those on any previous declarations.

Agency At ____ATLANTA, GEORGIA____

_____ALISON PADGETT_____ Agent

1. Remove the auto insurance rates worksheet (Form 9-1) from the Source Documents section of this *Instructions and Source Documents Booklet*. Visit two automobile insurance agents and compare their rates. Before interviewing the agents, determine the kinds of coverage you need or want. File the completed form in the Personal file labeled *Insurance*.

2. Check to see if your state has no-fault insurance laws. Request a copy of the laws from your Insurance State Commissioner. If you have Internet access, search for your state's Department of Insurance Web site. You can find information about your state's insurance laws there.

Examine the laws or information you gather, and make a report to the class.

3. Remove the sample renter's inventory record (Form 9-2) from the *Instructions and Source Documents Booklet*. This record provides a list of personal property commonly owned by renters. Record the date and purchase price for each item you own. File the record in the Personal file labeled *Insurance* for future reference.

Check Up

Having completed the Student Activities in this chapter, you should have mastered the skills listed below. Put a checkmark next to the skills you have mastered. If you aren't sure of a skill, review that section of the chapter.

☐ How to interpret risk factors in auto insurance policies

☐ How to determine the amount of auto protection needed

☐ How to keep auto insurance premiums to a minimum for adequate coverage

☐ How to interpret no-fault insurance laws

☐ What to do if you have an auto accident

☐ How to interpret home and property insurance policies

Now that you know all about auto and home insurance, move on to Chapter 10, *Looking at Transportation Options*.

Chapter

LOOKING AT TRANSPORTATION OPTIONS

PHOTO: © GETTYIMAGES/ PHOTODISC

Now Mark was getting really excited about the prospect of having his own car. The Smiths' car was not new and had over 100,000 miles on it, but it would be his. Now that he was sharing an apartment with Roberto, he could use the flexibility that a car would provide. If he decided to attend classes at City College, he would probably go at night. A car would enable him to stay at school late, after the buses stopped running.

He bumped into Kim at the corner sandwich shop that same afternoon. Practical Kim had the answers. "The best way to decide whether or not you can afford something is to write figures down on paper. You'll need to estimate the cost of owning and operating a car," she said.

How to Estimate Costs of Owning and Operating a Car

Kim talked, and Mark wrote down the costs. They divided the costs into two categories: **fixed expenses** and **variable expenses**. Mark remembered these two kinds of expenses from his experience preparing a budget. Fixed expenses remain essentially the same whether you drive the car two miles a day or forty miles a day. Under fixed expenses, Mark listed loan payments, auto insurance, car license tag, and state inspection fees.

Usually, variable expenses are directly related to the number of miles a car is driven. Under variable expenses, Mark listed gasoline, oil changes, and regular maintenance. Mark and Kim drew up an estimate of the yearly costs of owning and operating a new car. Then they divided each yearly amount by 12 months to estimate how much Mark would have to set aside each month to cover expenses. Their estimates are shown in Figure 10-1.

Note that depreciation is not included as an expense in Figure 10-1. Depreciation is a kind of expense. However, you do not make cash payments for depreciation. **Depreciation** is a decrease in the value of property as it becomes older. A new car decreases in value more rapidly in the first few years you own it. A new, large-size car may depreciate as much as 30 to 40 percent the first year, around 20 percent the second year, and at a decreasing percentage rate every year thereafter. Some reports suggest that a new car decreases by 20 percent the day you buy it and drive it off the lot.

Based on a 30-percent depreciation rate, a car that cost $15,000 new might be worth only $10,500 after the first year, even if it has been well maintained. This is the reason that a two- or a three-year-old used car is often a good buy. It's also the reason some buyers like to buy a demonstrator from a new car showroom. A **demonstrator** is a car that has been used by the dealer to demonstrate to customers how the car performs. Even though they are thought of as new cars, demonstrators have been driven and have depreciated in value. Therefore, they are sold at a discount.

Figure 10-1

Costs of Owning and
Operating an
Automobile

PERSONAL COSTS OF OWNING AND OPERATING AN AUTOMOBILE*

	Cost per Month	Cost per Year
Fixed Expenses		
Installment payment	$300.00	$ 3,600.00
Insurance	$ 66.67	$ 800.00
License fees (including drivers license, inspection fee, license tag; fees vary from state to state)	$ 3.33	$ 40.00
Other (parking fees, etc.)		
Total fixed expenses	$370.00	$ 4,440.00
Variable Expenses		
Gasoline	$ 60.00	$ 720.00
Oil changes	$ 2.08	$ 25.00
Tires (should last 3 years or up to 40,000 miles)		
Maintenance (parts, repairs, tune-ups)	$ 16.67	$ 200.00
Total variable expenses	$ 78.75	$ 945.00
Total fixed & variable expenses	$448.75	$ 5,385.00

*Depreciation is not included because it does not require a cash payment.
Adapted from the Money Management Institute booklet titled *Your Automobile Dollar*, published by the Money Management Institute of Household Finance Corporation, Prospect Heights, Illinois.

A Student Activity

1. Define depreciation. _____
   _____
   _____

2. Assume that a new car depreciates at an estimated 30 percent the first year and 20 percent the second year.

   a. How much would a $13,000 car be worth after one year? _____

   b. What would be the car's value after two years? _____
   _____

How to Shop for a New Car

When Mark returned to his apartment, he still had cars on his mind. Roberto said he also had been thinking about buying a new car. Several people had told Roberto to really do his homework before purchasing or even looking at a new car. They warned him that it's too easy to get pressured into a purchase if you're not prepared. Both Mark and Roberto agreed that the best way to approach buying a new car is to make most decisions at home, a safe distance away from the showroom and all the new cars and high-pressure salespeople. They first needed to learn as much as they could about the new models.

Learn About Models and Prices

That night they went to the public library to research some auto magazines. The librarian showed them *Consumer Reports* and explained that the April issue is devoted almost entirely to the purchase of cars. They looked at other magazines, such as *Motor Trend, Road & Track, Road Test,* and *Car and Driver.* There were lots of magazines available. *Gas Mileage Guide* gives a yearly report on gas mileage tests conducted on new cars, and *New Car Prices is* an auto-buying guide. The librarian said they could probably find more car-oriented magazines at a newsstand. He also suggested that the yearly copies of *Gas Mileage Guide* and *New Car Prices* can usually be found at new car dealerships.

The librarian recommended doing some research about cars on the Internet as well. Some sites, such as Edmunds (www.edmunds.com) and MSN Carpoint (http://carpoint.msn.com/homepage/), offer information about new and used cars, plus advice on how to evaluate and buy a car. You can find out the approximate worth of a used car at Kelley Blue Book (www.kbb.com). Some sites, such as www.carsdirect.com, enable you to buy online. Even if you don't order online, you can use the Internet to find out the invoice price (dealer's cost) of the vehicle and to learn about available options. When you've narrowed the search to two or three vehicles, you can get price quotes online. Price quotes and invoice prices will give you a basis for negotiation when you go to the dealership.

Mark and Roberto had plenty to read at the library. They read the magazines and used the library computer to study several Web sites. They learned a lot that night about buying a new car. Here is some of what they learned.

Select the Type of Car

When selecting the type of car you want, consider the rate of depreciation and cost of repairs and maintenance. Almost all cars depreciate, or lose value over time. However, different models depreciate at different rates. The rate of depreciation depends on customer demand for the model. For example, when gasoline prices are high, smaller cars with good gas mileage are in demand. As a result, smaller cars would depreciate less at that time than larger cars. If you choose a car that depreciates at a high rate, you will get less for it when you sell it than you would with another model that holds its value better.

The cost of repair and maintenance varies with the type of car. Some small cars are more expensive to repair than intermediate-size cars or even luxury cars. If involved in an accident, a smaller car usually sustains more damage than a larger, heavier car. Therefore, the repairs are more extensive and more expensive. Some kinds of foreign cars are more expensive to repair because the parts have to be ordered and are usually more costly than parts for American cars.

Look into the predicted reliability ratings of the models you are considering. These ratings reflect how often a particular model currently on the road has needed repair compared to other similar models. You can find predicted reliability ratings in *Consumer Reports* magazine.

Gas mileage is an important consideration as well. The more miles the car can go on a gallon of gas, the less you will spend on gasoline. You can find the miles per gallon (MPG) ratings in most car-oriented magazines and Web sites. Dealers also show the MPG on the window stickers of all new cars they have for sale.

Some experts suggest that the best way to select a car is to rent the one you like for a day or two. It's the best and least pressured way to test drive a car at your leisure.

Investigate Prices and Options

The price of a new car in a showroom is, with rare exception, negotiable. The price on the car window is called the **sticker price**. The sticker price is the full retail price, including all options already on that particular vehicle. In almost all cases, you should expect to pay less than the sticker price for the car.

The **invoice price** is the price the dealer paid the manufacturer for the car. This price does not appear on the sticker. However, you can find the invoice price online at several sites, including Edmunds. Usually a fair price lies somewhere between the sticker and invoice prices. The dealer's profit is the difference between the invoice price and the amount the buyer pays for the car. The dealer is supposed to make something on the car. However, if you know what the dealer paid (the invoice price), then you have more power to negotiate a price that includes a reasonable but not excessive profit.

Options are features not included in the base price. Some common options are air conditioning, CD player, leather upholstery, and electric windows and door locks. Options increase the price you will have to pay for the car. What may look like an economical buy in the library may quickly become expensive if you want a lot of options.

At the library, Roberto compiled a checklist of options to consider before going to look at new cars. He called the list his "What I Want Is Not Necessarily What I Get Chart." Figure 10-2 is a copy of the chart Roberto compiled.

Select a Dealer

Choose a reputable dealer and check out the service department before buying a new car. Even with a new car under warranty, the dealership is responsible for servicing and repairing any defects or problems with the car. It's also a good idea to check for customer complaints with the Better Business Bureau (BBB) before buying from a particular dealership. (Services offered by the BBB will be presented in Chapter 11.)

Other people who have purchased cars from the dealer are a good source of information about the service department. Also, find out the days and hours the

Figure 10-2

Roberto's Chart of Car Options

Car Options	What I Want	What I Need	What I Can Afford	What I Get (results: 2 out of 3)*
1. Automatic	✓		✓	✓
or				
Standard transmission		✓		
2. Small car	✓	✓	✓	✓
or				
Intermediate car				
or				
Large car				
3. Sports car	✓			
or				
Standard car		✓	✓	✓
4. 4 cylinder		✓	✓	✓
or				
6 cylinder	✓			
5. Cruise control	✓		✓	✓
or				
No cruise control		✓		
6. ABS brakes	✓			
or				
Standard brakes		✓	✓	✓
7. Air conditioning	✓		✓	✓
or				
No air conditioning		✓		
8. Standard radio		✓	✓	✓
or				
AM-FM stereo/cassette				
or				
AM-FM stereo/CD	✓			

*The option checked in the far right column is what Roberto thinks he should buy.

service department is open. If you work during the day, you need to be able to take your car in before or after work or on weekends.

Negotiate and Sign a Sales Agreement

Once you decide on a particular car, you negotiate and sign a sales agreement. A **sales agreement** is a contract between you and the dealer to purchase the car. The terms of the sales agreement are negotiable until both you and the sales manager have signed the agreement.

Before negotiating the terms of the sales agreement, you should be familiar with sales tactics a salesperson might use. Two of the most common tactics are lowballing and highballing.

Lowballing is used when the salesperson has no intention of selling the car at the low price offered, but wants to get you hooked on the car first. The tactic usually begins when the salesperson makes an offer to sell the car far below its sticker price. After the customer shows serious interest (or gets hooked), the salesperson takes the deal into the sales manager. The sales manager will not approve the offer but will sell the car at a higher price. The objective is that the customer is by now so in love with the car that she or he will agree to pay a price much higher than the original offer.

Highballing involves trading in a used car for a new car. A salesperson will offer a high price for the used car. After the price is agreed upon, the salesperson takes the offer into the sales manager, who says the offer is too high. The customer, who has his or her heart set on a new car, either agrees to accept a lower price for the used car or agrees to pay a higher price for the new car. Either way, the customer loses.

If you have done your homework, you should know the car's invoice price. You should also know the price that buyers are typically paying for this model with the same options. You should have a target price in mind before you make an offer. Start the negotiations by offering a price at or slightly above the invoice price. The salesperson's counteroffer will probably be above your offer but should be below the sticker price. Raise your offer, but don't go above your target price. In the end, if the salesperson is not willing to sell at a price you consider reasonable, be prepared to walk out.

In general, it is best to avoid signing a purchase agreement on the same day you find a car you like. Give yourself time to think about it. When you are ready to sign, the salesperson or a financing manager will try to sell you extras, such as rust proofing and extended warranties. Resist buying these last-minute add-ons. They are unnecessary and just add to the final price you pay. Some additional fees are legitimate, such as sales taxes and license and destination fees.

Trading in a Used Car

Before trading your used car, check its value on the Internet at sites such as Edmunds (www.edmunds.com), Kelley Blue Book (www.kbb.com), and Auto Trader (www.autotrader.com). You may also want to look at an automobile trade price book, found at libraries, dealerships, and banks, to determine its value. Also check newspaper ads for used cars that are similar to yours. Some owners prefer to sell their used cars themselves because they can often get a higher price than if they trade.

Discuss the price for your trade-in only after you've settled on the price of the new car. You have already determined the value of your used car, so you have an idea of a fair price. The value of a used car depends on several things, including the age and condition of the car, the number of miles it has been driven, and its optional features. Take these things into consideration when determining the price you think is fair.

Take the dealer's price, compare it with the prices offered outside the dealership, go home, and make comparisons. You may want to sell the car yourself if the dealer's price is far below the price of similar cars you see advertised for sale by private owners.

Understand the Warranty

Before signing a sales agreement, make sure you understand all aspects of the new car warranty. A **warranty** is a promise by a manufacturer or dealer that the product will perform up to expected quality standards over a given period of time. If the product or part breaks within the stated time period, the warranty covers the cost of repair or replacement. In a car warranty, the length of coverage is usually stated in months or mileage limits. For instance, a warranty may read like this: 12-month or 12,000 miles total warranty, with longer warranty periods for major parts, such as the engine.

However, warranties do differ. Be sure you know exactly what is covered and for how long. For instance, tires are usually covered by the tire manufacturer, but only for defects. The manufacturer will not replace a tire damaged by a nail. Also, be aware of what you are required to do in order to benefit from the warranty.

Apply for a Car Loan

When you don't have the cash to purchase the car, you have to apply for an installment loan. (You learned about installment loans in Chapter 5.) You borrow money for a specific period of time (12, 18, 24, 36, or 60 months). Then you pay back the principal (amount borrowed) plus interest (cost of using borrowed money) in regular monthly installments (payments).

The longer the loan period, the higher the interest rate. Your monthly payments will be lower for a 60-month loan than for a 24-month loan. However, you will pay more total interest on the longer loan because you are making more payments and paying a higher interest rate. Therefore, do not extend the loan any longer than you have to.

The interest rate makes a big difference in the cost of your car purchase, so shopping for an installment loan is important. The easiest place to get a car loan may be from the dealer, but it's not always the least expensive. Check the newspaper for current rates for car loans at various sources before buying a car. Sources of loans, in addition to car dealerships, are banks, savings and loan associations, and credit unions. Most car-buying Web sites also quote loan rates.

With a car loan, the car serves as collateral—property pledged as security for the loan. The lender holds the car's title (proof of ownership) until you pay the loan in full. If you fail to make your payments, the lender can take back the car.

When you apply for a car loan, the lender will usually require a down payment. The amount of the down payment will vary. If you apply for a loan from the car dealership, the dealer may suggest that your trade-in be used as the down payment. Be sure you have already negotiated the price of the trade-in before agreeing to this arrangement.

A copy of an auto installment loan contract is shown in Figure 10-3 on page 192. Before you sign a loan contract, make sure you understand the APR (annual percentage rate) and the total cost for financing the loan.

Your ability to get an auto loan at the lowest possible interest rate depends on your credit rating. Once again, you can see the importance of paying your bills on time and establishing a good credit rating.

Figure 10-3

Auto Installment Loan Contract

INSTALLMENT CONTRACT

Undersigned Buyer agrees to buy the property described below (hereafter called "Collateral") and Buyer acknowledges receipt thereof. Buyer promises to pay Seller, the unpaid part of this contract (Line 8) in the consecutive monthly installments commencing or the date indicated in the Terms of Payment or, if no date appears, one month from the date of this contract. Buyer hereby grants to Seller a security interest in the below described Collateral including all parts, accessories, equipment and any other additions or accessions, now or hereafter attached to and used in connection with said Collateral, to secure the payment of the Total of Payments (Line 8) and any delinquency charges including interest, any expenses of repossession and resale including costs of storage.

PURCHASER(S): *Mary C. Jones   111 Oak St.   Atlanta   Georgia*
(Print Full Name)   (No., Street or R.F.D)   (City)   (State)

SELLER: *Metro Auto Co.   201 Denton St.   Atlanta   Georgia*
(Dealer's Name)   (Correct Legal Address)   (City)   (State)

Seller does hereby sell, transfer and deliver unto Purchaser under the terms and conditions set forth herein, the following described property, delivery and acceptance of which in good order is hereby accepted by Purchaser.

NEW OR USED	YEAR	MAKE	BODY TYPE	SERIAL NO.	ODOMETER READING	LICENSE NO.
New	*20--*	*Ford Escort*	*4 Door*	*7B0890230040*	*15*	

Cash Price (including Sales Tax) .... $ *13,900.00* 1
Down Payment
(a) Cash (Down Payment) .... $ *3,000.00*
1(b) Trade-In $
    Less Amount Owed $
    Net Allowance $
    Total Down Payment .... $ *3,000.00* 2
Unpaid Balance of Cash Price .... $ *10,900.00* 3
Premiums for Property insurance, if any, for a term
    of _____ months .... $ *-* 4
Documentary Fees .... $ *-* 5
Unpaid Balance, i.e., Amount Financed (Add lines 3, 4, 5) $ *10,900.00* 6

FINANCE CHARGE (Interest) .... $ *545.00* 7

ANNUAL PERCENTAGE RATE _____ *5.0* _____ %
Total of Payments (Add lines 6 and 7) .... $ *11,445.00* 8

TERMS OF PAYMENT: _____ *60* _____ successive
monthly installments of $ *190.75*
and one final payment of $ *190.40*
commencing *January 3* , 20—

PROPERTY INSURANCE, if written in connection with this contract may be obtained by the Buyer through any person of his or her choice. If Buyer desires such insurance to be obtained through the Seller, the cost will be $_____ for the term of _____ year(s).

DEFAULT CHARGES: Seller shall be entitled to collect a deliquency charge on each installment in a default for a period of not less than 15 days of 5% of the unpaid amount of the installment. In the event Seller elects to accept delinquency and collection charges hereunder, all such payments from the Buyer shall be applied first to the current installment due, if any, then to delinquency charges, colllection charges, and unpaid installments.

Buyer acknowledges reading and receiving a copy of this contract in its completed form.

Executed at Atlanta, Georgia, this *12* day of *December* _____ 20--

J.J. Beal Sales Manager   *Mary C. Jones*
(Seller)   (Buyer)

[1] A trade-in can be counted toward total down payment.

 **Student Activity**

1. Mark and Roberto overheard the following conversation when they visited a new car dealership. Teresa, a customer, had her eye on a new silver sports car.

   Salesperson: What do you think?

   Teresa: It's a beauty, but a little high for my budget.

   Salesperson: You're in luck. We're clearing out the showroom this week to display the new models. Tell you what. We'll knock $2,000 off the sticker price.

   Teresa: Hey, that's a deal. Let's talk.

   Salesperson: Have a seat at my desk over there while I confirm this with the manager.

   (Salesperson returns from talking with the manager.)

   Salesperson: We have a bit of a problem here, but nothing we can't work out. The manager reminded me that the discount was effective on only certain model cars. But because you're so interested in this car—and it's an excellent buy without the discount—he's willing to knock off $500.

   Teresa: Well, that's quite a difference.

   Salesperson: We can work it out. Here, let's put paper and pencil to it. I know you like the car.

   a. What sales tactic is the salesperson using? _____
   _____

   b. Explain how this sales tactic works. _____
   _____
   _____
   _____

   c. List the mistakes Teresa probably made in shopping for a new car._____
   _____
   _____
   _____
   _____

   Continued

B Student Activity Continued

2. Answer true or false to the following statements:

_____ a. Almost all cars depreciate.

_____ b. The sticker price is usually a fair price for the car.

_____ c. You will probably pay more total interest on a 24-month car loan than on a 60-month car loan.

_____ d. A new car warranty usually covers specified parts for as long as you own the car.

_____ e. The higher a car's MPG, the less you will have to spend on gasoline.

3. After studying the auto installment loan contract, Figure 10-3, answer the following questions:

a. What APR is the loan based on? _____

b. What is the finance charge? _____

c. What is the amount of the down payment? _____

d. How long is the loan period?_____

4. Remove the chart of car options (Form 10-1) from the Source Documents section of this *Instructions and Source Documents Booklet.* Complete the chart for yourself. File it in the Personal file labeled *Automobile.* Use the chart when you shop for a new car.

5. Record the following transactions for Mark: On February 14, Mark received and deposited his paycheck. He deposited $240.01 and kept $85.00 in cash. Record the deposit in the check register. Record Mark's $325.01 income and the following cash expenditures for the week in the *Financial Management Records Booklet.* On February 14, Mark recorded the following cash amounts: food, $25.00; transportation, $10.00; personal, $10.00; entertainment, $35.00.

How to Shop for a Used Car

After looking at new car options with Roberto, Mark decided he wanted to look at some other used cars before buying his parents' car. His parents thought that was a good idea and recommended that he talk with a friend theirs, Mr. Howard, who taught automotive service at City College. Mark went to see Mr. Howard.

"It's always a good idea to know your options," said Mr. Howard. "Where you buy a used car is as important as what car you buy. You know your parents aren't going to cheat you, but you may find a car on a used-car lot that you think is much better. Now is a good time to learn how to shop for a used car."

Decide Where to Buy

Mr. Howard told Mark that used cars can be purchased from three major sources: a private seller (person), used-car dealers, and new-car dealers. He discussed the advantages and drawbacks of each source.

A private seller is a friend, acquaintance, or individual advertising to sell a car. The advantage of buying from a private seller is usually a lower price than asked by a dealership. Usually, the disadvantage is the absence of a warranty. The car may need an expensive repair, or it may have been in a serious accident and was never quite right after the repair. Therefore, if you don't know the history of the car, you take the chance of buying a car with a lot of problems.

An advantage of buying from a used-car dealer is a wide variety of cars from which to choose. Used-car dealers usually get their cars from private individuals and new-car dealers. Another advantage is that many dealers offer a limited warranty on certain parts of a used car. The disadvantage is the suspect reputations of some used-car dealers. You may be subjected to a hard-sell and/or not get a quality product. Know the reputation of the used-car dealer before you buy.

An advantage of buying from new-car dealers is the wide variety of newer automobiles that are usually offered. Because they have their own service departments, new-car dealers can make repairs themselves. Another advantage is that most dealers offer limited warranties. The disadvantage is that used cars purchased from a new-car dealership usually cost more than those purchased from the other two sources.

Gather Information About Used Cars

Mr. Howard mentioned the following sources of information on used cars and their prices:

1. National Automobile Dealers Association Official Used Car Guide

2. Red Book Official Used Car Valuations

3. Automotive Market Report

4. *Consumer Reports* April Issue

5. Kelley Blue Book

Guides 1-3 can be found in banks, some savings and loan associations, and car dealerships. These guides only estimate the cost since the price of a used car depends upon the condition and mileage on the car. Ads for used cars in newspapers are helpful sources for getting an idea about how much a specific type of used car should cost. According to Mr. Howard, the April issue of *Consumer Reports* is an excellent source.

The Internet is also a valuable source of information about prices on used cars. You can use the same sites you learned about for researching new cars.

Buying a used car can be a smart move because of the rapid depreciation on new cars. However, the condition of a used car is a tricky matter for most of us. The asking price for a used car will sometimes depend on how the seller judges your knowledge of the car's condition. If the seller thinks you don't know anything about cars, you may be taken for a higher purchase price. One source of general information about used cars is the *Guide to Used Cars,* published by Consumers Union each year.

The Federal Trade Commission (FTC) ruling of 1985 has improved the chances of a buyer getting a good used car. The FTC requires used-car dealers to inform buyers of exactly what auto parts the warranty covers. This does not mean you will get a used car without problems. It means you are entitled to know who will pay for what if something goes wrong. It's another advantage to buying a car from a dealer. A private seller is not bound by this ruling.

The FTC ruling requires the *Buyers' Guide* sticker, shown in Figure 10-4 (page 198), to be plainly visible on all used cars sold by a dealer. If the *As Is* block is checked, you have no warranty. If *Warranty* is checked, the dealer is obligated to pay for whatever items he or she has listed for the duration (length) of time a part is covered. In some cases, the dealer will check *Full Warranty,* meaning everything is covered for the amount of time designated.

Read the *Buyers' Guide* carefully. Verbal promises are difficult, if not impossible, to enforce.

Check the Condition of the Body and Accessories

Generally, if the previous owner took good care of the body, he or she probably kept the car well-maintained mechanically as well. Has the car been repainted? One way to tell is to lift the hood to see if the paint underneath matches the paint on the outside. If the car has been repainted, it could mean that it had been in a serious accident.

Check for rust spots around headlights, fenders, and bumpers. Look for damage in the upholstery, carpeting, and interior coverings. Make sure everything works and is in good condition. Check tires, lights, windshield wiper blades and washer, radio, tape or CD players, and speakers. If all that is in good condition, it is more likely that the parts you can't see are in good condition as well.

Check the Mileage

Check the odometer reading. The **odometer** measures the mileage a car has been driven. Years ago, many used-car dealers and car owners turned back the odometer to make a car appear to have lower mileage. In 1972 a law was passed to impose penalties on any seller who tampered with the odometer reading. According to the law, the seller must give written confirmation that the odometer reading has not been altered in any way.

Student Activity

You are looking for a used car for around $5,000. When pricing cars at a used car lot, you discover a six-year-old Honda with standard equipment priced at $5,000. A five-year-old Olds 98, loaded with options, is also priced at $5,000. When new, the Olds would have cost considerably more than the Honda.

1. Can you explain the similarity in price of the two used cars, even though the Olds was more expensive when new? Give possible reasons. _____
_____
_____
_____
_____

2. If you were choosing between these two used cars, what other issues would you consider before making a decision? _____
_____
_____
_____
_____

3. Which of the two cars would you buy? _____
Why? _____
_____
_____
_____
_____

4. If a similar model Honda was advertised in the paper by a private seller at $4,500, would you buy it? Give reasons for your decision. _____
_____
_____
_____
_____

Figure 10-4

Buyers' Guide Sticker

BUYERS' GUIDE

IMPORTANT: Spoken promises are difficult to enforce. Ask the dealer to put all promises in writing. Keep this form.

_____   _____   _____   _____
Vehicle Make   Model   Year   ID Number

WARRANTIES FOR THIS CAR

☐ **AS IS—NO WARRANTY**

YOU WILL PAY ALL COSTS FOR ANY REPAIRS. The dealer assumes no responsibility for repairs regardless of any oral statements about mechanical condition.

☐ **WARRANTY**

☐ FULL ☐ LIMITED WARRANTY. The dealer will pay _____ % of the total repair bill for the covered systems that fail during the warranty period. Ask the dealer for a copy of the warranty document, a full explanation of warranty coverage exclusions, and the dealer's repair obligations. Under state law, "implied warranties" may give you even more rights.

SYSTEMS COVERED: DURATION:

_____   _____

_____   _____

_____   _____

_____   _____

_____   _____

_____   _____

SERVICE CONTRACT. A service contract is available from _____ for $ _____ extra. This service contract adds to the dealer's responsibilities under any warranty. If you buy a service contract within 90 days of the time of sale, state law "implied warranties" may give you additional rights.

PRE-PURCHASE INSPECTION. ASK THE DEALER IF YOU MAY HAVE THIS CAR INSPECTED BY YOUR MECHANIC EITHER ON OR OFF THE LOT.

SEE THE BACK OF THIS FORM for important additional information, including a list of some major defects that may occur in used cars.

You may well be suspicious of odometer tampering if two of the numbers do not line up evenly or if the tenths counter vibrates when the car is moving. Another way to verify mileage is to look at the oil change sticker inside the car door or the state inspection sticker on the windshield. Both usually list the mileage. You can also ask a used-car dealer for the name and address of the previous owner. If you are refused, walk away. The previous owner should be able to answer questions regarding the use of the car.

According to a 2002 study by the National Highway Traffic Safety Administration, odometer tampering is again a major problem. Every year more than 450,000 people buy used vehicles with mileage gauges rolled back, spending thousands of dollars more than they should.

Here are some tips distributed by the federal odometer fraud program:

• Get a title history from the Department of Motor Vehicles and contact all previous owners. Ask them about the mileage of the vehicle when they sold it and how it ran.

• Take the vehicle to a reliable repair shop. A mechanic can usually tell if the vehicle's wear and tear is consistent with the odometer reading.

• Check with an independent vehicle history database, such as www.carfax.com, which will research vehicle histories for a fee.

• If your purchased vehicle is rolled back, return it to the seller and ask the seller to remedy the situation. Results are often possible without hiring an attorney.

Although mileage is important, low mileage doesn't always mean good maintenance. You probably don't want a car that has been driven 170,000 miles. At the same time, you may not want a car just because it has low mileage. A two-year-old car with 30,000 to 40,000 miles may be in better shape than a two-year-old car with 5,000 miles. The car with 5,000 miles on it was probably used for city driving, short distances, and at low speeds with stopping and starting. A car needs long distance driving on occasion in order to clean it of sludge and accumulation of acids in the lubrication system.

Check the Registration and Title

If you are purchasing a car from a stranger, ask to see the car's registration and title (proof of ownership). Check with the police or motor vehicle bureau to be sure the car is not stolen. If the car is stolen, you will not have legal title (ownership) and will have to give the car up and lose your money. Also, the title cannot be obtained until the loan is paid off completely. In other words; you need a confirmation of clear title to a car before buying.

Have a Mechanic Check the Car

Mr. Howard advised Mark to have a certified mechanic check the car before he decided to buy. Choose a mechanic that is not associated with the dealership. Most mechanics will do such a check for a reasonable fee. Reputable dealers will allow you to take the car to a shop to have it checked. Of course, you will be asked to leave some form of security at the dealership.

Mr. Howard showed Mark a diagram, Figure 10-5, that identifies areas where mechanical problems may occur. These areas should be checked by the mechanic.

Road Test the Car

Mr. Howard said buyers should always road test a car, taking a mechanic along if possible. A road test should not be a drive around the block. A worthwhile road test takes between 30 and 45 minutes. The test drive should include the items listed below:

1. Drive up hills and on bumpy road surfaces. Leave the window down to detect noises. Do not have the radio on. Test the radio later.

2. Run the car in all gears. An automatic transmission should shift easily without difficulty or slippage. A manual shift should not stick or slip.

3. Check acceleration. Pass a car on the highway or accelerate to enter a highway by an access road.

4. Test the brakes while driving slowly. When no other traffic is nearby, take your hands off the steering wheel and apply the brakes. If the car swerves or brakes too slowly, the car is dangerous.

5. Try the starter several times to make sure the car starts easily every time.

6. Listen for whines or other irregular noises while idling. Noises of this sort may indicate engine problems.

7. Drive a short distance with wet tires. If the car leaves four tire tracks instead of two, the frame of the car may be bent.

8. Park the car on a clean, smooth surface. Check for leaks. Transmission fluid is red. Engine oil is black.

9. At some point during the test drive, check the quality of air conditioning, heater, windshield wipers and washers, radio, and other accessories.

Figure 10-5

Possible Problem Areas

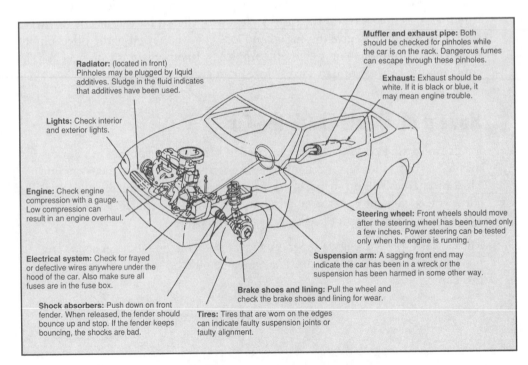

Radiator: (located in front) Pinholes may be plugged by liquid additives. Sludge in the fluid indicates that additives have been used.

Muffler and exhaust pipe: Both should be checked for pinholes while the car is on the rack. Dangerous fumes can escape through these pinholes.

Exhaust: Exhaust should be white. If it is black or blue, it may mean engine trouble.

Lights: Check interior and exterior lights.

Engine: Check engine compression with a gauge. Low compression can result in an engine overhaul.

Steering wheel: Front wheels should move after the steering wheel has been turned only a few inches. Power steering can be tested only when the engine is running.

Electrical system: Check for frayed or defective wires anywhere under the hood of the car. Also make sure all fuses are in the fuse box.

Suspension arm: A sagging front end may indicate the car has been in a wreck or the suspension has been harmed in some other way.

Brake shoes and lining: Pull the wheel and check the brake shoes and lining for wear.

Shock absorbers: Push down on front fender. When released, the fender should bounce up and stop. If the fender keeps bouncing, the shocks are bad.

Tires: Tires that are worn on the edges can indicate faulty suspension joints or faulty alignment.

Considering all he had learned about buying a used car from a private seller or a dealer, Mark decided to buy his parents' car if he could afford it. He knew he couldn't pay the full amount in one payment. He hoped they would let him pay a little each month.

D Student Activity

1. Answer the following questions about buying a used car:

   a. What might indicate that the car has been in a wreck?

   _____

   _____

   b. What may be a sign that the car has potential engine trouble? _____

   _____

   c. What are indications of odometer tampering? _____

   _____

   _____

2. Record the following transactions for Mark:

   a. On February 21, Mark received and deposited his paycheck. He deposited $240.01 and kept $85.00 in cash. Record the deposit in the check register. Record Mark's $325.01 income and the following cash expenditures for the week in the *Financial Management Records Booklet*. That same day, Mark recorded the following cash amounts: food, $30.00; T-shirt, $15.00; transportation, $12.00; fun, $20.00.

   b. The next day, February 22, Mark stopped at the Thrifty Grocery. He decided he needed to buy some food to eat at home for lunch because this eating-out business was costing him too much money. He wrote Check 119 for $45.00 for groceries. Record the transaction and write and file the check.

   c. Mark's parents said they wanted him to get health insurance before he bought the car. They didn't want him to put health insurance on the back burner. On February 23, Mark found a policy that offered very basic coverage at Best Health for a $65.00 premium per month. He wrote

Continued

Check 120 for $65.00. Record the transaction and write and file the check.

d. Mark's parents agreed to sell Mark their car for $600.00. They also agreed to let him pay them back in 12 monthly installments of $50.00 each. The best part of the deal was that they would not charge him interest if he made his payments on time. Mark remembered how he had agreed to buy his stereo without considering his budget. That could make paying for the car more difficult. He would not make that mistake again. Mark agreed to sign a promissory note for the loan from his parents. Remove the promissory note (Form 10-2) from the Source Documents section of this *Instructions and Source Documents Booklet.* Complete the note for Mark. He signed the note on February 25. He promised to pay his parents, Michael and Helen Smith, $600.00 in 12 consecutive monthly payments of $50.00 each. Payments are due on the 25th of each month. File the promissory note in the Outgoing File.

e. On February 25, Mark wrote Check 121 to Michael and Helen Smith for his first $50.00 car payment. Record the transaction and write and file the check.

f. Mark bought only liability property and bodily injury coverage from Every State Insurance Co. for $400.00 per year. He could pay his car insurance premium quarterly (every three months). If he paid in quarterly installments, he had to pay a $2.00 installment charge each quarter. Therefore, each quarterly payment was $102.00, for a total of $408.00 per year. On February 26, Mark wrote Check 122 for his first quarterly installment of $102.00 for car insurance. Record the transaction and write and file the check.

g. Mark had to pay a $30.00 fee to have the car title switched to his name and for car license tags. On February 27, Mark wrote Check 123 to the Georgia Bureau of Motor Vehicles for this fee. Record the transaction and write and file the check.

h. Remove Form 10-3 from the Source Documents section. Estimate how much Mark's car would cost him. He made a $50.00 monthly car payment for a total of $600.00 for the year. He would pay $408.00 per year for his car

Continued

D Student Activity Continued

insurance. Car tags and fees cost $40.00 once a year. He estimated he would spend $60.00 a month for gasoline. During the year he estimated that he would spend $25.00 for oil if he did the oil changes himself. Since it was an old car, he could expect more repairs than for a new car, so he estimated $300.00 a year for maintenance. Complete the form for Mark by recording his monthly and yearly fixed expenses. Calculate and total fixed expenses. Next, record his monthly and yearly variable expenses. Calculate the total variable expenses. Calculate the total fixed and variable expenses. File the form in the *Automobile* file.

Remove the diagram of possible problem areas in a used car (Form 10-4) from the Source Documents section of the *Instructions and Source Documents Booklet*. Identify the areas to be checked before buying a used car. File the completed diagram in the *Automobile* file. Use the diagram when you shop for a used car.

Check Up

Having completed the Student Activities in this chapter, you should have mastered the skills listed below. Put a checkmark next to the skills you have mastered. If you aren't sure of a skill, review that section of the chapter.

☐ How to estimate costs of owning and operating a car

☐ How to shop for a new car

☐ How to shop for a used car

Now that you know about buying a car, move on to Chapter 11, *Checking Out the Rights and Responsibilities of the Consumer.*

Chapter 11

CHECKING OUT THE RIGHTS AND RESPONSIBILITIES OF THE CONSUMER

PHOTO: © GETTYIMAGES/ PHOTODISC

Mark was enjoying his Sunday afternoon in his new apartment. Roberto was off somewhere, so he had the place to himself for a change. He felt good about himself and his accomplishments over the last several months. As he read the Sunday paper, an ad caught his attention. The headline read:

Get Your College Degree by Mail

Mark couldn't believe it. One of his dreams was to obtain a college degree. He was beginning to wonder if that would ever be possible. According to the ad, he could continue working at his job and get his college degree at the same time without attending any classes. He simply mailed in his assignments. He called Kim to tell her about the ad.

"It sounds too good to be true," Mark said.

"It probably is," Kim responded. "What kind of degree? Is the school accredited?"

"What does that mean?" Mark asked. He was disappointed in Kim's response.

"Accrediting agencies approve the curriculum and degrees offered by schools and colleges," Kim said. "If the institution isn't accredited by a recognized agency, you will have spent a lot of time and money on a 'degree' that isn't worth the paper it's written on. Also, certain schools use the word 'college' loosely."

"How do I find out?" Mark asked.

"There should be a phone number and address somewhere in the ad," she said. "Call and ask. And while you're at it, write down a lot of questions you'd like to ask. Like who are they? Where are they located? What's the name of the degree? Ask about the costs. Mark, no accredited school can offer an associate degree, not to mention a four-year college degree, in six weeks—no matter what the costs. Even legitimate, privately owned schools—like paralegal schools—can be very expensive. You may be able to get the same degree for a lot less at a local community college, like City College. You need a lot more information about this place."

How to Determine Your Rights as a Consumer

When you buy a product or a service, you are acting as a consumer. The marketplace depends on you to buy products. In recent years, consumers have become more aware of the influence they have on the types and quality of products being offered for sale. Health and good nutrition is a good example. You can't go to a grocery store anymore without seeing ads on product packages indicating low fat, low cholesterol, and high fiber. Companies developed these products to meet the growing consumer demand for healthier food choices.

Before 1962, consumers had little recourse if they weren't satisfied with a product they purchased. They were just stuck with a "lemon," as they put it. Today there are consumer laws that protect the rights of consumers in just about every area of the marketplace.

All consumers need to know their rights and responsibilities. Most of your rights are protected by state and federal laws. It is your responsibility to learn what these laws involve and complain when your consumer rights have been violated. In his State of the Union Address of 1962, President John F. Kennedy proposed a Consumer Bill of Rights that included the following areas:

1. *The right to safety*—Protection against the sale of products that are dangerous to life or health. (Product recalls are based on this law.)

2. *The right to choose*—Protection against unfair business practices that result in unreasonably high prices for goods and services.

3. *The right to be informed*—Protection against fraudulent and misleading advertising.

4. *The right to be heard*—Assurance of consumer representation in the formation of government policy and enforcement of consumer protection laws.

Since 1962, many consumer protection laws related to these four major areas have been passed. Some laws set rules related to telephone marketing, mail advertising, banking, schools and colleges, health products, and food marketing.

A Student Activity

1. What were the four areas covered by the 1962 Consumer Bill of Rights? _____
   _____
   _____

2. Which area of the 1962 Consumer Bill of Rights did Kim advise Mark to use? _____
   _____

3. Give examples of violations of each of the four areas covered by the 1962 Consumer Bill of Rights. _____
   _____
   _____
   _____
   _____
   _____

How to Use Consumer
Print and Online Publications

You can stay informed about consumer rights and responsibilities by reading consumer magazines and visiting consumer-oriented sites on the Internet. Numerous magazines and Web sites can help you make wiser decisions as a consumer. Two such magazines have been around for a long time: *Consumer Reports* and *Consumers' Research.* Both magazines are published by nonprofit organizations and have Internet sites.

Consumer magazines and Web sites save shopping time. You may remember that Mark and Roberto gathered a great deal of information about cars from *Consumer Reports* and www.consumerreports.org before they went shopping.

Let's say you're looking for a desktop computer. Numerous retail businesses, from computer stores to discount stores, sell computers. You can comparison shop by visiting each store in your community to look at computers. This method of shopping is loaded with consumer problems. Traveling from store to store can be very time consuming. Also, the stores may not offer all the brands or models. A salesperson may try to sell you a model the store offers, but not necessarily the model that best meets your needs for the lowest price. The salesperson may know very little about the actual performance of a particular computer model. Before going into the store, you need to know the features you want and the quality of different brands and models.

Consumers Union, which publishes *Consumer Reports,* has its own laboratories and testing facilities in which it tests and rates products on various aspects of quality. Consumers Union does not sell advertising space in its magazine or allow companies to use its ratings for the purpose of advertising. As a result, it can rate products objectively, free of pressure from advertisers to give their products high ratings. This objectivity makes *Consumer Reports* a reliable and respected source of consumer information.

Consumer Reports magazine is published monthly, January through December of each year. The issues are numbered 1-12. Consumers Union binds these 12 issues into one volume at the end of each year and sells these bound volumes to libraries and consumers. Each volume includes an index of articles for the past 12 issues. Every December, Consumers Union also publishes a special book called *The Consumer Reports Buying Guide Issue.* The *Buying Guide* is dated for the following year. For example, the December 2002 issue is dated *Buying Guide Issue, 2003.*

The *Buying Guide* is different in appearance from the other issues of *Consumer Reports.* It looks like a thick paperback book, rather than a magazine. The *Buying Guide* includes condensed versions of articles in the previous 12 issues of *Consumer Reports* and updated information that may not have been included in previous issues of the magazine. It also includes other items of interest, such as a list of addresses to which you can send complaints about products and an index of the contents.

Some consumers prefer the *Buying Guide* for quick information on products rated over the past year. If they want more detailed information, they can go to that particular issue of *Consumer Reports.*

The Consumers Union also offers its product reports online at www.consumer reports.org. Some of the information on the site is free, but most requires the purchase of a subscription. However, just as your community library has a subscription to the paper magazine, it may also subscribe to the Web site. You can search the site by product category or keyword to find articles on products of interest to you.

Magazines and Web sites like *Consumer Reports* are particularly helpful for complex products with many features to understand, such as a refrigerator. The articles and rating charts will help you learn about the features that make one model or brand different from another. You will also learn about which brands or models perform better than others in different quality categories. With this knowledge, you can narrow your choices to just a few that best meet your needs before you leave home to shop. Figure 11-1 is a *Consumer Reports* rating chart on refrigerator models and brands.

B Student Activity

1. What issue of *Consumer Reports* contains summaries of articles appearing in the past 12 issues? _____

2. How can you find an article about a particular product in a past issue of *Consumer Reports?* _____

   _____

3. Study the ratings in Figure 11-1, and answer the following questions:

   a. Are the models listed in alphabetical order or according to the overall quality rating?_____

   b. What does ○ symbolize?_____

   c. What does ◔ symbolize?_____

4. Choose a product rated in one of this year's issues of *Consumer Reports*. Write a report on your findings.

5. If you have Internet access, go to the *Consumer Reports* Web site at www.consumerreports.org. Read one of the free articles about cars. Write a brief list of the key points in the article.

Refrigerators

Ratings

Overall Ratings Within types, in performance order

Legend: Excellent ● Very good ◖ Good ◐ Fair ◗ Poor ○

Brand & Model (similar models in small type)	Price	Overall Score (0 P F G VG E 100)	Energy Cost/yr.	Energy Efficiency	Temp Tests	Noise	Ease of Use	Comments
TOP FREEZER MODELS (18-22 CU. FT.) The best-selling type, they're also the least expensive to run.								
Maytag MTB1956GE[W]	$825		$36	◐	◐	○	◐	Convenient features; crank-adjustable shelf. 67x30x29½ in. 18.5 cu. ft. (14.4 usable).
Kenmore (Sears) 7118[2] 7119[ ]	750		43	◐	◐	◐	○	66x32½x29½ in. 20.8 cu. ft. (16.9 usable).
Maytag MTB2156GE[W]	850		39	◐	◐	◐	◐	Convenient features; crank-adjustable shelf. 67x33x29 in. 20.7 cu. ft. (15.1 usable).
Kenmore (Sears) Elite 7120[2]	1,000		38	◐	◐	◐	○	Curved front; water dispenser with filter; speed icemaker. 66x33½x31½ in. 21.6 cu. ft. (15.8 usable).
Amana ART2107B[W]	800		38	◐	◐	○	○	69x30x32½ in. 20.6 cu. ft. (16.0 usable).
GE GTS18KCM[WW] GTS18KBM[ ], GTH18KBM[ ]	600		40	◐	◐	○	◐	66½x30x30½ in. 17.9 cu. ft. (14.0 usable).
Kenmore (Sears) 7198[2]	750		35	◐	◐	◐	○	Speed icemaker. 66x30x31 in. 18.8 cu. ft. (14.1 usable).
Frigidaire Gallery GLHT216TA[W] PLHT217TAC[ ]	680		38	◐	◐	○	○	Among the more repair-prone brands of top-freezers with icemakers. 69x30x32½ in. 20.6 cu. ft. (16.4 usable).
Kenmore (Sears) 7285[2] 7286[ ]	680		40	◐	◐	◐	○	66x30x30 in. 18.1 cu. ft. (14.1 usable).
Whirlpool Gold GR9SHKXK[Q]	940		37	●	◐	○	○	Curved front. 66x30x32 in. 18.8 cu. ft. (14.1 usable).
Frigidaire Gallery GLHT186TA[W] GLHT186TAC[ ]	680		40	◐	◐	○	○	Among the more repair-prone brands of top-freezers with icemakers. 66½x30x31 in. 18.3 cu. ft. (14.3 usable).
GE GTS22KCM[WW] GTS22KBM[ ]	650		44	◐	◐	○	◐	67½x33x31½ in. 21.7 cu. ft. (16.5 usable).
Whirlpool ET1FTTXK[Q]	800		43	◐	◐	○	○	Water dispenser with filter. 66x32½x30½ in. 20.8 cu. ft. (16.5 usable).
Whirlpool Gold GR2SHTXK[Q] GR2SHKXK[ ]	1,050		40	◐	◐	○	○	Curved front. Water dispenser with filter 66½x33x31½ in. 21.6 cu. ft. (15.9 usable).
Frigidaire FRT18P5A[W] FRT18HP5A[ ]	510		40	◐	◐	◐	○	No spill-guard shelves. Among the more repair-prone brands of top-freezers with icemakers. 66½x30x30 in. 18.4 cu. ft. (14.5 usable).
BOTTOM-FREEZER MODELS (18-22 CU. FT.) A small but growing part of the market, they're pricier than top-freezers.								
GE GBS22LB[WW]	1,050		48	◐	●	○	◐	68½x33x33 in. 21.7 cu. ft. (15.8 usable).
Amana ARB2117A[W]	1,300		45	◐	●	○	◐	69x33x31½ in. 20.5 cu. ft. (14.6 usable).
Amana BB20V1[W] BB20VIPS[ ]	1,700		47	◐	●	○	◐	Cabinet depth (requires door panels and 36-in.-wide opening). 69½x36½x27½ in. 19.7 cu. ft. (14.7 usable).
Amana Distinctions DRB1801A[W]	695		44	◐	◐	◐	○	No half-shelves. 67x30x31 in. 18.1 cu. ft. (13.3 usable).
Amana ARB2107A[W] BX21V[ ], BX21V2[ ]	1,040		45	◐	◐	○	◐	69x33x32 in. 20.5 cu. ft. (14.9 usable).
SIDE-BY-SIDE MODELS (20-28 CU. FT.) More expensive to buy and run, but they have a lot of features.								
Kenmore (Sears) 5255[2] 5256[ ]	1,400		52	◐	◐	●	◐	Speed icemaker. 69½x36x30 in. 25.5 cu. ft. (16.0 usable).
Kenmore (Sears) Elite 5260[2]	1,700		52	◐	◐	◐	◐	Curved front. Speed icemaker; digital controls, 1 half-shelf. 70x36x33 in. 25.6 cu. ft. (15.1 usable).
Amana ARSE66MB[B]	1,570		54	◐	◐	○	◐	1 half-shelf, beverage chiller. Among the more repair-prone side-by-side brands. 70x36x32 in. 25.6 cu. ft. (16.3 usable).

Figure 11-1

Rating Chart for Refrigerators

Figure 11-1
(continued)

Rating Chart for
Refrigerators

BRAND & MODEL SIMILAR MODELS IN SMALL TYPE	PRICE	OVERALL SCORE P F G VG E	ENERGY COST/YR.	ENERGY EFFICIENCY	TEMP TESTS	NOISE	EASE OF USE	COMMENTS
Frigidaire Gallery GLHS267ZA[W] PLHS267ZA[ ]	$1,275		$54	◐	◐	○	◐	Speed icemaker. Among the more repair-prone side-by-side brands. 69¹/₂x36x33¹/₂ in. 25.9 cu. ft. (17.5 usable).
GE Profile Arctica PSS29NGM[WW]	2,220		63	○	◐	◐	◐	Curved front with pebbled finish. Speed icemaker, digital controls, thaw-chill bin. 70x36x33¹/₂ in. 28.6 cu. ft. (17.3 usable).
Kenmore (Sears) 5275[2] 5276[ ]	1,800		55	◐	◐	◐	◐	Speed icemaker, 1 half-shelf. 70x36x32¹/₂ in. 27 cu. ft. (17.0 usable).
Kenmore (Sears) 5225[2] 5226[ ]	1,350		50	◐	◐	◐	◐	Speed icemaker. 66¹/₂x33x30¹/₂ in. 21.9 cu. ft. (14.2 usable).
Whirlpool gold GC5THGXK[Q] 🅓 GC5THGXL[ ]	2,300		53	◐	◐	◐	◐	Cabinet depth (requires door panels and 36-in.-wide opening). 72x35¹/₂x27¹/₂ in. 24.5 cu. ft. (14.7 usable).
KitchenAid Superba KSRG27FK[WH] KSRD27FK[ ]	1,700		55	◐	○	◐	◐	70x36x32 in. 26.8 cu. ft. (16.8 usable).
Maytag MSD2456GE[W]	1,210		52	◐	◐	○	◐	Crank-adjustable shelf. The most repair-prone side-by-side brand. 69x33x32 in. 23.6 cu. ft. (13.3 usable).
GE Profile Arctica PS123NGM[WW]	2,300		57	○	◐	○	◐	Cabinet depth (requires door panels and 36-in.-wide opening). Speed icemaker, digital controls, 1 half-shelf. 70¹/₂x36x27¹/₂ in. 22.6 cu. ft. (13.1 usable).
GE GSS25JFM[WW] A CR Best Buy GSS25JEM[ ]	890		60	◐	◐	◐	◐	70x36x31 in. 24.9 cu. ft. (16.9 usable).
Frigidaire Gallery GLRS237ZA[W] GLHS237ZA[ ]	1,100		57	○	○	◐	○	Speed icemaker. Among the more repair-prone side-by-side brands. 69¹/₂x33x33 in. 22.6 cu. ft. (14.6 usable).
Kenmore (Sears) 5106[2] 5104[ ]	1,200		56	○	◐	○	◐	66¹/₂x33¹/₂x29 in. 20 cu. ft. (13.2 usable).
Whirlpool ED2FHGXK[Q]	1,020		54	○	◐	○	◐	66¹/₂x33x31 in. 22 cu. ft. (13.3 usable).
Maytag Plus MZD2766GE[W]	1,500		55	◐	⊖	○	◐	Crank-adjustable shelf. The most repair-prone side-by-side brand. 70¹/₂x36x32 in. 26.8 cu. ft. (17.7 usable).
GE GSS20IEM[WW]	800		54	○	○	○	◐	No spill-guard shelves or water filter 67¹/₂x32x31¹/₂ in. 19.9 cu. ft. (13.3 usable).

BUILT-IN BOTTOM-FREEZER MODELS (20-21 CU. FT.) *The most expensive models, these fit flush with cabinets.*

BRAND & MODEL	PRICE	OVERALL SCORE	ENERGY COST/YR.	ENERGY EFFICIENCY	TEMP TESTS	NOISE	EASE OF USE	COMMENTS
Sub-Zero 650/F	4,600		42	◉	◉	○	○	2-yr. full warranty. Requires door panels and 36-in.-wide opening. Water filter. But no half-shelves. Among the more repair-prone brands. 84x36¹/₂x25¹/₂ in. 20.6 cu. ft. (15.4 usable)
GE Monogram ZIC360NM ZICS360NM[ ]	3,900		47	◐	◉	◐	○	2-yr. full warranty. Requires door panels and 36-in.-wide opening. 84x36¹/₂x25¹/₂ in. 20.6 cu. ft. (13.6 usable). Water filter.
KitchenAid KBRS36FKX[ ]	4,100		43	◉	◉	○	○	2-yr. full warranty. Requires door panels and 36-in.-wide opening. Water filter. 83¹/₂x36x25¹/₂ in. 20.9 cu. ft. (14.4 usable).
Viking DDBB363R[SS] DFBB363[ ], VCBB363[ ], DTBB363[ ]	4,800		47	◐	◉	○	○	2-yr. full warranty. Requires 36-in.-wide opening. Stainless steel. 83¹/₂x36x24¹/₂ in. 20.3 cu. ft. (15.0 usable).

How to Handle Complaints as a Consumer

A number of agencies provide services to consumers. Several agencies send out free pamphlets upon request, and most have Web sites as well. The computerized catalog in the library has information on numerous agencies and organizations. You can get consumer literature from the Consumer Federation of America (www.consumerfed.org), Department of Commerce (www.commerce.gov), National Consumers League (www.nclnet.org), Environmental Protection Agency (www.epa.gov), Federal Trade Commission (www.ftc.gov/ftc/consumer.htm), Food and Drug Administration (www.fda.gov), and your state's Office of Consumer Affairs, to name a few.

You can learn a lot by visiting your public or school library and checking out the sources for filing consumer complaints. There are federal, state, and local agencies as well as private organizations to which you can make complaints. Some non-government Web sites that handle complaints are www.badbusinessbureau.com, www.thecomplaintstation.com, www.egripes.com, and www.planetfeedback.com.

How and Where to Complain

Almost everyone has purchased a bad product at some time in their lives. If you buy a defective product from someone who refuses to repair or replace the product, it can be a frustrating experience. To complain about such treatment, you need to know how and where to complain successfully. Keep the following tips in mind if you want to complain about a product or service:

1. State your complaint to the local dealer where you bought the product. If the salesperson does not have the authority to handle your complaint, ask to speak to the manager. There is no need to get confrontational. Have with you the proper documentation, such as your receipt and warranty, if there is one. It's a good idea to keep all receipts of purchased products in your personal file for about six months to a year, depending on the kind of product and the warranty.

2. If the problem is not resolved to your satisfaction, contact the manufacturer in a letter. Again, keep the tone positve and friendly. State the facts. Don't exaggerate or be dishonest. Explain to the manufacturer what steps you have taken so far. Then simply state what you want: replacement, refund, or repair. Never use threats or sarcasm in a letter of complaint. You can find the addresses of manufacturers in the *Thomas Register of American Manufacturers* in most public libraries. You can also contact most manufacturers through their Web sites.

3. If you still get unsatisfactory results, contact a consumer interest group for aid. Figure 11-2 lists some major consumer organizations that offer services to consumers with complaints.

Letter of Complaint

Part of the process of successfully complaining is knowing how to write an effective letter of complaint. The letter should clearly state the action you want the receiver to take in order to resolve the problem. You should include all the essential information for the problem to be resolved:

1. Your name, address, and telephone number

2. Name and model number of the product

3. Place and date you purchased it

4. Brief but specific description of the nature of the problem

5. Description of your previous efforts to resolve the problem

Be sure to include a copy of your receipt and warranty coverage. The letter should be simple and direct. Take a look at Mark's letter of complaint in Figure 11-3 on page 212.

Figure 11-2

Where to Complain

Where to Complain	What to Complain About
City and county consumer protection agencies	Scams, frauds, false advertising, complaints about merchandise
Local media programs—action line	Unsatisfactory products/services
Local Food and Drug Administration office	Adulterated food, drugs, cosmetics and mislabeling of products
Regional office of Federal Trade Commission	Deceptive advertising, packaging, and selling
Local Better Business Bureau	Fraudulent business practices and advertising
Council of Better Business Bureaus 4200 Wilson Blvd., Ste. 800 Arlington, VA 22203	Same as above
State consumer office	Any type of consumer problem
State Office of Attorney General	Sales or business fraud
Office of Public Affairs and Consumer Services National Highway Traffic Safety Administration Dept. of Transportation 400 Seventh Street, S.W. Washington, DC 20590	Safety problems with cars and car accessories
Consumer Advocate U.S. Postal Service Rm. 5821, L'Enfant Plaza West S.W. Washington, DC 20260-2200	Postal service complaints, such as lost or damaged mail or packages
Consumer Product Safety Commission 5401 Westbard Ave Bethesda, MD 20207 Washington, DC 20207	Defective or unsafe products
Office of Consumer Affairs Dept. of Transportation 400 Seventh Street, S.W. 1825 Connecticut Avenue, N.W. Washington, DC 20500	Complaints related to air travel and shipments
U.S. Office of Consumer Affairs Dept. of Health and Human Services 300 Independence Ave., S W. Washington, DC 20201	Any type of consumer problem
Major Appliance Consumer Action Panel 20 N. Wacker Drive Chicago, IL 60606	Major appliance repair problems if dealer and manufacturer have not responded

Figure 11-3

Mark's Letter of Complaint

April 1, 20--

Ms. Charlene Williams
Manager, Customer Relations
LM Auto Parts
405 Industrial Row
Greenville, SC 29607-3971

Dear Ms. Williams,

On March 1, 20--, I purchased windshield wipers, model number AC251, and had them installed on my 1999 Monte Carlo at Enrique's Auto Shop, 1111 Misery Lane, Atlanta, GA 30333. The wipers have a 90-day warranty. It didn't rain for two weeks after I bought the wipers, so I didn't know they were defective. When it did rain, the wipers did not operate properly. They left smears that seriously impaired my vision of the road. They also banged against the edges of the windshield, making a lot of noise with each cycle. At times, they would stop altogether.

I went back to the dealer who sold and installed the wipers. He said I should have reported the defect earlier. When I said it had not rained and I had a 90-day warranty, he agreed to replace or repair them. When the dealer returned the car, I assumed the wipers were fixed. Now, a week and a half later, it rained again. The wipers performed the same way they did when they were first installed. I went back to the dealer. He said he had done all he could do and he could not help me any further. He said it was an old car and maybe that was the problem.

Old car or not, the wipers were new and under warranty as installed. Enclosed are copies of my receipt and warranty. I would like the defective wipers replaced with new ones. Please ship the new wipers to me. I will have them installed elsewhere. Thank you.

Sincerely,

Mark L. Smith

Mark L. Smith
333 College Drive, Apt. 3
Atlanta, GA 30322-3315
(470) 555-2370

Student Activity

1. Study the chart in Figure 11-2 and answer the following questions:

   a. To which agency might you report a defective refrigerator if you received no resolution from the dealer or manufacturer? _____

Continued

b. Where would you report a company that sold you a $300 camping trip to the Louisiana swamps? The trip does not exist._____

c. Where would you report a lost package mailed to a friend in Taiwan? _____

2. List five consumer publications in your school or public library.

_____

_____

_____

_____

3. Using your local telephone directory or one from a larger city nearby, list the names, addresses, and telephone numbers of consumer agencies in your area.

Agency	Address	Telephone #

4. Go to one of the Web sites mentioned in this section, or to another consumer-oriented site you find online. Write a one-page description of the consumer resources available at that site.

5. Look at Mark's letter of complaint in Figure 11-3 and answer the following questions:

a. Is Mark writing a consumer agency, the dealer, or manufacturer?_____

b. Is this the logical step to take at this point? _____

Give a reason for your answer._____

_____

c. What information does Mark provide in his letter? _____

_____

_____

_____

Is it sufficient for a successful resolution? _____

_____

6. Either use a real situation you have experienced in the past or make up one in which you are dissatisfied with a product or service. Write a letter of complaint to the proper source. File the letter in the Outgoing File.

Better Business Bureau

A business-sponsored agency that handles a lot of consumer complaints is the **Better Business Bureau (BBB)** (www.bbb.org). Many cities have Better Business Bureaus, which are a part of the national organization called the **Council of Better Business Bureaus**. The Better Business Bureau serves consumers by doing the following:

1. Informing them about complaints filed against a business

2. Assisting them in resolving disputes if they did not receive satisfaction from the business or manufacturer

3. Providing consumer information through BBB print and online publications

Kim had occasion to call the BBB at one point. She had signed up and paid a $100 deposit on a financial management course that was advertised in the paper. She sent in her deposit but never received further details about the course. The hotel where the course was supposed to have taken place knew nothing of the business or the course. Kim filed a complaint with the BBB.

The BBB had several complaints on file about this same company. According to the BBB, the company was a legitimate one. However, the company had a record of not returning deposits when they did not get enough participants in a course. Kim asked what she should do. The Bureau told her their role was not to take legal action with a company, but they would assist her in handling her complaint. When Kim asked for her refund with the backing of the BBB, she received it.

D Student Activity

1. Name three functions of the Better Business Bureau.

   _____

   _____

   _____

2. What might Kim have done before paying for the course on financial management? _____

   _____

   _____

3. How did the BBB help her? _____

   _____

   _____

4. Does the BBB take legal action against a business? _____

   _____

   _____

Small Claims Court

When two parties have failed to settle their dispute by other means, the BBB can arrange for a third party to help settle the dispute. A voluntary settlement through the BBB is a welcome alternative to taking the dispute to court.

However, sometimes you may have to take legal action against someone who has treated you unfairly. One means of taking legal action is through small claims court. **Small claims court** handles disputes involving small amounts of money. On average, you can sue for $2,000 to $5,000 in small claims court. Individual states determine the maximum amount handled by small claims court. The use of the small claims court has several advantages:

1. You do not need a lawyer.

2. Filing fees are minimal.

3. Cases are settled quickly. However, if you win the case, you have to collect the money awarded.

If you decide to use small claims court, you need to know the process. Before filing a case, send a letter by certified mail to the party being sued. The letter should cover the following:

1. How you have been harmed

2. Why the person or business is responsible

3. How much money you seek

Next, call the clerk of court in the county in which you will file your case or, better, go to the courthouse and ask what procedures you should follow. Have the following information with you.

1. Name and address of the person or company you want to sue

2. Product name, model number, year of purchase, and warranty coverage if you are complaining about a product

3. Proof of purchase (sales or charge slip, bill or canceled check)

4. History of your complaint (previous action taken, with names, dates, written correspondence, brief description of situation, and results of the complaint)

A Web site that offers a lot of assistance about procedures when going to small claims court is www.nolo.com. Here you will find state limitations on how much you can sue for in your particular state, as well as information on how to collect. *Everybody's Guide to Small Claims Court* (by Nolo Press) is a helpful book on the subject.

Going to small claims court should be your last resort, because going to any kind of court is never easy. You have to take off from work, wait for your turn, and sometimes end up with poor results. However, if you have determined that you have been unjustly treated, don't be intimidated by these difficulties. You should consider small claims court in the following circumstances:

1. The claim can be awarded in money. You cannot go to small claims court to recover stolen property or to require a specific act, such as an apology.

2. Some particular person is responsible for causing the complaint.

3. You have exhausted all other means of finding a resolution, such as direct complaints to the person or company involved, the BBB, or a consumer protection agency.

E Student Activity

You have learned about various consumer agencies, the BBB, and small claims court. If either of the following incidents happened to you, what would you do?

1. After informing the landlord several times that your front door did not close properly, let alone lock, the problem was not fixed. One day you came home to discover that the front door was wide open and you had been burglarized. When you told the landlord, he apologized but didn't pay for the cost of the stolen goods. What can you do? _____

_____

_____

_____

_____

_____

2. You entered a contest advertised in a flyer received in the mail. All it said to do was name five states east of the Mississippi River and pay a $10 entrance fee. Whoever answered correctly got a trip to the Bahamas. You named the correct five states but never heard from the company again. What can you do?

_____

_____

_____

_____

_____

How to Interpret Legal Agreements as a Consumer

Many consumer problems result from lack of communication or from not understanding the terms of the agreement. Understanding the legal agreement before you purchase can prevent problems later.

Contracts

Legal agreements are usually in the form of a contract. A **contract** is an agreement that establishes a legal obligation between two or more people. All agreements are not contracts. If Kim agrees to marry Mark this summer and changes her mind on May 31, she has not violated a contract. For a contract to be legal, five basic elements are involved:

1. There must be an offer and an acceptance of the offer.

2. The people involved must be **competent**—that is, capable of understanding the terms of the contract.

3. The subject of the agreement must be legal—that is, enforceable in a court of law.

4. There must be **consideration,** or payment for a product or a service performed.

5. The agreement must be in a legally acceptable form.

Contracts can be either oral or written. Usually an oral agreement is sufficient for transactions involving a small amount of money. Even then, the consumer should get a receipt for the transaction. In any case, oral contracts are risky. There have to be witnesses to the agreement for it to hold up in court. Even with witnesses, the contract may not be considered valid. A written contract can range from a short and simple agreement to a lengthy document with clauses, exceptions, and restrictions. A written contract should include the following:

1. The date and location of the agreement

2. The identification of the parties making the agreement

3. A statement of terms agreed upon

4. The signatures of both parties and their legal representatives

5. The signature of witnesses

Figure 11-4 is an example of a contract (written agreement) between Mark's parents and Plumbers Friends, Inc., for plumbing services.

Figure 11-4

Example of a Written Contract

This agreement is made on February 15, 20--, between Plumbers Friends, Inc., 2400 Pine Drive, Atlanta, GA 30301, the party of the first part, and Helen and Michael Smith, 1040 Peachtree Drive, Atlanta, GA 30319, the party of the second part.

The party of the first part agrees to install new plumbing in the home of the party of the second part at 1040 Peachtree Drive, Atlanta GA, by March 15, 20--, in accordance with the specifications attached hereto. In consideration of which the party of the second part agrees to pay the party of the first part $2,500 upon satisfactory completion of the job.

Doris Jones
_____
Doris Jones
Owner, Plumbers Friends, Inc.

Feb. 15, 20--
_____
Date

Helen Smith
_____
Helen Smith

Feb. 15, 20--
_____
Date

Michael Smith
_____
Michael Smith

Feb. 15, 20--
_____
Date

Bill of Sale

A **bill of sale** is a legal document that transfers title (ownership) of goods. It includes the name of the item purchased and the signatures of the seller and buyer. A bill of sale is usually written at the time ownership is transferred.

Possession of goods does not imply ownership. Stolen goods cannot be transferred. Always make sure the person has proof of ownership, such as a bill of sale, before purchasing an item from anyone. The bill of sale allows a person to legally transfer ownership of property. If stolen goods are purchased in good faith, they still must be returned to the rightful owner.

F Student Activity

Are the following contracts legal? If not, which element of a legal contract is missing?

1. Jose Mendez answered the door to find a salesperson selling a Home Study package on tax preparation skills. Jose cannot read English and can barely speak it, but he was interested in learning how to prepare his taxes. He signed the contract based on what the salesperson told him. Later, when he opened the package, the instructions were all in English. Was the contract legal? Explain. _____

_____

_____

_____

_____

2. Melissa Scott bought a lot of second-hand goods from a local shop called Used Furniture. She was always amazed at the good deals she got there. Last week, the owner of Used Furniture was arrested for selling stolen goods. The police found copies of several bills of sale to Melissa. They picked up her furniture. Was this police action legal? Explain. _____

_____

_____

_____

_____

3. You insist that Auto Soup-Up promised to install stereo speakers in the back doors of your car as well as in the front. The manager said he promised no such thing. You have no written contract. Is the manager legally bound to install the speakers in the back doors? Explain. _____

_____

_____

_____

_____

_____

Warranties

Before making a purchase, ask about the **warranty**. As you learned in Chapter 10, a warranty is a promise by a manufacturer or dealer that the product will perform up to expected quality standards over a given period of time. Warranties may be either express or implied. **Express warranties** are written guarantees of quality and performance that include instructions about replacement or repair. If the warranty is violated, consumers have legal grounds to have their rights fulfilled. An example of an express warranty is shown in Figure 11-5.

If there is no written warranty, some states have laws that require unwritten or implied warranties on all products sold to the public. An **implied warranty** guarantees the following:

1. *A product will do what it is supposed to do.* A lamp should turn on and off at the lamp switch.

2. *A product will perform as specified.* A car battery with a lifetime of three years should perform for three years.

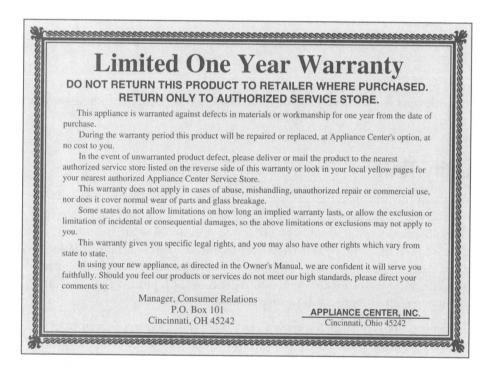

Figure 11-5

Express Warranty

Warranties should be examined carefully before you buy the product. Do not rely on newspaper ads. You might check the warranty for the answers to the following questions before purchasing an item:

1. What does the warranty cover? Parts and labor? Certain parts and not others? For how long?

2. Are there conditions under which the warranty is void or useless?

3. Do you have to mail in a card to confirm the date of purchase in order to be eligible for the warranty?

4. Whom do you contact if the product is defective?

According to the Magnuson-Moss Warranty Act of 1975, a warranty must be designated either *full* or *limited* if the product costs $10 or more. A full warranty must provide the following:

1. Repair within a reasonable time and without charge

2. Coverage for the initial purchaser *and* to anyone the original purchaser sells it to while the product is still under warranty

3. No unreasonable conditions for warranty service, such as shipping to the factory or sending the warranty card to the company in advance

4. Replacement of the defective product or a full refund if the product is still defective after a reasonable number of attempts to fix it

A limited warranty includes anything less than a full warranty, such as:

1. Coverage for parts but not labor

2. Partial refund instead of full refund on a defective product

3. Coverage for only the initial owner

4. Charges for shipping and handling a product sent to the manufacturer for repair

While a product is under warranty, you should file your receipt of purchase along with your warranty in a Personal file labeled *Warranties*. Both items will be needed if you want warranty services.

Identity Theft

Throughout the previous chapters, you have learned about various types of scams and fraud. The fastest growing consumer crime is **identity theft**. A criminal literally takes on your identity by obtaining your social security number, your credit card identification, your driver's license, and/or your checking account number. After all your hard work building a good reputation as a creditworthy person, the criminal uses your identity and good credit reputation to take out loans, open credit accounts, and make purchases.

In November, 2001, the U.S. Supreme Court ruled that victims of identity theft have no rights if two years have passed from the date of the original theft without a report. The trouble is you may not know until it's too late or you may neglect to take care of the matter. It is up to you to take charge of protecting your good reputation. If your privacy has been violated, you absolutely need to remedy the situation. This may take years, but be persistent. Here are a few important tips that will help:

• Do not put your social security number on your driver's license.

• Don't carry your checkbook. In general, pay by credit card or cash. Take the checkbook only when needed for a purchase.

• Pick up your newly ordered checkbooks at the bank. Do not have them mailed.

- Keep your checkbook and social security card in separate and secure places in your home.
- When you use a credit card, don't leave the receipt behind, especially at the gas pump.
- Don't order anything, by phone or over the Internet with a debit card, which immediately draws from your account. Use a credit card.
- Once a year, get a copy of your credit report from all three major credit agencies: Equifax, Experian, and TransUnion. It is important to get a report from all three because one credit agency may have information that another does not. Look for errors in those reports.
- Stop delivery of pre-approved credit cards to your mailbox by calling 1-888-50PT-OUT (1-888-567-8688).
- Buy a shredder and shred all receipts and identification documents.

If you have become a victim of identity theft, get busy cleaning up your reputation by doing the following:

- File a police report. You are required to do so by the Identity Fraud and Assumption Deterrence Act of 1998.
- Go to www.privacyrights.org to find out about steps to take to clear your name.
- Document all your efforts to clear your reputation.

It's a nightmare, but you can do it. You've got to clear your identity because if you don't, you will not be able to buy a car, buy a home, use your credit card, or write a check.

G Student Activity

1. Examine the copy of the warranty in Figure 11-5 and answer the following questions:

   a. When does the warranty expire? _____

   b. If the product is defective, who will replace or repair it?

   _____

   c. Will the company replace or repair the product in all circumstances? Explain. _____

   _____

   _____

   Continued

Student Activity Continued

    d. If the product is defective, how will you get it repaired or replaced?_____

2. What is identity theft?_____

_____

3. Record the following transactions for Mark:

    a. On February 28, Roberto told Mark that all the shared bills had arrived and were due. Roberto reminded Mark that the four tenants of the apartment shared monthly apartment bills equally. Roberto had accepted responsibility for paying the bills each month. When all the bills arrived, he divided the amounts by four and collected each tenant's share. This month, Mark's share was $155.00. Mark wrote Check 124 to Roberto Gonzalez for $155.00 for utilities. Record the transaction and write and file the check. Roberto told Mark that the $155.00 for utilities broke down by category as follows: electricity, $60.00; heating, $55.00; water and sewerage, $15.00; plus Mark's share of the TV cable, $15.00, and the phone, $10.00. Record the amounts in the proper categories in Mark's *Financial Management Records Booklet*.

    b. That same day, February 28, Mark received and deposited his paycheck. Earlier in the week, Mark had asked Kim out for Saturday night so they could have a chance to talk about something other than money. He would need extra cash for the evening. Therefore, he deposited $225.01 in his checking account and kept $100.00 in cash. Record the deposit in the check register. Record Mark's $325.01 income and the following cash expenditures for the week in the *Financial Management Records Booklet*. On February 28, Mark recorded the following cash amounts: food, $15.00; transportation, $10.00; personal, $10.00; entertainment, $25.00.

    c. On February 28, Mark received his bank statement dated February 24. Remove the bank statement (Form 11-1) and canceled checks (Form 11-2) from the Source Documents section of this *Instructions and Source Documents Booklet*. Verify Mark's bank statement against the check register and complete the reconciliation form on the back of the bank statement. Record the $4.00 bank service charge in Mark's check register and *Financial Management Records Booklet* for February 24, the date of the charge on the statement. (If you need to review the procedures for reconciling a bank

Continued

Student Activity

statement, refer to Chapter 2.) File the canceled checks in the *Checking Account—Canceled Checks* file.

4. Total Mark's February expenditures in his *Financial Management Records Booklet*. Then record his monthly budget figures for each category from Figure 3-8, page 44. Calculate the amounts by which Mark was over or under budget for each category. Take a look at the items in which Mark was over budget for February, and answer the following questions.

a. In what categories was Mark over budget (+)? _____

_____

b. Below is a list of some of Mark's budget categories. For each category, explain what you think Mark should do, if anything, to either adjust his budget or change his spending habits to stay within his budget. For example, in February Mark spent less on clothing than he had budgeted. Should he spend more on clothes next month, or move some of that budgeted amount to another category where he needs it more?

Total Expenditures: _____

_____

Food: _____

_____

Clothing: _____

_____

Rent or Mortgage: _____

_____

Electricity/Heating/Water and Sewerage: _____

_____

Personal/Household: _____

_____

Transit/Auto Expense: _____

_____

Home Furnishings: _____

_____

Entertainment: _____

_____

Medical: _____

_____

Mark will continue to monitor his expenditures and budget carefully for the remainder of the year. He may find it necessary to make some additional adjustments later. Although his finances will be tight for awhile, Mark feels confident that he can live within his budget, and he knows so much more about what living on a budget means.

On Your Own *For Life*

You have now completed *On Your Own: A Personal Budgeting Simulation*. As you helped Mark become organized and financially independent, you were learning skills to use in your own life.

1. You established a basic filing system for organizing your financial and personal records.

2. You established your list of goals to use in preparing your personal budget.

3. You learned about banking, credit, careers, housing, and insurance.

4. You learned how to be a responsible consumer.

You now possess skills that will help you succeed when you are *on your own for life*. Use them wisely.

Check Up

Having completed the Student Activities in this chapter, you should have mastered the skills listed below. Put a checkmark next to the skills you have mastered. If you aren't sure of a skill, review that section of the chapter.

☐ How to determine your rights as a consumer

☐ How to use consumer print and online publications

☐ How to handle complaints as a consumer

☐ How to interpret legal agreements as a consumer

On Your Own

Source Documents Section

FOLDER LABELS

Green (Financial) Labels

Banking

Bills to Be Paid

Budget

Checking Account

Checking Account—
ATM Receipts

Checking Account—
Bank Statements

Checking Account—
Canceled Check Records

Credit

Credit—
Bank Card

Income Records

Savings Account

Tax Records

Red (Personal) Labels

Automobile

Housing

Insurance

Job Search

Resume

Yellow (Self Improvement) Labels

Careers

Goals and Objectives

Blue (Leisure) Label

Leisure

FILE INDEX

FINANCIAL (green)
  Banking
  Bills to Be Paid
  Budget
  Checking Acount
  Checking Account—ATM Receipts
  Checking Account—Bank Statements
  Checking Account—Canceled Check Records
  Credit
  Credit—Bank Card
  Income Records
  Savings Account
  Tax Records

PERSONAL (red)
  Automobile
  Housing
  Insurance
  Job Search
  Resume

SELF IMPROVEMENT (yellow)
  Careers
  Goals and Objectives

LEISURE (blue)
  Leisure

_____

STATEMENT OF NET WORTH

Assets		**Liabilities**	
Cash in Checking Account	$_____	Loan Balance	$_____
Cash in Savings Account	_____	Current Bills:	
Cash Value of Life Insurance	_____	Apartment Rent	_____
Car (depreciated value)	_____	Credit Card	_____
Furniture (depreciated value)	_____	Edison Electric	_____
Personal Items	_____	City Gas	_____
		City Water/Sewerage	_____
		TV Cable	_____
		Internet	_____
		GA Telephone	_____
		Cell Phone	_____
Total Assets	$_____	Total Liabilities	$_____

Assets - Liabilities = Net Worth $_____

Food

Costs

_____

_____

_____

_____

_____

_____

_____

_____

_____

_____

_____

_____

_____

_____

_____

_____

_____

_____

Total _____

Personal/Household

Costs

_____

_____

_____

_____

_____

_____

_____

_____

_____

_____

_____

_____

_____

_____

_____

_____

_____

_____

Total _____

BUDGET RECORD

Month of _____ 20 _____ Income _____

Budget Categories	Budgeted Spending	Actual Expenditures	Over + or Short −
_____	_____	_____	_____
_____	_____	_____	_____
_____	_____	_____	_____
_____	_____	_____	_____
_____	_____	_____	_____
_____	_____	_____	_____
_____	_____	_____	_____
_____	_____	_____	_____
_____	_____	_____	_____
_____	_____	_____	_____
_____	_____	_____	_____
_____	_____	_____	_____
_____	_____	_____	_____
_____	_____	_____	_____
_____	_____	_____	_____

SAVINGS ACCOUNT DEPOSIT SLIP

Form 4-1

NAME _____

ACCT. NO. _____

Date _____ 20 ____

For Classroom Use Only

ALL ITEMS ARE ACCEPTED SUBJECT TO THIS INSTITUTION'S RULES
AND REGULATIONS PERTAINING TO SAVINGS ACCOUNTS

NATIONAL BANK
Atlanta, GA

	Dollars	Cents
Currency		
Coin		
Checks		
LESS CASH BACK		
Total Deposit		

Form 4-2

SAVINGS ACCOUNT REGISTER

Account No: _____

DATE	WITHDRAWALS	DEPOSITS AND INTEREST	BALANCE

Form 4-3

NATIONAL BANK
Atlanta, GA

CARD NO.
773304452294

DATE   TIME
01/05/--   11:05

TERMINAL   TRANSACTION
0013   0780

CHECKING WITHDRAWAL $350.00
04452294

NEW BALANCE $568.86

THANK YOU

Lacy's Department Store
Atlanta, Georgia

```
SALE  0611   01/13/--   06:08 PM

05016  MENS SHIRT                29.99
               SUBTOTAL          29.99
               6% TAX             1.80
               TOTAL             31.79

VISA        31.79
ACCOUNT NUMBER 00011222  09/--
AUTHORIZATION NUMBER 0335
```

I AGREE TO PAY IN ACCORDANCE WITH THE
TERMS OF THE ACCOUNT INDICATED.

x _Mark L. Smith_

CUSTOMER SIGNATURE

Lacy's Department Store
Atlanta, Georgia

```
SALE  0425   01/13/--   05:20 PM

763  COLOGNE                     15.00
               SUBTOTAL          15.00
               6% TAX              .90
               TOTAL             15.90

VISA        15.90
ACCOUNT NUMBER 00011222  09/--
AUTHORIZATION NUMBER 0312
```

I AGREE TO PAY IN ACCORDANCE WITH THE
TERMS OF THE ACCOUNT INDICATED.

x _Mark L. Smith_

CUSTOMER SIGNATURE

Britches Department Store
Atlanta, Georgia

```
SALE  0035   01/07/--   06:15 PM

0059286  SLACKS                  29.99
0059344  SLACKS                  29.98
               SUBTOTAL          59.97
               6% TAX             3.60
               TOTAL             63.57

VISA        63.57
ACCOUNT NUMBER 00011222  09/--
AUTHORIZATION NUMBER 0274
```

I AGREE TO PAY IN ACCORDANCE WITH THE
TERMS OF THE ACCOUNT INDICATED.

x _Mark L. Smith_

CUSTOMER SIGNATURE

Form 5-4

NATIONAL BANK
Atlanta, GA

| NEW BALANCE ▶ | 111.26 |

| MINIMUM PAYMENT DUE ▶ | 15.00 |

Mark L. Smith
1040 Peachtree Drive
Atlanta, GA 30319-1396

AMOUNT ENCLOSED _____

_ _ _ TO INSURE PROPER CREDIT DETACH AND RETURN THIS TOP PORTION _ _ _ _ _ _ _ _ _ _ _ _ _ _ _ _ _ _

ACCOUNT NUMBER	LINE OF CREDIT	STATEMENT DATE	PAYMENT DUE DATE
00011222	1,000.00	01/20/--	02/20/--

AVERAGE DAILY BALANCE SUBJECT TO FINANCE CHARGE	FINANCE CHARGE	CASH ADVANCES MADE THIS BILLING CYCLE	FINANCE CHARGE
.00	.00	.00	.00
ANNUAL PERCENTAGE RATE	18.00%	CASH ADVANCE AMOUNT ANNUAL PERCENTAGE RATE	.00%

MAKE CHECKS PAYABLE TO NATIONAL BANK

DATE POSTED	REFERENCE NUMBER	DESCRIPTION OF TRANSACTION	AMOUNT
01/07	02043	Britches Department Store	63.57
01/13	04578	Lacy's Department Store	15.90
01/13	04578	Lacy's Department Store	31.79

PREVIOUS BALANCE		PAYMENTS AND CREDITS		TOTAL FINANCE CHARGES		NEW TRANSACTIONS		NEW BALANCE
.00	−	.00	+	.00	+	111.26	=	111.26
.00	−	.00	+		+	.00	=	.00

LOAN APPLICATION

Form 5-5

PERSONAL

NAME-LAST, FIRST, MIDDLE		DATE OF BIRTH	SOCIAL SECURITY NO.	DEPENDENTS

MAIL ADDRESS - STREET OR BOX	CITY, STATE, ZIP CODE

HOW LONG	PARISH	HOME PHONE	MARITAL STATUS: DO NOT COMPLETE UNLESS YOU RESIDE IN A COMMUNITY PROPERTY STATE. ☐ MARRIED ☐ UNMARRIED ☐ SEPARATED

RESIDENCE ADDRESS (DIFFERENT FROM MAILING)	PARISH

PREVIOUS ADDRESS (WITHIN 2 YEARS)	HOW LONG

NAME OF RELATIVE NOT LIVING WITH YOU	ADDRESS	RELATIONSHIP	HOME PHONE

NAME OF RELATIVE NOT LIVING WITH YOU	ADDRESS	RELATIONSHIP	HOME PHONE

EMPLOYMENT

EMPLOYER'S NAME	ADDRESS	HOW LONG

POSITION OR DEPARTMENT	BADGE OR I.D.	SUPERVISOR'S NAME	SALARY $	☐ MONTH ☐ SEMI-MONTH ☐ ANNUAL	BUSINESS PHONE

PREVIOUS EMPLOYER (WITHIN 3 YEARS)	ADDRESS	HOW LONG

Alimony, child support, or separate maintenance income need not be revealed if you do not wish to have it considered as a basis for repaying your obligation.

Alimony, child support, separate maintenance received under: ☐ court order ☐ written agreement ☐ oral understanding

SOURCE OF OTHER INCOME	AMOUNT $	☐ MONTH ☐ SEMI-MONTH ☐ ANNUAL	HOW LONG

CREDIT

NAME OF BANK	ADDRESS	ACCOUNT NO.	SERVICES ☐ CHK. ☐ SAV. ☐ C.D.	☐ COML. LN. ☐ CONS. LN.

MORTGAGE HOLDER OR LANDLORD ☐ BUYING ☐ RENTING	ADDRESS	ACCOUNT NO.	COST	MO. PAY	BALANCE

CREDIT: LIST ALL LOANS, CREDIT CARDS AND REVOLVING CHARGE ACCOUNTS WHICH ARE IN YOUR NAME OR THE NAME OF YOUR SPOUSE WHICH MAY BE SATISFIED OUT OF YOUR INCOME.

CREDITOR'S NAME AND ADDRESS	ACCOUNT IN NAME OF	COLLATERAL	MO. PAY	BALANCE

CO-APPLICANT
(ADDITIONAL CO-APPLICANTS MUST COMPLETE SEPARATE APPLICATION FORMS)

IF ☐ SPOUSE OR ☐ OTHER WILL BE CONTRACTUALLY LIABLE, COMPLETE THIS SECTION. IF APPLICANT RELIES ON COMMUNITY PROPERTY, SPOUSE'S INCOME, ALIMONY, CHILD SUPPORT OR MAINTENANCE PAYMENTS FROM A SPOUSE OR FORMER SPOUSE, FOR REPAYMENT OF THIS LOAN, FILL IN THIS SECTION ABOUT YOUR SPOUSE OR FORMER SPOUSE.

NAME-LAST, FIRST, MIDDLE	DATE OF BIRTH	SOCIAL SECURITY NO.	DEPENDENTS

MAIL ADDRESS - STREET OR BOX	CITY, STATE, ZIP CODE

HOW LONG	PARISH	HOME PHONE	MARITAL STATUS: DO NOT COMPLETE UNLESS YOU RESIDE IN A COMMUNITY PROPERTY STATE. ☐ MARRIED ☐ UNMARRIED ☐ SEPARATED

PREVIOUS ADDRESS (WITHIN 2 YEARS)	HOW LONG

NAME OF RELATIVE NOT LIVING WITH YOU	ADDRESS	RELATIONSHIP	HOME PHONE

EMPLOYER'S NAME	ADDRESS	HOW LONG

POSITION OR DEPARTMENT	BADGE OR I.D.	SUPERVISOR'S NAME	SALARY $	☐ MONTH ☐ SEMI-MONTH ☐ ANNUAL	BUSINESS PHONE

PREVIOUS EMPLOYER (WITHIN 3 YEARS)	ADDRESS	HOW LONG

Alimony, child support, or separate maintenance income need not be revealed if you do not wish to have it considered as a basis for repaying your obligation.

Alimony, child support, separate maintenance received under: ☐ court order ☐ written agreement ☐ oral understanding

SOURCE OF OTHER INCOME	AMOUNT $	☐ MONTH ☐ SEMI-MONTH ☐ ANNUAL	HOW LONG

NAME OF BANK	ADDRESS	ACCOUNT NO.	SERVICES ☐ CHK. ☐ SAV. ☐ C.D.	☐ COML. LN. ☐ CONS. LN.

MORTGAGE HOLDER OR LANDLORD ☐ BUYING ☐ RENTING	ADDRESS	ACCOUNT NO.	COST	MO. PAY	BALANCE

CREDIT: LIST ALL LOANS, CREDIT CARDS AND REVOLVING CHARGE ACCOUNTS WHICH ARE IN YOUR NAME OR THE NAME OF YOUR SPOUSE WHICH MAY BE SATISFIED OUT OF YOUR INCOME.

CREDITOR'S NAME AND ADDRESS	ACCOUNT IN NAME OF	COLLATERAL	MO. PAY	BALANCE

WARRANTY OF APPLICANT(S)

THE UNDERSIGNED APPLICANT(S) WARRANTS AND REPRESENTS THAT ALL STATEMENTS MADE HEREON ARE TRUE AND CORRECT AND ARE GIVEN TO INDUCE THIS BANK TO APPROVE THIS CREDIT APPLICATION. THE UNDERSIGNED APPLICANT(S) AUTHORIZES OUR TOWNE BANK TO MAKE WHATEVER CREDIT INQUIRIES IT DEEMS NECESSARY IN CONNECTION WITH THIS APPLICATION AND AGREES THAT THIS APPLICATION SHALL REMAIN IN THE PROPERTY OF THE BANK WHETHER OR NOT THE LOAN IS EXTENDED.

APPLICANT'S SIGNATURE	DATE	CO-APPLICANT'S SIGNATURE	DATE

Form **1040EZ**

Department of the Treasury—Internal Revenue Service

Income Tax Return for Single and Joint Filers With No Dependents (99) **20--**

OMB No. 1545-0675

Label

(See page 12.)

Use the IRS label. Otherwise, please print or type.

Presidential Election Campaign (page 12)

L A B E L H E R E

Your first name and initial | Last name | Your social security number

If a joint return, spouse's first name and initial | Last name | Spouse's social security number

Home address (number and street). If you have a P.O. box, see page 12. | Apt. no.

City, town or post office, state, and ZIP code. If you have a foreign address, see page 12.

▲ **Important!** ▲

You **must** enter your SSN(s) above.

Note. Checking "Yes" will not change your tax or reduce your refund.
Do you, or spouse if a joint return, want $3 to go to this fund? . . . . ▶

You | Spouse
☐ Yes ☐ No | ☐ Yes ☐ No

Income

Attach Form(s) W-2 here.
Enclose, but do not attach, any payment.

1 Total wages, salaries, and tips. This should be shown in box 1 of your W-2 form(s). Attach your W-2 form(s). | 1

2 Taxable interest. If the total is over $400, you cannot use Form 1040EZ. | 2

3 Unemployment compensation, qualified state tuition program earnings, and Alaska Permanent Fund dividends (see page 14). | 3

4 Add lines 1, 2, and 3. This is your **adjusted gross income.** | 4

Note. You **must** check Yes or No.

5 Can your parents (or someone else) claim you on their return?
Yes. Enter amount from worksheet on back. ☐
No. If **single,** enter 7,450.00. If **married,** enter 13,400.00. ☐
See back for explanation. | 5

6 Subtract line 5 from line 4. If line 5 is larger than line 4, enter 0. This is your **taxable income.** ▶ | 6

Credits, payments, and tax

7 Rate reduction credit. See the worksheet on page 14. | 7

8 Enter your Federal income tax withheld from box 2 of your W-2 form(s). | 8

9a **Earned income credit (EIC).** See page 15. | 9a

b Nontaxable earned income. | 9b

10 Add lines 7, 8, and 9a. These are your **total credits and payments.** ▶ | 10

11 **Tax.** If you checked "Yes" on line 5, see page 20. Otherwise, use the amount on **line 6 above** to find your tax in the tax table on pages 24–28 of the booklet. Then, enter the tax from the table on this line. | 11

Refund

Have it directly deposited! See page 20 and fill in 12b, 12c, and 12d.

12a If line 10 is larger than line 11, subtract line 11 from line 10. This is your **refund.** ▶ | 12a

b Routing number

c Type: ☐ Checking ☐ Savings

d Account number

Amount you owe

13 If line 11 is larger than line 10, subtract line 10 from line 11. This is the **amount you owe.** See page 21 for details on how to pay. ▶ | 13

Third party designee

Do you want to allow another person to discuss this return with the IRS (see page 22)? ☐ **Yes.** Complete the following. ☐ **No**

Designee's name ▶ | Phone no. ▶ ( ) | Personal identification number (PIN) ▶

Sign here

Under penalties of perjury, I declare that I have examined this return, and to the best of my knowledge and belief, it is true, correct, and accurately lists all amounts and sources of income I received during the tax year. Declaration of preparer (other than the taxpayer) is based on all information of which the preparer has any knowledge.

Joint return? See page 11.

Keep a copy for your records.

Your signature | Date | Your occupation | Daytime phone number ( )

Spouse's signature. If a joint return, **both** must sign. | Date | Spouse's occupation

Paid preparer's use only

Preparer's signature ▶ | Date | Check if self-employed ☐ | Preparer's SSN or PTIN

Firm's name (or yours if self-employed), address, and ZIP code ▶ | EIN

Phone no. ( )

For Disclosure, Privacy Act, and Paperwork Reduction Act Notice, see page 23.

Cat. No. 11329W

Form **1040EZ** (2001)

Use this form if	• Your filing status is single or married filing jointly.

• Your filing status is single or married filing jointly.
• You (and your spouse if married) were under 65 on January 1, 20--, and not blind at the end of 20--.
• You do not claim any dependents.
• Your taxable income (line 6) is less than $50,000.
• You do not claim a student loan interest deduction (see page 8) or an education credit.
• You had **only** wages, salaries, tips, taxable scholarship or fellowship grants, unemployment compensation, qualified state tuition program earnings, or Alaska Permanent Fund dividends, and your taxable interest was not over $400. **But** if you earned tips, including allocated tips, that are not included in box 5 and box 7 of your W-2, you may not be able to use Form 1040EZ. See page 13. If you are planning to use Form 1040EZ for a child who received Alaska Permanent Fund dividends, see page 14.
• You did not receive any advance earned income credit payments.

If you are not sure about your filing status, see page 11. If you have questions about dependents, use TeleTax topic 354 (see page 6). If you **cannot use this form,** use TeleTax topic 352 (see page 6).

Filling in your return

For tips on how to avoid common mistakes, see page 30.

If you received a scholarship or fellowship grant or tax-exempt interest income, such as on municipal bonds, see the booklet before filling in the form. Also, see the booklet if you received a Form 1099-INT showing Federal income tax withheld or if Federal income tax was withheld from your unemployment compensation or Alaska Permanent Fund dividends. **Remember,** you must report all wages, salaries, and tips even if you do not get a W-2 form from your employer. You must also report all your taxable interest, including interest from banks, savings and loans, credit unions, etc., even if you do not get a Form 1099-INT.

Worksheet for dependents who checked "Yes" on line 5

(keep a copy for your records)

Use this worksheet to figure the amount to enter on line 5 if someone can claim you (or your spouse if married) as a dependent, even if that person chooses not to do so. To find out if someone can claim you as a dependent, use TeleTax topic 354 (see page 6).

A. Amount, if any, from line 1 on front . . . . +_____250.00 Enter total ▶ **A.**_____

B. Minimum standard deduction . . . . **B.**_____750.00

C. Enter the **larger** of line A or line B here . . . . **C.**_____

D. Maximum standard deduction. If **single,** enter 4,550.00; if **married,** enter 7,600.00 . . . . **D.**_____

E. Enter the **smaller** of line C or line D here. This is your standard deduction . . . . **E.**_____

F. Exemption amount.
  • If single, enter 0.
  • If married and—
    —both you and your spouse can be claimed as dependents, enter 0.
    —only one of you can be claimed as a dependent, enter 2,900.00.
  F._____

G. Add lines E and F. Enter the total here and on line 5 on the front . . . . **G.**_____

If you checked "No" on line 5 because no one can claim you (or your spouse if married) as a dependent, enter on line 5 the amount shown below that applies to you.
• Single, enter 7,450.00. This is the total of your standard deduction (4,550.00) and your exemption (2,900.00).
• Married, enter 13,400.00. This is the total of your standard deduction (7,600.00), your exemption (2,900.00), and your spouse's exemption (2,900.00).

Mailing return

Mail your return by **April 15, 20--.** Use the envelope that came with your booklet. If you do not have that envelope, see the back cover for the address to use.

a Control number			OMB No. 1545-0008	Safe, accurate, FAST! Use **IRS e-file**		Visit the IRS Web Site at **www.irs.gov**.

b Employer identification number 10-00000		1 Wages, tips, other compensation 5,250.05	2 Federal income tax withheld 501.93
c Employer's name, address, and ZIP code Antwan's Auto Parts 7890 Makeshift Drive Atlanta, GA 30317-6247		3 Social security wages 5,250.05	4 Social security tax withheld 325.52
		5 Medicare wages and tips 5,250.05	6 Medicare tax withheld 76.18
		7 Social security tips	8 Allocated tips
d Employee's social security number 636-00-4854		9 Advance EIC payment	10 Dependent care benefits
e Employee's first name and initial Last name Mark L. Smith 1040 Peachtree Drive Atlanta, GA 30319-1396		11 Nonqualified plans	12a See instructions for box 12 Code
		13 Statutory employee ☐ Retirement plan ☐ Third-party sick pay ☐	12b Code
		14 Other	12c Code
			12d Code
f Employee's address and ZIP code			

15 State	Employer's state ID number	16 State wages, tips, etc.	17 State income tax	18 Local wages, tips, etc.	19 Local income tax	20 Locality name
GA	10-000 00	5,250.05	121.29			

Form **W-2** Wage and Tax Statement   20--   Department of the Treasury—Internal Revenue Service

Copy B To Be Filed with Employee's FEDERAL Tax Return.

20-- Tax Table

Caution. Dependents, see the worksheet on page 20.

Example. Mr. Brown is single. His taxable income on line 6 of Form 1040EZ is $26,250. First, he finds the $26,250-26,300 income line. Next, he finds the "Single" column and reads down the column. The amount shown where the income line and filing status column meet → is $3,941. This is the tax amount he should enter on line 11 of Form 1040EZ.

At least	But less than	Single	Married filing jointly
		Your tax is—	
26,200	26,250	3,934	3,934
26,250	26,300	(3,941)	3,941
26,300	26,350	3,949	3,949
26,350	26,400	3,956	3,956

If Form 1040EZ, line 6, is— / And you are—

At least	But less than	Single	Married filing jointly
		Your tax is—	
0	5	0	0
5	15	2	2
15	25	3	3
25	50	6	6
50	75	9	9
75	100	13	13
100	125	17	17
125	150	21	21
150	175	24	24
175	200	28	28
200	225	32	32
225	250	36	36
250	275	39	39
275	300	43	43
300	325	47	47
325	350	51	51
350	375	54	54
375	400	58	58
400	425	62	62
425	450	66	66
450	475	69	69
475	500	73	73
500	525	77	77
525	550	81	81
550	575	84	84
575	600	88	88
600	625	92	92
625	650	96	96
650	675	99	99
675	700	103	103
700	725	107	107
725	750	111	111
750	775	114	114
775	800	118	118
800	825	122	122
825	850	126	126
850	875	129	129
875	900	133	133
900	925	137	137
925	950	141	141
950	975	144	144
975	1,000	148	148

1,000

At least	But less than	Single	Married filing jointly
1,000	1,025	152	152
1,025	1,050	156	156
1,050	1,075	159	159
1,075	1,100	163	163
1,100	1,125	167	167
1,125	1,150	171	171
1,150	1,175	174	174
1,175	1,200	178	178
1,200	1,225	182	182
1,225	1,250	186	186
1,250	1,275	189	189
1,275	1,300	193	193
1,300	1,325	197	197
1,325	1,350	201	201
1,350	1,375	204	204
1,375	1,400	208	208
1,400	1,425	212	212
1,425	1,450	216	216
1,450	1,475	219	219
1,475	1,500	223	223

At least	But less than	Single	Married filing jointly
		Your tax is—	
1,500	1,525	227	227
1,525	1,550	231	231
1,550	1,575	234	234
1,575	1,600	238	238
1,600	1,625	242	242
1,625	1,650	246	246
1,650	1,675	249	249
1,675	1,700	253	253
1,700	1,725	257	257
1,725	1,750	261	261
1,750	1,775	264	264
1,775	1,800	268	268
1,800	1,825	272	272
1,825	1,850	276	276
1,850	1,875	279	279
1,875	1,900	283	283
1,900	1,925	287	287
1,925	1,950	291	291
1,950	1,975	294	294
1,975	2,000	298	298

2,000

At least	But less than	Single	Married filing jointly
2,000	2,025	302	302
2,025	2,050	306	306
2,050	2,075	309	309
2,075	2,100	313	313
2,100	2,125	317	317
2,125	2,150	321	321
2,150	2,175	324	324
2,175	2,200	328	328
2,200	2,225	332	332
2,225	2,250	336	336
2,250	2,275	339	339
2,275	2,300	343	343
2,300	2,325	347	347
2,325	2,350	351	351
2,350	2,375	354	354
2,375	2,400	358	358
2,400	2,425	362	362
2,425	2,450	366	366
2,450	2,475	369	369
2,475	2,500	373	373
2,500	2,525	377	377
2,525	2,550	381	381
2,550	2,575	384	384
2,575	2,600	388	388
2,600	2,625	392	392
2,625	2,650	396	396
2,650	2,675	399	399
2,675	2,700	403	403
2,700	2,725	407	407
2,725	2,750	411	411
2,750	2,775	414	414
2,775	2,800	418	418
2,800	2,825	422	422
2,825	2,850	426	426
2,850	2,875	429	429
2,875	2,900	433	433
2,900	2,925	437	437
2,925	2,950	441	441
2,950	2,975	444	444
2,975	3,000	448	448

3,000

At least	But less than	Single	Married filing jointly
		Your tax is—	
3,000	3,050	454	454
3,050	3,100	461	461
3,100	3,150	469	469
3,150	3,200	476	476
3,200	3,250	484	484
3,250	3,300	491	491
3,300	3,350	499	499
3,350	3,400	506	506
3,400	3,450	514	514
3,450	3,500	521	521
3,500	3,550	529	529
3,550	3,600	536	536
3,600	3,650	544	544
3,650	3,700	551	551
3,700	3,750	559	559
3,750	3,800	566	566
3,800	3,850	574	574
3,850	3,900	581	581
3,900	3,950	589	589
3,950	4,000	596	596

4,000

At least	But less than	Single	Married filing jointly
4,000	4,050	604	604
4,050	4,100	611	611
4,100	4,150	619	619
4,150	4,200	626	626
4,200	4,250	634	634
4,250	4,300	641	641
4,300	4,350	649	649
4,350	4,400	656	656
4,400	4,450	664	664
4,450	4,500	671	671
4,500	4,550	679	679
4,550	4,600	686	686
4,600	4,650	694	694
4,650	4,700	701	701
4,700	4,750	709	709
4,750	4,800	716	716
4,800	4,850	724	724
4,850	4,900	731	731
4,900	4,950	739	739
4,950	5,000	746	746

5,000

At least	But less than	Single	Married filing jointly
5,000	5,050	754	754
5,050	5,100	761	761
5,100	5,150	769	769
5,150	5,200	776	776
5,200	5,250	784	784
5,250	5,300	791	791
5,300	5,350	799	799
5,350	5,400	806	806
5,400	5,450	814	814
5,450	5,500	821	821
5,500	5,550	829	829
5,550	5,600	836	836
5,600	5,650	844	844
5,650	5,700	851	851
5,700	5,750	859	859
5,750	5,800	866	866
5,800	5,850	874	874
5,850	5,900	881	881
5,900	5,950	889	889
5,950	6,000	896	896

6,000

At least	But less than	Single	Married filing jointly
		Your tax is—	
6,000	6,050	904	904
6,050	6,100	911	911
6,100	6,150	919	919
6,150	6,200	926	926
6,200	6,250	934	934
6,250	6,300	941	941
6,300	6,350	949	949
6,350	6,400	956	956
6,400	6,450	964	964
6,450	6,500	971	971
6,500	6,550	979	979
6,550	6,600	986	986
6,600	6,650	994	994
6,650	6,700	1,001	1,001
6,700	6,750	1,009	1,009
6,750	6,800	1,016	1,016
6,800	6,850	1,024	1,024
6,850	6,900	1,031	1,031
6,900	6,950	1,039	1,039
6,950	7,000	1,046	1,046

7,000

At least	But less than	Single	Married filing jointly
7,000	7,050	1,054	1,054
7,050	7,100	1,061	1,061
7,100	7,150	1,069	1,069
7,150	7,200	1,076	1,076
7,200	7,250	1,084	1,084
7,250	7,300	1,091	1,091
7,300	7,350	1,099	1,099
7,350	7,400	1,106	1,106
7,400	7,450	1,114	1,114
7,450	7,500	1,121	1,121
7,500	7,550	1,129	1,129
7,550	7,600	1,136	1,136
7,600	7,650	1,144	1,144
7,650	7,700	1,151	1,151
7,700	7,750	1,159	1,159
7,750	7,800	1,166	1,166
7,800	7,850	1,174	1,174
7,850	7,900	1,181	1,181
7,900	7,950	1,189	1,189
7,950	8,000	1,196	1,196

8,000

At least	But less than	Single	Married filing jointly
8,000	8,050	1,204	1,204
8,050	8,100	1,211	1,211
8,100	8,150	1,219	1,219
8,150	8,200	1,226	1,226
8,200	8,250	1,234	1,234
8,250	8,300	1,241	1,241
8,300	8,350	1,249	1,249
8,350	8,400	1,256	1,256
8,400	8,450	1,264	1,264
8,450	8,500	1,271	1,271
8,500	8,550	1,279	1,279
8,550	8,600	1,286	1,286
8,600	8,650	1,294	1,294
8,650	8,700	1,301	1,301
8,700	8,750	1,309	1,309
8,750	8,800	1,316	1,316
8,800	8,850	1,324	1,324
8,850	8,900	1,331	1,331
8,900	8,950	1,339	1,339
8,950	9,000	1,346	1,346

Continued on page 25

VALUES-INTERESTS WORKSHEET

Work vs. Play

1. Work and play are an important part of our lives. Next to the word *Work*, write any words that you associate with work. Next to the word *Play*, write any words that you associate with play.

   Work: _____

   Play: _____

2. Here are four descriptions of jobs, each providing different sources of satisfaction. *Rank* these in order of their appeal to you (4 = high appeal, 3 = some appeal, 2 = little appeal, 1 = no appeal). Which job would you take first? Be honest with yourself. For example, would you really reject the secure, dull job if it paid well?

Rank

_____ a. *Secure* but rather dull job. You will always be sure of having your job and getting salary raises. It is possible that you can build some excitement into this job if you are imaginative enough, but that will take a lot of effort.

_____ b. *Exciting* but very risky job. You're never sure from one month to the next whether you will have a job. You learn a great deal in this job and are always being challenged, but the uncertainties worry you day and night.

_____ c. *Prosperous.* This is a job where you can learn a lot, attain prestige, and have a great deal of power and responsibility for decisions. You are so busy earning money, however, that you really do not have time to learn new ideas or move the company in the direction you'd like to see it go.

_____ d. *Free Time and Fringe Benefits.* This job is the least demanding of all the jobs. The pay is low, and you do not learn very much that is new to you. You can travel to many places, however, and arrange your working hours to suit yourself. You have a company car, work only 30 hours a week if you like, and you don't have to produce much to satisfy your boss.

3. Would you work if you didn't have to? Why or why not?

   _____

   _____

4. Name three people whose work you admire. Tell why you admire the kinds of work they do.

   _____

   _____

   _____

   _____

   _____

   _____

(continued on back)

VALUES-INTERESTS WORKSHEET (cont'd)

5. In what kinds of work situations would you be willing to work for less than the normal pay? What rewards from work are more important than money?

    _____

    _____

    _____

    _____

6. Complete this sentence: People who work with me think I am _____

    _____

    _____

    _____

    _____

7. *Rank* these sources of work satisfaction from 1 to 5 according to their importance to you (5 = very important; 1 = not important).

    _____ Money

    _____ Prestige

    _____ Security

    _____ Recognition

    _____ Independence

Lacy's Department Store
Atlanta, Georgia

```
SALE  0925   01/22/--   07:05 PM

03275  TOWELS                        22.58
              SUBTOTAL               22.58
              6% TAX                  1.35
              TOTAL                  23.93


VISA       23.93
ACCOUNT NUMBER 00011222   09/--
AUTHORIZATION NUMBER 0418
```

I AGREE TO PAY IN ACCORDANCE WITH THE
TERMS OF THE ACCOUNT INDICATED.

x *Mark L. Smith*
CUSTOMER SIGNATURE

ABILITIES WORKSHEET

1. Answer the following questions on your subjects:

   a. List the subjects you like best.   Why?
      _____   _____
      _____   _____

   b. List the subjects you dislike.   Why?
      _____   _____
      _____   _____
      _____   _____

   c. List the subjects in which you make   Why?
      the best grades.
      _____   _____
      _____   _____
      _____   _____

   d. List the subjects in which you make   Why?
      the worst grades.
      _____   _____
      _____   _____
      _____   _____

(continued on back)

ABILITIES WORKSHEET (con't)

2. Name the things you do best. You may consider them talents or skills. They need not be related to a particular job or career. Name and define them as specifically as possible.

a. _____

_____

b. _____

_____

c. _____

_____

d. _____

_____

e. _____

_____

f. _____

_____

JOB APPLICATION

GENERAL INFORMATION

Name _____

Date _____

Street Address _____

Phone Number _____

City _____ State _____ ZIP _____

Social Security Number _____

Work Desired

Full-time _____
Part-time _____
Seasonal _____
Temporary _____

RECORD OF EDUCATION

High School	_____ _____ _____	Coll. Prep. ☐ Business ☐ Other Voc. ☐	9 10 11 12	Yes ☐* No ☐ *Year _____	
Community College	_____ _____ _____		1 2 3 4	Yes ☐* No ☐ *Year _____	
College	_____ _____ _____		1 2 3 4	Yes ☐* No ☐ *Year _____	Major Area:

WORK EXPERIENCE

List all present and past employment, including part-time or seasonal, beginning with the most recent.

Company	Employment Dates and Salary	Describe the work you did in detail	Reason for leaving
Name _____ Address _____ Phone _____ Supervisor _____	From: _____ To: _____ Salary _____		
Name _____ Address _____ Phone _____ Supervisor _____	From: _____ To: _____ Salary _____		
Name _____ Address _____ Phone _____ Supervisor _____	From: _____ To: _____ Salary _____		

MEDICAL HISTORY

Do you have any impairments, physical, mental, or medical, which would interfere with your ability to perform the job for which you have applied?   Yes _____   No _____

If yes, describe such impairments and specific work limitations.

_____

UNITED STATES MILITARY SERVICE

Veteran YES _____ NO _____   Service Branch _____
Service Dates: FROM _____   TO _____

Please indicate other abilities, experience, skills or special knowledge which you particularly feel would qualify you for the type of work for which you are now applying, such as experience in the Armed Forces, volunteer work, etc.

_____

_____

_____

_____

_____

I authorize investigation of all statements in this application, and I understand that any false statements or deliberate omissions on this application will be cause for my discharge.

_____
Signature of Applicant

Form 6-8

NATIONAL BANK
Atlanta, GA

STATEMENT OF ACCOUNT

Mark L. Smith
1040 Peachtree Drive
Atlanta, GA 30319-1396

| ACCOUNT NUMBER | 04452294 |
| STATEMENT DATE | Jan. 27, 20-- |

BALANCE LAST STATEMENT	TOTAL AMOUNT WITHDRAWALS	NO. OF WITHDRAWALS	NO. OF DEPOSITS	TOTAL AMOUNT DEPOSITS	SERVICE CHARGE	BALANCE THIS STATEMENT
613.15	516.85	5	5	1100.05	4.00	1192.35

CHECK	AMOUNT	DEPOSITS	DATE	BALANCE
			12/26	613.15
		240.01	12/27	853.16
107	59.10		1/2	794.06
108	15.21	140.01	1/3	918.86
	350.00 ATW		1/5	568.86
		240.01	1/10	808.87
109	18.00		1/14	790.87
		240.01	1/17	1030.88
110	74.54	240.01	1/24	1196.35
	4.00 SC		1/27	1192.35

SC – SERVICE CHARGE
CC – CHECK CHARGE
MC – MISCELLANEOUS CHARGE
RT – RETURNED CHECK
ATD – AUTOMATED TELLER DEPOSIT
ATW – AUTOMATED TELLER WITHDRAWAL

YOU CAN EASILY
BALANCE YOUR CHECKBOOK
BY FOLLOWING THIS PROCEDURE

FILL IN THE FOLLOWING AMOUNTS FROM YOUR CHECKBOOK AND BANK STATEMENT.

BALANCE SHOWN ON
BANK STATEMENT $ _____

BALANCE SHOWN IN
YOUR CHECKBOOK $ _____

ADD DEPOSITS
NOT ON STATEMENT $ _____

_____

ADD ANY DEPOSITS NOT
ALREADY ENTERED
IN CHECKBOOK $ _____

_____

TOTAL $ _____

TOTAL $ _____

SUBTRACT CHECKS ISSUED
BUT NOT ON STATEMENT

NO.	AMOUNT
_____	$ _____
_____	_____
_____	_____
_____	_____
_____	_____
_____	_____
_____	_____
_____	_____
_____	_____
_____	_____

SUBTRACT CHECKS, SERVICE
CHARGES AND OTHER BANK
CHARGES NOT IN CHECKBOOK

ITEM	AMOUNT
_____	$ _____
_____	_____
_____	_____
_____	_____
_____	_____
_____	_____

TOTAL $ _____

BALANCE $ _____

TOTAL $ _____

BALANCE $ _____

THESE TOTALS REPRESENT THE CORRECT AMOUNT OF MONEY YOU HAVE IN THE
BANK AND SHOULD AGREE. DIFFERENCES, IF ANY, SHOULD BE REPORTED TO THE BANK
WITHIN TEN DAYS AFTER THE RECEIPT OF YOUR STATEMENT.

Mark L. Smith
1040 Peachtree Drive
Atlanta, GA 30319-1396

107

December 30 20 -- 15-77/250

PAY TO THE
ORDER OF Service Merchandise $ 59.10/100

Mark L. Smith
1040 Peachtree Drive
Atlanta, GA 30319-1396

108

December 31 20 -- 15-77/250

PAY TO THE
ORDER OF Fay's Drugstore $ 15.21/100

Mark L. Smith
1040 Peachtree Drive
Atlanta, GA 30319-1396

109

January 9 20 -- 15-77/250

PAY TO THE
ORDER OF Fay's Drugstore $ 18.00/100

Mark L. Smith
1040 Peachtree Drive
Atlanta, GA 30319-1396

110

January 21 20 -- 15-77/250

PAY TO THE
ORDER OF Great Fi-Buys $ 74.54/100

Seventy-four 54/100 _____ DOLLARS

For Classroom Use Only

NATIONAL BANK
Atlanta, GA

FOR Down payment on stereo   Mark L. Smith

⑆025000779⑆ 0445229⑆

CONDITION REPORT OF APARTMENT _____

General Condition	Dirty Yes	No	Damaged Yes	No
Walls	___	___	___	___
Floors	___	___	___	___
Ceilings	___	___	___	___
Ceiling Fixtures	___	___	___	___
Carpet	___	___	___	___
Drapes/Curtains	___	___	___	___
Door Key/Lock	___	___	___	___
Windows	___	___	___	___
Window Screens	___	___	___	___
Mailbox	___	___	___	___
Thermostat	___	___	___	___

Kitchen	Dirty Yes	No	Damaged Yes	No
Stove	___	___	___	___
Refrigerator	___	___	___	___
Garbage Disposal	___	___	___	___
Kitchen Cabinets	___	___	___	___
Dishwasher	___	___	___	___

Bathroom				
Towel Racks	___	___	___	___
Medicine Cabinet	___	___	___	___
Tub/Shower	___	___	___	___
Toilet	___	___	___	___

_____   Date: _____
Signature of Tenant

_____   Date: _____
Signature of Landlord

NATIONAL BANK
Atlanta, GA

CARD NO.
7730452294

DATE   TIME
02/01/--   10:22

TERMINAL   TRANSACTION
0013   1162

CHECKING WITHDRAWAL $300.00

04452294

NEW BALANCE $981.79

THANK YOU

RENTER'S CHECKLIST

	Apt. 1	Apt. 2
Address	_____	_____
Is the apartment close to work?	_____	_____
What is the monthly rent?	_____	_____
How many bedrooms?	_____	_____
Is it unfurnished?	_____	_____
What is the length of the lease?	_____	_____
Options for breaking the contract?	_____	_____
Can you sublet?	_____	_____
What is the amount of the security deposit?	_____	_____
Who pays utilities?	_____	_____
Average monthly cost?	_____	_____
Who pays water?	_____	_____
Average monthly cost?	_____	_____
Are pets allowed?	_____	_____
Are there extra fees for:		
Storage space?	_____	_____
Parking space (outdoor, indoor, covered)?	_____	_____
Is there a resident manager or superintendent?	_____	_____
What are the garbage disposal facilities?	_____	_____
Is there laundry equipment in the unit?	_____	_____
Is the laundry room safe?	_____	_____
Are laundry room hours assigned?	_____	_____
What are the provisions for mail and parcel delivery?	_____	_____

RENTER'S CHECKLIST (cont.)

	Apt. 1	Apt. 2
What are the security provisions?	_____	_____
Is there a security guard?	_____	_____
Are there safe fire exits?	_____	_____
Is there a smoke detector system?	_____	_____
Is the general layout of the unit good?	_____	_____
Is the bathroom in good condition?	_____	_____
Is there adequate hot water?	_____	_____
Will the unit be painted or decorated before you move in?	_____	_____
Are there "house rules"(for example, no loud music at certain times)?	_____	_____
Is there adequate closet space?	_____	_____
Is there a dead-bolt lock on the door?	_____	_____
A peephole?	_____	_____
Can you install your own lock?	_____	_____
Is the kitchen in good condition?	_____	_____
Adequate storage?	_____	_____
Appliances included?	_____	_____
Exhaust fan?	_____	_____
Are window treatments included?	_____	_____
Are there sufficient electrical outlets (2-3 per room)?	_____	_____
Is there adequate ventilation?	_____	_____
Is there insulation?	_____	_____
Can windows be opened?	_____	_____
Are there screens?	_____	_____
Are there storm windows?	_____	_____
Will the outside of the windows be cleaned by building maintenance?	_____	_____
What are the other tenants like (age, children)?	_____	_____
Other (comments, impressions)	_____	_____

SOCIAL SECURITY ADMINISTRATION
Application for a Social Security Card

Form **8-1**
Form Approved
OMB No. 0960-0066

1

NAME ──────────▶
TO BE SHOWN ON CARD

First	Full Middle Name	Last

FULL NAME AT BIRTH IF OTHER THAN ABOVE

First	Full Middle Name	Last

OTHER NAMES USED

2

MAILING ADDRESS ──────────▶
Do Not Abbreviate

Street Address, Apt. No., PO Box, Rural Route No.

City	State	Zip Code

3 **CITIZENSHIP** ──────────▶
(Check One)

☐ U.S. Citizen   ☐ Legal Alien Allowed To Work   ☐ Legal Alien **Not** Allowed To Work (See Instructions On Page 1)   ☐ Other (See Instructions On Page 1)

4 **SEX** ──────────▶

☐ Male   ☐ Female

5 **RACE/ETHNIC DESCRIPTION** ──────────▶
(Check One Only - Voluntary)

☐ Asian, Asian-American or Pacific Islander   ☐ Hispanic   ☐ Black (Not Hispanic)   ☐ North American Indian or Alaskan Native   ☐ White (Not Hispanic)

6 **DATE OF BIRTH** _____ Month, Day, Year

7 **PLACE OF BIRTH** _____ (Do Not Abbreviate)   City   State or Foreign Country   FCI

Office Use Only

8

A. MOTHER'S MAIDEN NAME ──────────▶

First	Full Middle Name	Last Name At Her Birth

B. MOTHER'S SOCIAL SECURITY NUMBER ──────────▶

☐☐☐ – ☐☐ – ☐☐☐☐

9

A. FATHER'S NAME ──────────▶

First	Full Middle Name	Last

B. FATHER'S SOCIAL SECURITY NUMBER ──────────▶

☐☐☐ – ☐☐ – ☐☐☐☐

10 Has the applicant or anyone acting on his/her behalf ever filed for or received a Social Security number card before?

☐ Yes (If "yes", answer questions 11-13.)   ☐ No (If "no", go on to question 14.)   ☐ Don't Know (If "don't know", go on to question 14.)

11 Enter the Social Security number previously assigned to the person listed in item 1. ──────────▶

☐☐☐ – ☐☐ – ☐☐☐☐

12 Enter the name shown on the most recent Social Security card issued for the person listed in item 1. ──────────▶

First	Middle Name	Last

13 Enter any different date of birth if used on an earlier application for a card. ──────────▶

_____ Month, Day, Year

14 **TODAY'S DATE** _____ Month, Day, Year

15 **DAYTIME PHONE NUMBER** (___) _____ Area Code   Number

I declare under penalty of perjury that I have examined all the information on this form, and on any accompanying statements or forms, and it is true and correct to the best of my knowledge.

16 **YOUR SIGNATURE**
▶

17 **YOUR RELATIONSHIP TO THE PERSON IN ITEM 1 IS:**
☐ Self   ☐ Natural Or Adoptive Parent   ☐ Legal Guardian   ☐ Other (Specify)

DO NOT WRITE BELOW THIS LINE (FOR SSA USE ONLY)

NPN			DOC	NTI	CAN			ITV
PBC	EVI	EVA	EVC	PRA	NWR	DNR	UNIT	

EVIDENCE SUBMITTED

SIGNATURE AND TITLE OF EMPLOYEE(S) REVIEWING EVIDENCE AND/OR CONDUCTING INTERVIEW

_____ DATE

DCL _____ DATE

Request for Social Security Statement

☐ Please check this box if you want to get your statement in Spanish instead of English.

Please print or type your answers. When you have completed the form, fold it and mail it to us. (If you prefer to send your request using the Internet, contact us at *www.ssa.gov*)

1. Name shown on your Social Security card:

_____ ____
First Name   Middle Initial

_____
Last Name Only

2. Your Social Security number as shown on your card:

☐☐☐ - ☐☐ - ☐☐☐☐

3. Your date of birth (Mo.-Day-Yr.)

☐☐ - ☐☐ - ☐☐

4. Other Social Security numbers you have used:

☐☐☐ - ☐☐ - ☐☐☐☐

☐☐☐ - ☐☐ - ☐☐☐☐

5. Your Sex: ☐ Male   ☐ Female

For items 6 and 8 show only earnings covered by Social Security. Do NOT include wages from State, local or Federal Government employment that are NOT covered for Social Security or that are covered ONLY by Medicare.

6. Show your actual earnings (wages and/or net self-employment income) for last year and your estimated earnings for this year.

A. Last year's actual earnings: *(Dollars Only)*

$ ☐☐☐ , ☐☐☐ . ☐ ☐

B. This year's estimated earnings: *(Dollars Only)*

$ ☐☐☐ , ☐☐☐ . ☐ ☐

7. Show the age at which you plan to stop working.

☐☐
(Show only one age)

8. Below, show the average yearly amount (not your total future lifetime earnings) that you think you will earn between now and when you plan to stop working. Include performance or scheduled pay increases or bonuses, but not cost-of-living increases.

If you expect to earn significantly more or less in the future due to promotions, job changes, part-time work, or an absence from the work force, enter the amount that most closely reflects your future average yearly earnings.

If you don't expect any significant changes, show the same amount you are earning now (the amount in 6B).

Future average yearly earnings: *(Dollars Only)*

$ ☐☐☐ , ☐☐☐ . ☐ ☐

9. Do you want us to send the statement:

- To you? Enter your name and mailing address.
- To someone else (your accountant, pension plan, etc.)? Enter your name with "c/o" and the name and address of that person or organization.

_____
"C/O" or Street Address (Include Apt. No., P.O. Box, Rural Route)

_____
Street Address

_____
Street Address (If Foreign Address, enter City, Province, Postal Code)

_____
U.S. City, State, Zip code (If Foreign Address, enter Name of Country

NOTICE:
I am asking for information about my own Social Security record or the record of a person I am authorized to represent. I understand that if I deliberately request information under false pretenses, I may be guilty of a Federal crime and could be fined and/or imprisoned. I authorize you to use a contractor to send the Social Security Statement to the person and address in item 9.

▲

Please sign your name (Do Not Print)

_____
Date   (Area Code)   Daytime Telephone No.

AUTO INSURANCE RATES

	Company A	Company B
Name of company	_____	_____
Name of agent	_____	_____

Types of Coverage	**Premiums**	**Premiums**
Liability Limits _____/ _____/ _____	_____	_____
Collision Deductible _____	_____	_____
Comprehensive Deductible _____	_____	_____
Medical Limit _____	_____	_____
Uninsured-motorist	_____	_____
Other coverages	_____	_____
_____	_____	_____
_____	_____	_____
Total premium	_____	_____

RENTER'S INVENTORY RECORD

Living Room	Date Purchased	Purchase Price
Rugs	_____	$_____
Couch	_____	_____
Chairs	_____	_____
Tables	_____	_____
Drapes	_____	_____
Lamps	_____	_____
Other (list)		
_____	_____	_____
_____	_____	_____

Dining Room	Date Purchased	Purchase Price
Rugs	_____	$_____
Table	_____	_____
Chairs	_____	_____
China Cabinet	_____	_____
Drapes	_____	_____
Silverware	_____	_____
China	_____	_____
Stemware	_____	_____
Other (list)		
_____	_____	_____
_____	_____	_____

Kitchen	Date Purchased	Purchase Price
Small Appliances	_____	$_____
Pots & Pans	_____	_____
Dishes/Glasses	_____	_____
Utensils	_____	_____
Other (list)		
_____	_____	_____
_____	_____	_____

Bathroom	Date Purchased	Purchase Price
Shower Curtain	_____	$_____
Towels	_____	_____
Rug	_____	_____
Hair Dryer	_____	_____
Other (list)		
_____	_____	_____
_____	_____	_____

Bedroom	Date Purchased	Purchase Price
Rugs	_____	$_____
Bed	_____	_____
Mattress	_____	_____
Dresser	_____	_____
Night Table	_____	_____
Lamps	_____	_____
Sheets	_____	_____
Blankets	_____	_____
Other (list)		
_____	_____	_____
_____	_____	_____

Clothing	Date Purchased	Purchase Price
Coats	_____	$_____
Suits	_____	_____
Sweaters	_____	_____
Shirts/Blouses	_____	_____
Skirts	_____	_____
Slacks	_____	_____
Dresses	_____	_____
Underwear	_____	_____
Shoes	_____	_____
Jewelry	_____	_____
Other (list)		
_____	_____	_____
_____	_____	_____

Electrical Equipment	Date Purchased	Purchase Price
Television	_____	$_____
Radio	_____	_____
Stereo	_____	_____
VCR	_____	_____
DVD Player	_____	_____
Computer	_____	_____
Tapes/Discs	_____	_____
Other (list)		
_____	_____	_____
_____	_____	_____
Total Inventory		$_____

Car Options	What I Want	What I Need	What I Can Afford	What I Get (results: 2 out of 3)
1. Automatic · · or · · · · Standard transmission				
2. Small car · · or · · · · Intermediate car · · or · · · · Large car				
3. Sports car · · or · · · · Standard car				
4. 4 cylinder · · or · · · · 6 cylinder				
5. Cruise control · · or · · · · No cruise control				
6. ABS brakes · · or · · · · Standard brakes				
7. Air conditioning · · or · · · · No air conditioning				
8. Standard radio · · or · · · · AM-FM stereo/cassette · · or · · · · AM-FM stereo/CD				

PROMISSORY NOTE

On this date, _____ , I promise to pay to the order of

_____ the amount of

_____ dollars

($_____) in _____ consecutive monthly payments of $_____ each

on the 25th day of each month until this loan is paid in full.

Signed _____

PERSONAL COSTS OF
OWNING AND OPERATING AN AUTOMOBILE

	Cost per Month	Cost per Year
Fixed Expenses		
Installment payment	_____	_____
Insurance	_____	_____
License and inspection fees	_____	_____
Other	_____	_____
Total fixed expenses	_____	_____
Variable Expenses		
Gasoline	_____	_____
Oil	_____	_____
Tires	_____	_____
Maintenance	_____	_____
Total variable expenses	_____	_____
Total fixed & variable expenses	_____	_____

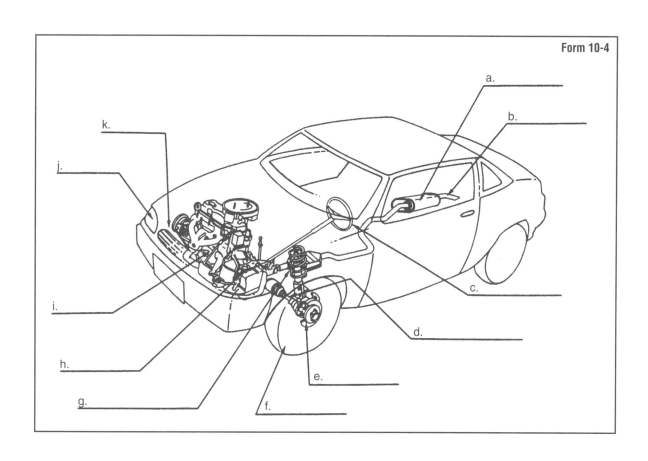

NATIONAL BANK
Atlanta, GA

STATEMENT OF ACCOUNT

Mark L. Smith
1040 Peachtree Drive
Atlanta, GA 30319-1396

ACCOUNT NUMBER	04452294
STATEMENT DATE	Feb. 24, 20--

BALANCE LAST STATEMENT	TOTAL AMOUNT WITHDRAWALS	NO. OF WITHDRAWALS	NO. OF DEPOSITS	TOTAL AMOUNT DEPOSITS	SERVICE CHARGE	BALANCE THIS STATEMENT
1,192.35	1,478.50	12	4	960.04	4.00	669.89

CHECK	AMOUNT	DEPOSITS	DATE	BALANCE
			1/27	1,192.35
	50.00 ATW		1/29	1,142.35
111	48.00		1/30	1,094.35
112	52.57	240.01	1/31	1,281.79
	100.00 ATW		2/1	1,181.79
	300.00 ATW		2/3	881.79
113	400.00		2/5	481.79
115	67.00		2/6	414.79
114	160.00	240.01	2/7	494.80
	50.00 ATW		2/9	444.80
116	120.00		2/11	324.80
118	111.26		2/13	213.54
117	19.67	240.01	2/14	433.88
		240.01	2/21	673.89
	4.00 SC		2/24	669.89

SC – SERVICE CHARGE
CC – CHECK CHARGE

MC – MISCELLANEOUS CHARGE
RT – RETURNED CHECK

ATD – AUTOMATED TELLER DEPOSIT
ATW – AUTOMATED TELLER WITHDRAWAL

YOU CAN EASILY
BALANCE YOUR CHECKBOOK
BY FOLLOWING THIS PROCEDURE

FILL IN THE FOLLOWING AMOUNTS FROM YOUR CHECKBOOK AND BANK STATEMENT.

BALANCE SHOWN ON BANK STATEMENT	$ _____	BALANCE SHOWN IN YOUR CHECKBOOK	$ _____
ADD DEPOSITS NOT ON STATEMENT	$ _____	ADD ANY DEPOSITS NOT ALREADY ENTERED IN CHECKBOOK	$ _____
	_____		_____
	_____		_____
TOTAL	$ _____	TOTAL	$ _____

SUBTRACT CHECKS ISSUED BUT NOT ON STATEMENT

NO.	AMOUNT
_____	$ _____
_____	_____
_____	_____
_____	_____
_____	_____
_____	_____
_____	_____
_____	_____
_____	_____

SUBTRACT CHECKS, SERVICE CHARGES AND OTHER BANK CHARGES NOT IN CHECKBOOK

ITEM	AMOUNT
_____	$ _____
_____	_____
_____	_____
_____	_____
_____	_____
_____	_____

TOTAL	$ _____	TOTAL	$ _____
BALANCE	$ _____	BALANCE	$ _____

THESE TOTALS REPRESENT THE CORRECT AMOUNT OF MONEY YOU HAVE IN THE BANK AND SHOULD AGREE. DIFFERENCES, IF ANY, SHOULD BE REPORTED TO THE BANK WITHIN TEN DAYS AFTER THE RECEIPT OF YOUR STATEMENT.

Mark L. Smith
1040 Peachtree Drive
Atlanta, GA 30319-1396

111

January 25 20 -- $\frac{15\text{-}77}{250}$

PAY TO THE
ORDER OF Carl Jones $ 48.00/100

Mark L. Smith
1040 Peachtree Drive
Atlanta, GA 30319-1396

112

January 25 20 -- $\frac{15\text{-}77}{250}$

PAY TO THE
ORDER OF Thrift Drugs $ 52.57/100

Mark L. Smith
1040 Peachtree Drive
Atlanta, GA 30319-1396

113

February 1 20 -- $\frac{15\text{-}77}{250}$

PAY TO THE
ORDER OF College Park $ 400.00/100

Mark L. Smith
1040 Peachtree Drive
Atlanta, GA 30319-1396

114

February 3 20 -- $\frac{15\text{-}77}{250}$

PAY TO THE
ORDER OF Aruna Nazami $ 160.00/100

Mark L. Smith
1040 Peachtree Drive
Atlanta, GA 30319-1396

115

February 3 20 -- $\frac{15\text{-}77}{250}$

PAY TO THE
ORDER OF Thrift Drugs $ 67.00/100

Mark L. Smith
1040 Peachtree Drive
Atlanta, GA 30319-1396

116

February 9 20 -- $\frac{15\text{-}77}{250}$

PAY TO THE
ORDER OF Thrifty Grocery $ 120.00/100

Mark L. Smith
1040 Peachtree Drive
Atlanta, GA 30319-1396

117

February 9 20 -- $\frac{15\text{-}77}{250}$

PAY TO THE
ORDER OF Great Zi-Buys $ 19.67/100

Mark L. Smith
1040 Peachtree Drive
Atlanta, GA 30319-1396

118

February 9 20 -- $\frac{15\text{-}77}{250}$

PAY TO THE
ORDER OF National Bank $ 111.26/100

One hundred eleven 26/100 ————————— DOLLARS

For Classroom Use Only

NATIONAL BANK
Atlanta, GA

FOR 00011222

Mark L. Smith

⑆025000779⑆ 04452294 ⑇